The Art of Programming
Embedded Systems

THE ART OF PROGRAMMING EMBEDDED SYSTEMS

Jack G. Ganssle

Softaid, Inc.
Columbia, Maryland

Academic Press
San Diego New York Boston
London Sydney Tokyo Toronto

Find Us on the Web!   http: //www.apnet.com

This book is printed on acid-free paper. ∞

Copyright © 1992 by ACADEMIC PRESS

All Rights Reserved.
No part of this publication may be reproduced or transmitted in any form or by any
means, electronic or mechanical, including photocopy, recording, or any information
storage and retrieval system, without permission in writing from the publisher.

ACADEMIC PRESS
525 B Street, Suite 1900, San Diego, California 92101-4495

United Kingdom Edition published by
Academic Press Limited
24–28 Oval Road, London NW1 7DX

Library of Congress Cataloging-in-Publication Data

Ganssle, Jack G.
    The art of programming embedded systems / Jack G. Ganssle.
      p. cm.
    Includes bibliographical references and index.
    ISBN 0-12-274880-8
    1. Embedded computer systems--Programming. I. Title.
QA76.6.G334 1991
005.1--dc20
                                       91-24153
                                       CIP

PRINTED IN THE UNITED STATES OF AMERICA
97 98 IBT 9 8 7 6 5 4 3

This book is dedicated to
Cathy, Graham, and Kristina

Contents

Preface

DeMarco and Lister, in their wonderful book *Peopleware*, complain that too many software people just don't read technical publications. What a frightening thought! No other industry is so characterized by constant and profound change. Somehow, we embedded programmers must access every scrap of information in the fight to stay up to date.

In the embedded world it seems most of us learn via on-the-job training. While many colleges offer embedded programming courses, few go beyond descriptions of the sort of simple projects even a high-school hacker might build.

With embedded systems ranging in size from a few hundred lines for a trivial controller to multi-million-line tracking systems, it's impossible to cover all of the issues encountered in designing embedded systems in one or even a dozen volumes. In this book I've tried to address the subject from three different approaches: design, solutions to practical problems, and planning.

While we're all familiar with the tenets of top-down design, far too little has been written on the subject of designing code that is debuggable and useful in the production environment that our embedded code is targeted toward. Chapters 4 and 5 deal with these subjects.

Much of the book is taken up with algorithms and techniques for solving a number of problems common to many embedded systems. Chapters 6 through 10 address these system problems, with example solutions to each.

Finally, perhaps an underlying theme throughout the book is the concept of the software engineer as a manager. "Coders" worry about writing software, period. I believe that true software engineers should be concerned with every aspect of the system, from its high-level design to the low-level code, even to business issues that affect the end-product's marketability. What will adding a floating-point package do to the cost of goods? How does time-to-market impact the product's viability? When we select a processor, what business issues are important, perhaps even as important as the technical trade-offs? Although Chapters 1, 2, and 11 specifically deal with these questions, this also pervades most of the rest of the book.

Acknowledgments

Academic Press came up with the idea and inspiration for the book. Randy Gilleland read the manuscript quite a few times, in all its various forms, and contributed code, ideas, and enthusiasm. Scott Rosenthal made numerous suggestions about the book's technical content.

The stories and experiences that make up so much of this book all stem from work I've done with hundreds of others over the years. I can't acknowledge the individuals, but thanks to y'all.

Thanks to my three-year-old son Graham for not destroying the temptingly huge stacks of files associated with this project.

Finally, special thanks to my wife Cathy for taking care of the kids while I worked on this book and for encouraging and supporting the project through eighteen months of effort.

CHAPTER 1

Introduction

These are the days of miracles and wonders.—Paul Simon
I just can't get no respect.—Rodney Dangerfield

How many of us designing microprocessor-based products can explain our jobs at a cocktail party? To the average consumer the word "computer" conjures up images of mainframes or PCs. Most consumers blithely disregard or perhaps are unaware of the tremendous number of little processors that are such an important part of everyone's daily life. We wake up to the sound of a computer-generated alarm, eat a breakfast prepared with a digital microwave, and drive to work in cars with an electronic dashboard. Perhaps a bit fearful of new technology, we'll tell anyone who cares to listen that a pencil is just fine for writing, thank you; computers are just too complicated.

So many products that we take for granted simply couldn't exist without an embedded computer! Thousands owe their lives to sophisticated biomedical instruments like CAT scanners, implanted heart monitors, and sonograms. Ships as well as pleasure vessels navigate by LORANs and SATNAVs that tortuously iterate nonlinear position equations. State-of-the-art DSP chips in traffic radar detectors attempt to thwart the police, playing a high-tech cat-and-mouse game with the computer in the authority's radar gun. Compact disc players give perfect sound reproduction using high-integration devices that provide error correction and accurate track seeking.

It seems somehow appropriate that, like molecules and bacteria, we disregard computers in our day-to-day lives. The microprocessor has become part of the underlying fabric of late twentieth-century civilization. Our lives are being subtly changed by the incessant information processing that surrounds us.

Microprocessors offer far more than minor conveniences like the TV remote control. One ultimately crucial application is reduced consumption of limited natural resources. Smart furnaces use solar input and varying user demands to efficiently maintain comfortable temperatures. Think of it—a fleck of silicon saving mountains of coal! Inexpensive programmable sprinklers make off-peak water use convenient, reducing consumption by turning the faucet off even when forgetful humans are occupied elsewhere. Most industrial processes rely on some sort of computer control to optimize energy use and to meet EPA discharge restrictions. Electric motors are estimated to use some 50% of all electricity produced—cheap motor controllers that net even tiny efficiency improvements can yield huge power savings. Short of whole new technologies that don't yet exist, smart, computationally intense use of resources may offer us the biggest near-term improvements in the environment.

What is this technology that has so changed the nature of the electronics industry? Programming the VCR or starting the microwave, you invoke the assistance of an embedded microprocessor—a computer built right into the product.

Embedded microprocessor applications all share one common trait: the end product is not a computer. The user may not realize that a computer is included; certainly no three year old knows or cares that a processor drives her Speak and Spell. The teenager watching MTV is unaware that embedded computers control the cable box and the television. Mrs. Jones, chatting long distance, probably made the call with the help of a simple embedded controller in her phone. Even the "power" computer user may not know that his PC is really a collection of processors; the keyboard, mouse, and printer all include at least one embedded microprocessor.

For the purpose of this book, an embedded system is any application where a dedicated computer is built right into the system. While this definition can apply even to major weapon systems based on embedded VAXes, here I address the perhaps less glamorous but certainly much more common applications using 4-, 8-, and 16-bit processors.

As embedded systems designers, we pursue a career many don't understand (we "just can't get no respect"), but our business is part of a huge industry. By 1990 a total of about 45 million recognizable computers (i.e., PCs, Macintoshes, even CP/M systems) were in place. Yet over 1 billion microprocessors and microcontrollers were shipped in that year alone!

Although the microprocessor was not explicitly invented to fulfill a demand for cheap general-purpose computing, in hindsight it is apparent that an insatiable demand for some amount of computational power sparked its development. In 1970 the minicomputer was being harnessed in thousands of applications that needed a digital controller, but its high cost restricted it to large industrial processes and laboratories. The microprocessor almost immediately reduced computer costs by a factor of a thousand. Some designers saw an opportunity to replace complex logic with a cheap 8051 or Z80. Others realized that their products could perform more complex functions and offer more features with the addition of these silicon marvels.

Back in 1980 Intel estimated that over a million different products incorporated some sort of micro—primarily low-end, high-volume processors. Thirty-two-bit CPU's, though widely touted as the future of computers, will continue to represent only a miniscule fraction of the market. Certainly we'll see many of these high-performance engines included in workstations and personal computers or in complex embedded environments (like laser printers) where a lot of horsepower is needed. In general, most embedded systems will always use 4-, 8-, and 16-bit CPUs, the workhorses of the industry.

This, then, is the embedded systems industry. In two decades we've seen the microprocessor proliferate into virtually every piece of electronic equipment. The demand for new applications is accelerating.

The goal of this book is to offer approaches to dealing with common embedded programming problems. While all college computer science courses teach traditional programming, few deal with the peculiar problems of embedded systems. As always, schools simply cannot keep up with the pace of technology. Again and again we see new programmers totally baffled by the interdisciplinary nature of this business. There is often no clear distinction between the hardware and software; the software in many cases is an extension of the hardware; hardware components are replaced by software-controlled algorithms. Many embedded systems are real time—the software must respond to an external event in some number of microseconds and no more. We'll address many design issues that are traditionally considered to be the exclusive domain of hardware gurus. The software and hardware are so intertwined that the performance of both is crucial to a useful system; sometimes, programming decisions profoundly influence hardware selection.

One of the themes of this book is the software person as an engineer. Engineers are trained to make trade-offs between performance and cost, unlike university-trained computer science majors. Now programmers are often called software engineers, a refreshing moniker that suggests that this distinction is ending. The embedded systems programmer is part engineer (with some knowledge of the hardware), part systems analyst, and part traditional programmer.

Historically, embedded systems were programmed by hardware designers, since only they understood the detailed bits and bytes of their latest creation. With the paradigm of the microprocessor as a controller, it was natural for the digital engineer to design as well as code a simple sequencer. Unfortunately, most hardware people were not trained in design methodologies, data structures, and structured programming. The result: many early microprocessor-based products were built on thousands of lines of devilishly complicated spaghetti code. The systems were unmaintainable, sometimes driving companies out of business.

The increasing complexity of embedded systems implies that we'll see a corresponding increase in specialization of function in the design team. Perhaps a new class of firmware engineers will fill the place between hardware designers and traditional programmers. Regardless, programmers developing embedded code will always have to have detailed knowledge of *both* software and hardware aspects of the system.

On the Algorithm Collection

It's ludicrous that we software people reinvent the wheel with every project. We have so few resources to draw on! Wise programmers make an ongoing effort to build an arsenal of tools for current and future projects.

Nickolas Wirth described programs as a combination of data structures and algorithms. Data structures, crucial to efficient program designs, are addressed in every programming course. Algorithms receive short shrift.

The field of mathematics is a good model for us. Centuries of work produced a huge variety of techniques for solving almost every conceivable problem. Applied mathematicians would never dream of reinventing an iterative polynomial approximation. They have hundreds of proven techniques to draw from.

Make an investment in collecting algorithms for future use. When a crisis hits there is no time to begin research; you should have the information available *now*. Embedded systems people sometimes claim their work is all real-time control and they don't use conventional algorithms. This is rubbish. How much time have you spent debugging a fast multiply? Did you save it? Embedded systems are becoming more complex and address much more difficult problems. In the future you can expect to be dealing with sophisticated noise cancellation routines, domain transformations (like the Fourier transform), and the like. As a young engineer I spent months developing curve fitting routines only to discover later that elegant solutions were already well known. Fortunately, my boss was as ignorant as I!

Collect algorithms. Look for ways of solving the sort of problems you work on but remember that few of us stay in one job for our whole career. Use a wide net, sweeping in algorithms that look useful. The few minutes you spend at it will possibly save months on some other job in the future.

The average technical person is inundated with information, much of it trivial, much worthless, but with occasional gems hidden in the rough. Develop the mindset of the collector. When reading trade journals, books, or even popular computer publications, stay alert for algorithms.

It's surprising where good ideas come from. The electronics press, such as *EDN*, *Electronic Design*, and *Computer Design*, frequently run articles about purely programming issues. In the past they've described Booth's algorithm for fast multiplies, dozens of fast Fourier transforms, and quite a few unusual approximations. It's important to look for algorithms even when disguised as something else—in these magazines you'll find fascinating ideas buried in code for obscure calculators and in manufacturers' self-serving promotional pieces. It is important to read past the articles' titles. Look for the method used to solve the problem.

Byte magazine contains all sorts of algorithms, from completely coded math packages to error detection code and picture processing ideas. *Dr. Dobbs Journal* regularly publishes useful code fragments, including complete compilers and interpreters. *Embedded Systems Programming* and *Personal Engineering and Instrumentation News* both target embedded systems in particular.

Technical books are a wonderful source of information. The Bibliography contains a number of references. Look in unusual places: the *CRC Standard Math Tables* includes series expansions for many transcendental calculations as well as sometimes forgotten trig relationships that are essential to many computations.

Knuth's four volume set *The Art of Computer Programming* is an expensive shelf filler, but it is the standard reference for much of our profession. Some malign its theoretical approach, but if you take the time to understand the concepts, you'll have a firm foundation for applying almost any algorithm.

Manuals are an overlooked gold mine. DEC's *RSX-11M Fortran Manual* contains an appendix that lists all of the approximations used in the language's library. Tandy's basic manual for the ancient TRS-80 includes program listings for similar approximations. Manuals for HP's calculators (especially for the optional libraries) include particularly complete sets of engineering and financial algorithms. In general, older computers and calculators with limited capabilities were accompanied by lots of useful ways to circumvent their shortcomings.

Users' groups are the old standby for disseminating approaches to solving particular problems. Many of these groups supply complete program listings. Intel's Insite Library for the 8008 and later the 8080 contained hundreds of generally simple, concise listings for a wide range of problems. (The 8008 needed all the help it could get!) Even today, many chip vendors have extensive applications notes with advice for their products. Intel's 8085 software UART applications note is probably still the best general description of this concept. Even if you are not using a particular chip, the approach to the problem may be worthwhile.

Embedded programmers can never stray far from the hardware. This is nowhere more apparent than in signal conditioning. For decades this has been the realm of the analog engineer, yet now even *it* is giving way to digital processing. Analog designers have developed a huge knowledge base for analyzing signals. The data books often include tremendously useful application notes describing aliasing, smoothing, integration, and other important techniques. What could be more algorithmic than a successive approximation analog-to-digital converter?

The Association of Computing Machinery (ACM), possibly the largest formal organization for programmers, has made an effort to collect and collate algorithms. Puzzlingly, their collection contains little applicable to embedded systems. In the collection's two decades ACM members have no doubt solved literally millions of problems. Yet only 500 contributions have been made.

ADA proponents promote the concept of reusable packages, but the language by itself will not make this happen—only daily effort and discipline can yield the documented, filed, and published reusable modules the industry needs.

This is surely a throwaway society. Recycle your algorithms! Someday a smart organization will distribute algorithms on CD ROM, cross-referenced via hypertext. Until then, use whatever means are at hand but start collecting them now. A shoebox full of ripped-out articles is better than nothing, but it's a good idea to organize them at least a bit. Three-ring binders (divided by subject) and file folders are both good ways of saving and sorting the collection.

Make use of your company's clerical support staff. Mark interesting algorithms and have a secretary copy and file them. Some engineering groups use secretaries to maintain an "EEM" file—a cabinet full of vendor brochures sorted by categories developed by the publishers of *Electronic Engineer's Master*. Convince your boss that the algorithm collection is just as important. Keep a personal copy for when you change jobs!

Never take an algorithm at face value, especially if it is from public domain code, the bane of our profession. Analyze it critically. Does it make sense? What happens at the boundary conditions? Many of the best approximation routines work only over limited argument ranges; are these documented?

At first, collecting algorithms is discouraging. The collection will grow slowly, particularly until you develop the habit of being constantly on the prowl for new techniques, new problem-solving approaches. Over months and years the files will fatten. The minutes per month of maintenance will be repaid a hundred times over whenever you extract a useful idea from it.

Corporate Knowledge

In any company larger than just a few people, "corporate knowledge" is a valuable asset that should be managed and guarded just like the cash balance in the bank and the business's investment portfolio. This expertise, painfully acquired through years of mistakes and successes, is fundamental to the business's operation. In traditional industries this might be no more than where the keys to the executive washroom are kept. In a technology company it is represented as conventional drawings and disk files and, even more important, by the experiential knowledge of "this way works."

Have you ever wondered how cars are designed? The automobile companies have accumulated nearly a century of dos and don'ts related to every aspect of autos. What materials work well in door gaskets? What gas tank placements cause lawsuits? How should seats be designed for maximum comfort? Do they pass this wisdom down by word of mouth? How is it organized and collected?

We hear constantly that this is an information economy, yet these words ring hollow. Do we guard this information? Do we actively inventory and organize it? If information is so valuable, why does any business tolerate data losses from sloppy backup procedures?

Company knowledge, which doesn't appear on any balance sheet, is probably a greater asset than all manufacturing plants put together. This is represented by algorithms, circuits, and even the lore passed down from senior designer to newcomers. Perhaps someday the bean counters will add "information" to the company's valuation.

As programmers, we should think in terms of maintaining the information: minimize entropy! This is the value of the algorithm collection.

To beat an old drum, write modular, self-documented code. Remember that five or ten years from now you or another programmer will want to modify it or extract its essence into new code. Think ahead.

Of one thing we can be sure: When the world truly wakes up to the value of information, it will be taxed.

Basic Assumptions

This book is aimed at programmers working on embedded development projects who wish to hone their skills. The generic term "programmers" includes the hardware engineers who are currently responsible for much of today's microprocessor-based code. This book is not a tutorial, but it can serve as an introduction for experienced programmers wishing to learn more about the field.

This book focuses on approaches to solving embedded problems. Most of the example code is presented in C, which is rapidly becoming the *lingua franca* of the industry. While I've tried to avoid assembly language, in a few places it was necessary to illustrate some low-level concepts. Every embedded programmer should be proficient with at least one assembly language and certainly should have at least a working knowledge of C.

The best embedded programmers are those who have at least some understanding of hardware. A number of texts give useful introductions to microprocessor design. One of the best is by Lipovski (see the Bibliography). Some of the subjects addressed might seem the exclusive province of hardware designers, but it is important that the software engineers understand the constraints placed on their code by the hardware.

CHAPTER 2

Initial Considerations

"Begin at the beginning," the King said, gravely, "and go on till you come to the end: then stop."—Alice in Wonderland, Lewis Carroll.

Business Issues

Engineering is expensive. High salaries, pricey capital equipment, and low productivity all contribute to outrageous design costs. The accountants who write our paychecks refer to these as nonrecurring engineering (NRE) expenses. With the exception of poor planning–induced redesigns, NRE costs are incurred only once in the life of a project. On the other hand, recurring costs are those expenditures required to manufacture the product—parts, subcontract labor, and the like.

The trade-off between NRE and recurring costs often defines the marketability of the product. Obviously, high recurring costs imply a high sales price regardless of volume. Even a few extra cents in a high-volume item like an electronic greeting card can be a disaster. Often a huge amount of NRE is invested to drive recurring costs down. At the other end of the spectrum, NRE must be minimized in low-volume products unless the product's price is so high (like a spacecraft's) that lots of engineering can be justified.

Some organizations view engineering as an overhead expense and never properly allocate it to each project. Regardless of how a business accounts for engineering, a reckoning ultimately takes place. The numbers are simple: the price of the widget must include NRE costs amortized over the volume produced during some payback period. If the product is not priced to include these very real costs, it will be a guaranteed money-loser.

Consider the automobile industry: a billion dollars spent on engineering and tooling, amortized over, say, 10 million cars, means the price of each of those cars *must* go up at least $100. Or, look at software products. It costs nothing to duplicate the disks and manuals; the $500 charged for a database program covers marketing and engineering costs.

The implications are crucial to programmers and engineers in the trenches. Every decision you make will be reflected in the product's viability and the company's success. Spend too little time compressing code in a mass-marketed toy and the extra ROM costs will leave a window sure to be capitalized on by a Taiwanese importer. Work inefficiently and your extra time will be reflected in higher NRE costs that *must* cause some end-product price increase. It sometimes seems like a no-win situation: you must work fast to keep engineering costs under control, but you must also work long hours to reduce recurring costs.

The converse is equally true. Who cares if there is an extra ROM in something your company will sell 10 of? All too often programmers elect to code entire projects in assembly, when performance is not an issue, or they endlessly tune a routine to squeeze out one more byte when memory is not a constraint. In low-volume products NRE accounts for a high percentage of the sales price. Find a way to do the job quickly, even if more hardware is needed.

Surveys indicate that embedded systems are getting much more complex. Between 1985 and 1989 the average embedded program doubled in size and presumably doubled in NRE investment. The electronics industry thrives on declining hardware costs resulting from high integration levels. Someday soon increasing engineering expenses will offset these gains, driving product prices up even as recurring costs continue to plummet.

The engineer is usually the company's technology manager. Use technology to reduce NRE costs. Just shifting from assembly language to C will net a huge productivity improvement. Recycling old code and algorithms is just as effective. Study new aids like CASE. Don't necessarily buy the latest fad; wait for the dust to settle and evaluate it in the cold light of experience—someone else's, if possible. Never work on one project at a time. Plan ahead and assume that the work you are doing today will be reused sometime in the future. Inadequate specifications are the biggest cause of huge NRE overruns; don't start coding until the project is well defined. Finally, write good code!

The user interface is always a source of great frustration. Marketing usually abdicates the design of this critical part of the system, yet no other section so influences the user's perception about the product's quality. In the absence of input, software engineers design an interface that is invariably unacceptable to everyone else. Try storyboarding it. If a CRT is involved, use one of the screen prototyping programs like Dan Brinklin's *Demo* to give all participants a feel for the product's ultimate behavior, without spending too much time writing code that will likely be discarded.

Picking the Processor

In most organizations the hardware designers select a processor that meets certain performance criteria and cleanly interfaces to the rest of the system. Software concerns are just as important as hardware issues and should be just as influential.

A crucial decision must be made—can you reuse your old code? If 70% of the system can be stolen from current projects, especially if coded in assembly, fight to keep the current architecture! The software is probably the biggest part of the NRE budget—preserve your investment.

Some aspects of CPU selection are entirely unrelated to technical issues. The product's marketability is a function of its total life-cycle costs, including hard-to-measure yet critical expenses like inventory handling. If your company used Z80s and Z80 peripherals in all of its products, do you really want to stock another family of components? Inventory is costly, inventory is taxed, and inventory management requires yet more money.

What experience does the design team have? Retraining an army of 8088 programmers in the intricacies of the 68000 is bound to be expensive. They'll be learning while doing, struggling with new hardware, instruction sets, and tools; and making mistakes while the project's meter is running. The production, repair, and support groups will need additional equipment and training. If, however, the company's long-range plans involve a move to the new architecture, then taking the plunge is unavoidable. Try to pick a simple project for starters and budget enough time to overcome the inevitable learning curve.

Intangibles play an important part. Does the chip, and all of its associated peripherals, have reliable second sources? Is it really available, in quantity? If the part is old, will it continue to be available in the future? If you can't buy the part, you can't ship product. How hard will the CPU be to program? While there is a way around every shortcoming, do you have the time to fight an inadequate architecture? The old 1802 didn't have call and return instructions, the 6805's index register is only 8 bits long, and the 8008's stack was only 7 bytes deep. A high-level language can mask hardware deficiencies but only at the expense of bigger and slower code. If the processor has limited stack manipulations instructions (like the 8051), then a C compiler will generate a lot of code to handle automatic variables.

Using a new processor is generally a mistake unless there are compelling technical and business reasons to do so. Engineers want to work with cutting-edge components—we're all victims of a sort of high-tech lust. Subordinate emotional decisions to cold, analytical analysis.

COSTS

The cost of tools is an important consideration. Even if you ultimately decide to use the same processor employed in all of the company's products, the start of a project is a good time to reevaluate the development environment. Maybe now is the time to move from assembly to C or to upgrade to an ANSI compatible compiler. Are the debuggers adequate? Should you try a source code management program? Programmer time is hideously expensive—look for ways to spend a few bucks up front to save lots of time downstream.

Hardware engineers should look at their equipment as well. Do you use an emulator to bring up the prototypes? Better be sure it handles the CPU and its clock rates. Reevaluate the logic analyzer; is it fast enough?

Obviously the cost of the processor itself is important but don't be lulled into looking at its price alone. Total system cost is the issue—the half-dollar CPU that needs a twenty-dollar UART is no bargain.

I once tried to convince a friend to use the 647180X, a Z80-like microcontroller, on his latest project. The $15 chip could replace a CPU, serial controller, counter, ROM, and RAM and yet preserve his considerable investment in Z80 code. He explained that cost was the overriding concern, and the Z80 and its peripherals totalled only about $3. The microcontroller was a neat solution but just didn't stand up to a cost analysis. He had obviously done his homework and was right.

It's interesting that in the 8- and 16-bit worlds new CPU architectures have generally been failures. Most embedded systems are designed using chips whose ancestors reach almost all the way back to the beginning of recorded microprocessor history. The Z80 was introduced in 1976, the 6800 in 1975, the 8088 in 1978, and the 8048 (the 8051's precursor) in 1977. These processors and their derivatives continue to account for most embedded designs. Perhaps the tremendous demand for some sort of computing power, however little, was largely satisfied by this generation of processor. Most new architectures have failed or at least have failed to gain significant market share.

To harness the industry's fantastic ability to cram ever more transistors on a chip but continue to sell old (i.e., successful) processor architectures, the vendors have developed a number of high-integration components. The Z80 family is a prime example. The 64180/Z180 is a Z80 at heart with lots of on-board peripherals (counters, DMA, UARTs, etc.). The chip can often replace quite a few system components, yet the software is still Z80 machine code. Another example is the 8051, which early on became a very broad family with a chip for every purpose. Dozens of proliferation chips let you select an 8051 core that includes just the right peripheral mix for your application. Similarly, Intel positioned the 8088 family in the embedded controller market with the 80188 and 80186. After years of legal wrangling, NEC emerged as an important provider of other variants of the 8088 (the V series). Even the 68000 has entered the high-integration fray: both Motorola and Signetics sell single-chip versions. In all of these cases new life is being breathed into old chips; using tried and true backbones, more and more peripherals (and in some cases memory) are being moved onto the CPU.

These high integration parts are excellent choices for embedded designs. Most of the trade-offs are exclusively hardware concerns, like reducing printed circuit board real estate, power consumption, and the like, but important software issues are involved.

Carefully analyze the peripheral selection included on the chip. Is it really adequate? In an interrupt-driven environment, be sure that the interrupt structure is useful. If the device is a microcontroller, does it include enough RAM and ROM? This may impact language selection.

Fast data transfers are sometimes important. The on-board DMA controllers are frequently used to move memory data around. If this is a requirement, be sure that the chip supports memory-to-memory DMA. Some restrict DMA to memory-to-I/O cycles.

A lot of embedded systems depend on a real-time operating system. Context switching is sequenced by a regular timer interrupt. Does the chip have a spare timer? Don't let the hardware team allocate all spare timers to their more visible needs. Few realize that these types of hardware resources are sometimes needed to make the software run.

ADDRESS SPACE

Whether a microcontroller or microprocessor is used, one of the biggest software issues in processor selection is the CPU's address space. Will your program fit into memory?

Microcontrollers have only miniscule amounts of on-board memory, sometimes only a few thousand bytes. Remember: once the chip choice is made, you are committed to making the code work on that CPU. A simple remote data logger might be coded in a high-level language, while complex applications can be a nightmare to shoehorn in. Be very sure about memory needs before casting the processor choice in concrete!

The huge address spaces of 16-bit microprocessors are more than adequate for most programs. This is not the case in the 8-bit world, which usually limits addresses to 64k. Once this seemed like an unlimited ocean we could never fill. Embedded projects are getting bigger, and less efficient tools are regularly used to reduce the NRE costs. 64k might not be enough.

Some designs use bank switching schemes or memory management units (MMUs) to let the program disable one section of RAM or ROM and bring in another. While potentially giving access to immense memory arrays, neither of these approaches yields the nice huge linear address space we all yearn for. (The same could be said about segmentation on the 80x88.) A number of important trade-offs (presented in Chapter 6) come into play, not the least of which is your compiler—will it support the MMU? Few compilers automatically use the memory manager to squeeze a big program into the project's virtual address space. In general you'll have to handle the MMU manually, perhaps tediously issuing lots of MMU commands throughout the code. Still, the memory manager does offer a reasonable way out of the memory constraints imposed by a 16-bit address bus.

PERFORMANCE

In selecting the processor, most companies first look at performance, the industry's elusive but hotly pursued Holy Grail. Semiconductor vendors are happy to ship you crateloads of comparative benchmarks showing how their latest CPU outperforms the competition. Drystones, Whetstones, MIPs, and Linpacks—their numbers are legion, baffling, and usually meaningless. An embedded CPU needs just enough horsepower to solve its one, specific problem. Only two questions are relevant: (1) Will this processor get the job done within specified time constraints? and (2) Will it satisfy performance needs imposed on the product or its derivatives in the future? The answers are sometimes not easy to determine.

If the project is an incremental upgrade of an existing product, consider instrumenting the current code to measure exactly how much free processor time exists. The results are always interesting and sometimes terrifying. Hardware performance analyzers will nonintrusively show the percentage of time spent in each section of the code, particularly the idle loop. You can do the same with an oscilloscope. Add code to set an I/O bit high only when the idle loop is running (don't forget to bring it low in the interrupt service routines). The scope will immediately show the bit's state; it's a simple matter to then compute the percentage of CPU utilization. In a performance-critical application, it's a good idea to build in this code from the beginning. It can be IFed out prior to shipment but easily reenabled at any time for maintenance.

Consider making these measurements to close the feedback loop on the design process when you finish a project. Just how accurate were your performance estimations? If, as is often the case, the numbers bear little resemblance to the original goals, then find out where the errors were and use this information to improve your estimating ability. Without feedback, you work forever in the dark. Strive to learn from your successes as well as the failures.

Most studies find that 90% of a processor's time is spent executing 10% of the code. Identify this 10% in the design (*before* writing code) and focus your energies on this section.

Modeling the critical sections is always a good idea. Try writing similar code on a PC, being sure to use the same language as in the final system. Set up an experiment to run the routine hundreds or thousands of times, so you can get accurate elapsed time measurements.

The trick is to port these execution figures to estimates on the target hardware. Well-heeled companies buy a development board for each of the CPUs being evaluated. Smaller firms can use simulators (although these cost as much as the boards!), or you can "guestimate" a conversion factor. Compare instruction sets and timing. Include wait states and DMA activity. You can get quite accurate numbers this way, but a wise designer will then add in another 50% in the interest of conservative design.

Model real-time operations, especially those synchronized to external devices, the same way. The PC has an extensive interrupt structure—use it! Its software interrupts can be used to simulate external hardware events.

Use this opportunity to debug the algorithms. A PC or other system with a friendly interface makes it easy to work out conceptual bugs while also estimating the code's performance. It is surprising how often actually making something work will turn up problems that demand much more memory or performance. Hardware engineers prototype hardware; we should prototype software.

Sometimes your code will have to respond to very fast external devices that stretch the processor's capability to the limit. Success depends on confining the fast code to a single small routine that can be studied carefully and accurately before proceeding. You may have little choice but to write assembly code on paper and count instruction execution times. The great peril in this is proceeding under the assumption that the code will work—it seldom does. Have an associate evaluate the code, no matter how simple it may be. If this critical section has a bug in it, then the entire project might collapse like a house of cards.

Forget about computing timing with complex processors. Some, like the H16 and Z280, have on-board cache, prefetchers, and other hardware that make it all but impossible to measure instruction times. The timing tables included in the manufacturer's data books seem to be designed to obfuscate.

When making the trade-offs, be sure to factor in special processor features. A multiply instruction can speed the code up considerably— if it is useful. Sometimes the highly touted multiply or divide runs surprisingly slowly. Check the timing! It's also common to find that the math instructions work with very limited precision. The 64180's MUL and DIV take only 8-bit arguments.

Once we ported a BASIC compiler coded in 8085 assembly language to a new 16-bit processor. The customer fell in love with an instruction designed to speed multitasking—in under a microsecond it saved and reloaded all 16 registers. While the instruction worked perfectly, the concept was flawed. Every context switch needed a lot of rather complex code to decide what task to run next. Preserving and saving

Inventory costs
Second sources for CPU and the peripherals
Availability
Can you reuse your old code?
Retraining costs and time
   Engineers, production and support crew
Tool costs
Total system cost: CPU and all peripherals
High-integration parts
   Adequate I/O and memory?
   Reasonable on-board peripherals?
   Timer for context switching?
Memory address space
Performance
   Will you need special hardware, like an FPU?

Figure 2.1 Processor selection trade-offs.

the context represented only a tiny part of the computational overhead. It was an example of being seduced by an apparently fantastic feature that in practice turns out to be not quite such a problem solver after all.

If you are working in C, does the language support the CPU's special features? Even in the highly standardized environment of the 8088, some Cs make no provision for 8087 numeric coprocessors.

Picking the processor is not easy. Consider using a feature matrix with weighting factors scaled to the project's trade-offs. When there is no clear deciding factor between competing CPUs, it makes sense to just make the best possible decision without agonizing over it. (See Fig. 2.1.)

Estimating Memory Requirements

Those software engineers lucky enough to be consulted about memory needs early in the design invariably seem to reply with one of two answers: "Uh, as much as you can fit on the board," or an off the cuff "How about xxxK?" Both answers are wrong.

If recurring costs are a consideration, then asking for too much memory is unfair to the company and reflects poorly on your ability as a system designer. Just adding spare sockets that will probably be unpopulated adds hidden costs. The board will be bigger and thus more costly. Decoupling capacitors will certainly be loaded for the empty sockets. The extra wiring might force a change to more board layers or could create additional noise problems.

Extra sockets thrown in through lazy design are a problem to justify and a mistake. Extra sockets added because of a careful analysis of current and future needs are appropriate. These are the same sockets—what's the difference?

Risk. A good design always minimizes risk. After all, "as much memory as possible" might not be enough! Discovering this after writing 20,000 lines of code could destroy the project and your own job.

Analyze how much RAM and ROM will be needed. Remember that the project's specification is likely incomplete and that additional demands will be made on it. Make allowances for changes and unexpected problems. Creeping featurism is common and unavoidable.

RAM

Most of the time it's pretty easy to estimate a project's RAM needs. RAM has fixed requirements, comprising data arrays, the stack, temporary and permanent small variables, and compiler overhead.

RAM is mostly allocated to data storage. Input and output buffers are fairly obvious, but don't forget transient data. Do you need to store a copy of a big array while manipulating it? Interrupt service routines often queue data—make sure adequate queue space exists. Sometimes the array requirements are crippling. Consider using sparse matrices if most of the elements are not used or are a fixed value.

Always allow plenty of room for the stack (and heap, if used), especially if using C. C stores the automatic variables on the stack. Interrupt handling, especially if lots of fast interrupts are running, can use stack space at a prodigious rate. Compute a worse case interrupt scenario and add stack accordingly. Stack overflows are easily avoided but are a nightmare to find.

Every program makes use of a number of pointers, temporaries, and small data variables. Careful top-down design will identify most of these. The CPU's architecture will dramatically impact the use of temporaries—the 6800 has practically no registers, so lots of memory is a must. Interestingly, in analyzing several hundred thousand lines of code written for quite a few different computers, I've found a personal trend—typically, I use one small variable per 50 to 100 lines of code. This number is much smaller in C, since the automatics exist on the stack only for the scope of the function and take no permanent memory.

Assemblers produce no RAM overhead, but C compilers certainly do. The amount varies widely and relates to the number and type of library routines you use. Measuring this involves writing small programs that use all of the compiler features you'll need in the final project. Add up memory needs. Then double the program's size and see how more RAM is used. Extrapolate these results to the size of the final project.

ROM

Many embedded projects exhaust their ROM space in development or later during maintenance. Squeezing a few bytes out of a program to make things fit is a thankless chore.

It is always important to learn from the past. If the product is a variant or upgrade of an existing one, use the older device as a model to study its ROM requirements. Of course, nothing is stagnant in this industry; a new product might be recoded in C, invalidating much of what could be learned. Modern C compilers are very efficient—most vendors peg their code generation at only 25% less miserly than assembly language.

It's hard to accurately estimate ROM needs of entirely new products. A good design starts with top-down decomposition; as a result you should have a handle on the number of individual modules and their average size. No routine should exceed two or three pages! From this you can get a quick estimate of the number of lines of code involved. Whether written in assembly language or C, you can convert this to code size by writing a few hundred lines and compiling. It is helpful to determine a conversion factor from number of lines to number of bytes (which varies a bit with programming style and commenting standards). Then you can quickly estimate the impact of additions and changes.

Of course, top-down design doesn't always work. (If it did there would be no software crisis!) In C, consider prototyping much of the code on a cross development system (e.g., a PC). You won't have to wait for the hardware to be ready to start testing, and you can start to get a handle on code size (in terms of the number of lines) and other problems early, when hardware changes are still possible.

We decided to introduce a new instrument at a big show in Boston. An analysis of the schedule showed that we had to freeze the hardware design and all software risk factors (which meant that most of the software had to be coded and tested) by early March, only three months after starting design. Obviously impossible! The schedule dictated the CPU selection—a PC-compatible processor would let us code and debug in parallel with the hardware design. We used an 80188 and the Turbo-C compiler, wrote a very simple hardware simulator (under a hundred lines), and started coding in parallel with the schematic design. By the end of January the prototype was being manufactured and the program's structure was coded and tested. During hardware checkout the rest of the hardware-independent code was debugged. Final integration of the hardware and software was a bit rocky, as it always is, but by early March the system worked and we released it to the PC show. Prototyping really paid off.

Always try to break the problem down into pieces you have already solved—reusing old code will save a lot of time. Make use of your algorithm collection! Never reinvent the wheel.

Plan for being wrong. Few estimates are accurate; don't code yourself into an escape-proof corner. Both in engineering and business, a good plan includes some provision for problems. With a microcontroller that has built-in ROM, you have no choice—your ROM estimate *must* be correct. There is no way to expand that memory, so be sure to prototype the code. Larger systems typically use bytewide PROMs. If the design calls for 27256 PROMs and cost is not an overriding concern, con the hardware engineers into using 32-pin sockets. The extra cost is minuscule, and it will let you expand from the 32k plan to much larger devices. Bytewide memories come in standard, JEDEC-approved packages. Even if a particular size doesn't exist, a JEDEC standard probably defines what the pinout will be when it is finally introduced. Whether 28- or 32-pin memories are included, be sure that address lines for the largest JEDEC package are wired in so you can change PROM sizes within the family.

Never start a project where memory requirements are already tight. You will certainly need more than initially assumed. Unfortunately, experience comes painfully in this business. Every old programmer wears a scar from battles with ROM size. Squeezing code is a time-consuming, bug-inducing nightmare. Plan ahead to avoid it altogether.

Selecting I/O Devices

Just because the I/O requirements are dictated by the application doesn't mean you should abdicate your role in selecting chips and interfaces. Far too often programmers are content to accept a completed design and code around the problems they encounter. The hardware team needs the expert advice you can provide; they often must decide between several different chips that satisfy the same application.

Lousy hardware design can make the software complex and the final application less than adequate. Thousands of examples abound. The PC's CGA card stands high on the list of poor hardware/software interfaces. In the interest of saving a few pennies the designers made writing to the screen very, very slow. To avoid generating snow, writes must be restricted to the infrequent retrace intervals. This design is now in tens of millions of computers, all of which have this crippling flaw.

High-integration technology applies to I/O devices as well as processors. For example, Zilog sells a "Killer I/O" part (some marketing person saw too many Rambo films) that includes a cornucopia of serial, parallel, timers, and other ports. The silicon die is huge compared to a Z80 or 6800. It's interesting that CPUs are now far simpler than their I/O.

In some cases the software trade-offs are very clear; an 8-bit latched output is easy to code for. Most A/D converters are just not very hard to read.

Communications interfaces are one glaring exception. SCSI, IEEE-488, HDLC, and other acronym-ridden protocols are hard to write code for and harder to debug. Data sheets for the controller chips are 50 to 100 pages long, yet are cryptic and incomplete. Astonishingly, the chip's vendors continue to push these hardware "solutions" without offering useful software help. Why are so few really good programming application notes written for these parts? Why don't the manufacturers offer a disk with the code already written?

It's not unusual for a floppy disk controller, SCSI, or IEEE-488 chip to use several thousand lines of code that is tough to debug, since dozens of internal registers must be set correctly before anything happens. Programmers unite! Demand more applications help!

Applications notes, if they exist, usually address only one aspect of the chip. We used a Western Digital SCSI controller in one project where speed was important (as it always is with SCSI). The data sheet was accompanied by about a thousand lines of code demonstrating the chip in its simplest, slowest, and least useful mode. We were forced to recreate from scratch a DMA interface that Western Digital *must* have written to test the chip in the first place.

Faced with the choice between two competing controller chips, by all means use the one with the most software support. Beg, borrow, or steal driver code. Remember that it will take weeks to become adept at the intricacies of some of these protocols. Look for a canned solution! Be sure the code uses the chip in a useful mode. Routines organized around polling will be hard to adapt to an interrupt driven structure. DMA transfers might mean a completely different chip setup.

Using an unknown, devilishly complex I/O device represents a significant risk factor in scheduling. Writing the code can be tough, but debugging is always worse. Leave time for surprises.

High integration does offer some interesting solutions to writing low-level code. All of the I/O on a big chip is well defined; there are only so many modes it can work in. In 1989, Intel started distributing a free software package for the 80196 that automatically writes I/O drivers. The program asks questions about the application's operation, working down through a tree of menus, refining the selections. Using timer 0? Reload or timeout? Interrupt on end? By the time all questions are answered, the program completely understands your needs and writes a file of 80196 I/O code. Certainly this must represent a significant investment for Intel—several megabytes of code are involved. Just as certainly it makes the 80196 a much more attractive CPU. We can only hope that this is a harbinger of the future.

It's shocking just how much time it can take to code and debug low-level handlers. A few lines of code can take an inordinate amount of time to debug—I once spent two weeks speed-tuning a four-instruction sequence that transferred data to a tape drive. When analyzing a problem, replace your natural *joie de vivre* with a pessimistic, worst-case attitude. Then, get happy again! But gird yourself for a tough debugging battle.

One of the fun parts of designing embedded systems is replacing hardware with software. Recurring costs are replaced with additional NRE. Be sure this is a sensible trade-off. If recurring costs are not an issue, by all means shift the burden back to the hardware.

Languages: The HLL Dilemma

A mind boggling array of languages is used in embedded systems. Assembly is finally giving way to high-level languages (HLLs). C is supplanting both assembly and most other HLLs. ADA, mandated by the Department of Defense for many of their projects, will probably become an important language; but it is so big and so complex that it will not be influential in small systems. PL/M, introduced by Intel for the 8008 in the early 1970s, is the original embedded HLL. It refuses to die but is rarely used in new projects. And then there's Forth, whose advocates' ardor is matched only by the skepticism of the rest of the software community.

It's important to select an HLL that promises to be widely used over the project's entire life cycle. Will PL/M programmers be available in 10 years to maintain the code? Probably not. Prognosticating the future is difficult in this rapidly changing business, but C (including its derivative, C++) and ADA seem to be languages with long lives ahead.

Despite the stampede to C, assembly continues to be a crucially important embedded language. Current compilers are just not as efficient as a competent assembly programmer. This is particularly true in smaller systems like microcontrollers and 8-bit microcomputers. Strongly consider C for any new project; the reduction in coding time is substantial.

Regardless of language, you'll certainly use some amount of assembler code, if only for interrupt handling or low-level I/O drivers. Much of any embedded system involves lots of bit twiddling, something assembly is particularly adept at. All assemblers are not created equal—carefully evaluate the tools before starting coding.

ASSEMBLER SELECTION

Most projects are now developed in a cross-development environment. A PC or workstation serves as the host computer; code is edited, assembled and/or compiled, and linked on this platform regardless of the architecture of the target CPU. The software tools generate code in the target computer's machine language, even though the tools are written for the host.

A wide range of PC-hosted assemblers and linkers are sold. Little compatibility exists between them. Pseudo-operators and even instruction mnemonics differ between assemblers, so code written for one may not assemble on another. Preserving old code is always important, but variances in assembler syntaxes usually require at least some amount of source file editing to bring the old code in line with the new tool's standards.

Usually a handful of global edits to replace differing pseudo-ops will cure this source compatibility problem, but in some cases there is no good solution. NEC's V-series of processors are high-integration clones of the Intel 80x88 family. For some inscrutable reason (probably having to do with litigation), NEC elected to standardize these chips on a new set of mnemonics that resembles not at all Intel's standard. Fortunately, Intel's mnemonics work just fine with these parts, promoting a level of standardization despite the vendor. Similarly, years ago a number of quite different dialects of Z80 assembly language were common, prompting a proliferation of not particularly accurate translation utilities.

Software tools cannot keep up with the new processors. It's not uncommon to use a derivative CPU with new, perhaps important, instructions that haven't been implemented in the assembler. An efficient macro facility is therefore essential on any nontrivial project. New addressing modes are hard to implement in macros, but it's easy to code new instructions. Macros also let you replace cryptic OUT 23,44 forms with a much more readable TURN_ON_ERROR_LIGHT, while costing nothing in execution speed or code size.

Being in the emulator business, we see just about every toolset used in the industry. Some are frightening. In 1988 a customer called confused about the built-in disassembler. He didn't understand its purpose. After further discussion we discovered that he had never used an assembler or compiler—he handcoded all projects in hex! Variations on this theme are not uncommon. Another customer wrote about 30,000 lines of Z280 code using an 8085 assembler. It's bad enough that the mnemonics were nonstandard, but the code was liberally laced with Z280 instructions entered in hex via "define byte" pseudo-ops. IBM was right with their admonition: THINK.

A sizable project might use 20 or more separate source files with several INCLUDEs and perhaps hundreds of external references between modules. Are the linker and assembler both reasonably fast? Some products are notoriously slow. Can they handle huge files and symbol tables?

MS-DOS host computers have rather limited memory space for storing symbol tables and compiled code, yet many linkers continue to use memory-resident tables. Unless the project is small, demand a virtual linker (one that writes intermediate tables to disk). It's hard enough to shoehorn the code into ROM; you don't want to also wrestle with memory limitations on the development platform.

Some assemblers automatically optimize code generation. In the Intel 80x88 family, both long and short jumps are supported. Most assemblers will compact a long jump to a short one if the destination is close.

We wrote one of the first H16 embedded systems. The assembler and linker had been ported from a VAX platform to the PC and were far from bug free. We lost a lot of time because the assembler tried to optimize all address references—sometimes incorrectly. It would occasionally, with no apparent pattern, insert a short reference where a long one was needed. No real solution existed; we had to wait till the vendor fixed the assembler.

Debugging information (discussed in more detail in the next section) is an important concern. Does the assembler provide a debugging file? If you mix C and assembly, will the assembly be as debuggable as the C? As I write this, two of the most popular 8-bit C compiler/assembler packages specifically do not provide assembly debugging records in the link file.

C COMPILERS

It's hard to beat C for a large embedded project. Everyone admits that it is less efficient than assembly, but C will reduce software NRE costs by a factor of three or more. In almost any product other than one based on a microcontroller (where memory is very limited), the savings in design, coding, and maintenance quickly justify the extra memory expenses. Ask yourself: Where is the crossover between NRE and recurring costs? How many units will I have to sell before the 25% larger ROM costs more than the extra $50, $100, or $150 thousand in NRE?

Moore's law states that every two years the silicon wizards will double the number of transistors on a chip. Therefore memory is cheap and gets ever cheaper as densities increase. Never base NRE versus recurring decisions on today's component prices; plan ahead to when the unit will be in production. Most memory vendors will be happy to give you pricing for one to two years in the future.

On one project we agonized over selection of a very large, fast static RAM. At $180 per chip there was no way to make a profit on our product. A very knowledgeable friend in the memory business assured us that prices would tumble. We took the gamble. Three months after introducing the product the RAMs cost $50 each; a year later they were down to just over $20.

C's rapid proliferation spawned dozens of compilers targeted to embedded systems. Their quality ranges from nearly perfect to downright unusable. Sometimes the compiler's caliber is inversely proportional to the data sheet's gloss and the product's cost. Unfortunately, the best characteristics are apparent in the vendor's advertising, and the worst don't show up until you've used it for some time.

Code size and speed are usually uppermost programming concerns, especially to cynical dyed-in-the-wool assembly programmers being dragged into an HLL for the first time. I hesitate to add to the hype about efficiency except to say that C code is slower and larger than comparable assembly—but not by much. In most cases the difference is only about 25%. Some pathological cases do exist. The 6800 has no real stack, so automatic variables (i.e., ones stored on the runtime stack) must be laboriously manipulated using the CPU's entirely inadequate 8-bit index register. In this sort of situation perhaps it makes sense to adapt to the processor's architecture and use static variables everywhere. At the other end of the spectrum, the 68000 is a C programmer's dream platform, since stack relative addressing is fast and easy.

Any machine translator works best for target CPUs with lots of resources. On the 80x88, 68000, and similar machines compilers do a remarkable job. The 6800 and 8051 families force convoluted approaches to C data handling, resulting in much less efficiency. Evaluate your application. How much speed is really needed? You can always code critical subroutines in assembly. How much ROM will the code require? Buy a compiler, write some code, and measure its performance.

All compilers will perform some amount of optimization to minimize code size or increase speed. Some are truly remarkable, removing constant expressions from loops and the like. This may not be a virtue; extensive optimization makes the code impossible to debug. No one yet knows how to tie optimized code to a debugger. All meaningful references between the object code and the original source lines are lost when the compiler moves source around, so all debugger vendors insist that you debug with optimizations turned off. There is an easy solution: write good code! Don't leave a constant assignment inside a loop where it will be executed thousands or millions of times. Don't ask the compiler to convert needlessly between floating point and integer. Do a little precompiling in your head.

Compilers designed for nonembedded programming usually are very poor at dividing memory into separate RAM and ROM sections. They invariably assume that the address space is all RAM. Embedded programs reside in ROM and the data is stored in a remote RAM area, so the ability to specify separate starting addresses for code and data is crucial. But this is far from enough—the ideal compiler will let you divide your code and data even further. Suppose the target system sports memory-mapped I/O; it's essential that these I/O ports, although looking like RAM variables to the compiler, be assigned to the proper absolute addresses. The compiler/linker must thus support segments for variables and ports, each of which is set to different absolute addresses.

The code area is often divided into several segments. Some processors, like the 80x88 family, power up to an address in high memory. You may need code at the end just for the reset jump. Interrupt vectors are stored at fixed locations on all CPUs; the compiler/linker must let you define these at absolute addresses distinct from the rest of the code.

How fast does the compiler translate a program? Be sure to look at link speeds as well, since most C programs consist of lots of little modules. Turbo C's blazing compilations put cross compilers to shame. In our evaluations we measured compile/link times for a 1000-line program, ranging from Turbo's few seconds to over 20 minutes (on the most expensive compiler tested). Expect to use your tools a lot. Demand reasonable translation times.

Many cross compilers are not virtual, incorrectly assuming the "huge" address space of the host development system will be adequate. On a PC much of 640k address space is taken up with the compiler itself, DOS, network drivers, and TSRs. Many compilers are limited to very small source programs. Virtual products, which write intermediate tables to disk, support programs of any size.

Now that an ANSI standard finally exists for the C language, how important is it that the compiler conforms to this specification? If the product will be reused many times by other engineering groups, portability is vital. There is a lot to be said for using at least a close facsimile of the ANSI standard so the product can survive a midstream compiler change. In any event, be sure that the compiler supports function prototyping. It's a simple way of automatically checking parameter lists and will eliminate many hours of debugging.

If the system uses C-coded multitasking or interrupt handlers, be sure that the library is reentrant. Some aren't. Manuals rarely allude to reentrancy. Try compiling a tiny "do nothing" program and measure RAM use. Then add library calls without adding variables. Be suspicious if more RAM is linked in.

On the subject of libraries, does the compiler include all of the functions you'll need? While many embedded systems make no runtime calls, others depend on extensive library support. Evaluate your requirements.

Will you need special CPU resources? Does the compiler support these? Most compiler companies use a common parser and simply re-place code generation modules when building variants for different processors. Therefore, register variables, for example, may not really use registers.

A few compilers support memory management units. If your design requires extended memory that can be accessed only via an MMU, be sure that the compiler gives you some sort of MMU control. Some com-pilers will even automatically remap it and insert C functions into in-dividual maps. Chapter 6 contains more information about memory management with compilers and assemblers.

Is the compiler compatible with the assembler? Compiled C code must be combined with assembled files via a common linker. Almost every linker takes a different object file format, essentially guaranteeing problems in combining tools from different vendors. In some cases the tools from a single vendor are incompatible. This problem underscores the importance of insuring that the assembler can handle the scope of your project; don't expect to work around a weak assembler by substi-tuting one from another software house.

Don't forget that once the code is written you'll have to debug it. Plan to use a source-level debugger (SLD). Be sure that the compiler is compatible with the debugger. Prior to the widespread use of C, it was common to mix and match tools; the assembler, linker, and debugger could all come from different vendors yet work together with a minimum of trouble. The symbol and hex files might have needed a trivial amount of conversion to get the tools to work well together, but that was expected and was really not a lot of trouble. The biggest problem lay in getting symbol file documentation from the vendors.

Block-structured languages like C have changed all of this. Tools are sometimes like the construction workers on the Tower of Babel. Few are now really compatible with one another.

Source-level C debugging requires a tremendous amount of infor-mation about the program's organization. C is not just an extension of assembly; line number records and symbol addresses, while sufficient for programs created with an assembler, are only a fraction of what is needed for C. Usually, most of the difficulty lies with data representa-tions. Is a variable local to one function? How is its scope defined in the debug file? Is it a static that has an absolute memory address or, as for an automatic type, is it assigned as an offset from the stack? Is it a register variable? All of these questions get even more complicated if the variable is an array or structure.

Unfortunately, many compilers produce little or no debug information, rendering them all but useless in an embedded environment where troubleshooting by adding print statements just doesn't work.

The 8-bit arena is especially chaotic. While a number of standards for expressing source debug information have been proposed (such as IEEE-695 and COFF), few languages produce these; those that do often add their own extensions. The quality of information varies widely and changes almost daily as the vendors scramble to get their products into better competitive positions. The files are far more complex than a simple symbol file, so generating conversion utilities is a difficult and time-consuming process. SLD vendors must think long and hard before supporting a particular format.

The moral of the story is to ask hard questions from each of your development tool vendors. Make no assumptions about compatibility. Once you have a text file of C code, it must be compiled, linked, perhaps located, and debugged through an SLD and emulator. Will each of these tools work together? Will you get full source debug functionality, like local variables, scope tracking, and C line-number support, or will some important feature be compromised?

Finally, try to insure that the compiler is reliable. Talk to people who have successfully completed sizable embedded projects with the tool. How often did the compiler crash, miscompile, or unexpectedly cost engineering time?

A friend told of a large embedded programming job he was involved in during 1989 and 1990. The Navy mandated the use of the obscure language CMS2. At great expense my friend's company acquired a DOD approved VAX cross compiler that was so unreliable they were forced to write code in small sections, compile it,

Code size
Code speed
Compile and link times
Reasonably standard dialect
Memory segmentation
Virtual compile and link
Reentrant libraries
Library completeness
CPU specific features
MMU support
Object file compatibility
Debug information
Reliability

Figure 2.2   Compiler selection factors.

and examine all of the compiler's assembly output. If the translation was obviously wrong, the programmers made a more or less random source change and tried again. Your tax dollars at work.

A lot of factors go into compiler selection (see Fig. 2.2). When you finally make a decision, buy the product and immediately run tests to evaluate the product's usefulness. A few days of testing can reveal many fatal flaws. Return it if it is unacceptable—reputable companies will always take a return if made within the first week or two.

Transitioning to ROM

"Putting it all together" to make a working system is a lot harder with an embedded program than with conventional mainframe and PC-hosted code. You can't rely on an intelligent linker and loader to magically bring a compiled program into play. ROMed code requires a different mindset and different programming procedures. For example, self-modifying code just won't work in ROM.

As discussed earlier, code and data must be carefully separated; the program sections are relocated at absolute addresses that are a function of the hardware design. Addresses can range from the mundane to the bizarre; in some systems ROM and RAM chips alternate throughout the address space. The traditional Von Neumann architecture is violated by numerous systems; it's not uncommon to find code and data sharing the same logical addresses, the distinction being drawn by hardware that differentiates the type of access being made.

All embedded systems require at least three memory segments: data, code, and vectors. A typical configuration places interrupt vectors (and sometimes the power-up jump) at or near location 0. Code and data areas follow in some order and are usually not contiguous. Memory-

high   Memory-mapped I/O
        (unassigned address space)
        RAM
        (unassigned address space)
        Code
        Interrupt vectors
0000   Power-up jump to code (sometimes in high memory)

Figure 2.3   Typical memory map.

mapped I/O, if used, is more often than not located at a very high address (see Fig. 2.3).

How will you insert fixed address items like the power-up jump and interrupt vectors? If your linker doesn't support multiple segments, you might have to patch these every time you burn a ROM or every time you download the code to an emulator. Sometimes you can cobble up a batch file to automate the process or build a separate load module of absolute items then burn or download both modules with each iteration. Regardless, *something* will have to be absolute to facilitate building links between both load modules.

The first address in the code module can be a jump to the start of the code followed by jumps to each interrupt service routine. The jumps are fixed in size and can be declared sacred; you make the rule that none can be inserted or deleted. Although the start addresses of the routines they reference will change, the start of the jumps will not. This approach is a good idea in any event. Fixed addresses that point to important routines can be useful when in the field without your development tools. The program has its own built-in "symbol table" (if the order of jumps is documented). Regardless of version, it is then possible to look at these jumps and find subroutines. (See Fig. 2.4.)

Somehow the compiled code must eventually be burned into PROMs or at least downloaded to an emulator for test. Most linkers generate some sort of absolute or pseudoabsolute binary format accepted by few emulators and PROM programmers. If a straight binary image of the code is generated, as is the case with most 8-bit linkers, then the program in Fig. 2.5 will convert the binary output file to Intel hex, a de facto standard for many tools.

The 80x88 compilers and linkers usually generate .EXE files, which contain each segment's code origined at 0. The MS-DOS loader resolves

```
Module 1:   Assembled at an absolute address
                    JMP    start
                    JMP    vector 1
                    JMP    vector 2
                    etc.
        Module 2:   Relative address
            start:  code
           vector:  code
           vector:  code
```

Figure 2.4   Where needed, assemble one module with jumps at an absolute address.

```
#include "stdio.h"
#include "ctype.h"
#define TRUE 1
#define FALSE 0
main
() {
  char infile[13],evenfile[13],oddfile[13];
  int index,even_index,odd_index,length,value;
  int even_checksum,odd_checksum,status,split;
  int line_cnt,even_line[0x20],odd_line[0x20];
  int hex_size,done;
  FILE *in_fp,*even_fp,*odd_fp;

  printf("\n\nThis program converts a binary .COM file into a standard");
  printf("\nhex format file. If desired, two hex files will be produced");
  printf("\n(even and odd files) for use in 16 bit applications.");
  printf("\n\nSpecify the input file name without an extension. This");
  printf("\nprogram assumes the file was created with the extension
.COM.");
  printf("\nIt will produce a file with the same name, but the
extension");
  printf("\n.HEX. If even and odd files are produced, the extensions
will");
  printf("\nbe .EVN and .ODD.");
  printf("\n\n");
  printf("Input filename? : ");
  scanf("%s",infile);

  for (index=0; isalpha(infile[index])
    || isdigit(infile[index]); index++ {
    if (islower(infile[index]))
      infile[index] =infile[index] - 0x20;
    evenfile[index] =oddfile[index] =infile[index];
    }

  infile[index] =evenfile[index] =oddfile[index] =NULL;

  strcat(infile,".COM");
  in_fp = fopen(infile,"rb");
  if ( in_fp == NULL ) {
    printf("Could not open %s\n",infile);
    return;
    }

  printf("Separate into even and odd files? ⟨Y or N⟩ : ");
  value = getch ();
  if (value == 'Y' || value == 'y') {
```

Figure 2.5 Hex build code. (*Figure continues.*)

```
      printf("Yes\n");
      split = TRUE;
      }
  else {
    printf("No\n");
    split = FALSE;
    }

  if (! split)
    strcat(evenfile,".HEX");
  else {
    strcat(evenfile,".EVN");
    strcat(oddfile,".ODD");
    }

  even_fp = fopen(evenfile,"w");
  if ( even_fp == NULL ) {
    printf("Could not open %s\n",evenfile);
    return;
    }

  if (split) {
    odd_fp = fopen(oddfile,"w");
    if ( odd_fp == NULL ) {
      printf("Could not open %s\n",oddfile);
      return;
      }
    }

  printf("Starting offset in input file       (HEX) : ");
  scanf ("%x",&index);
  printf("Starting offset of hexfile          (HEX) : ");
  scanf ("%x",&even_index);

  if (split) odd_index = even_index;

  hex_size = 0;
  done = FALSE;

  do {

    for (line_cnt=0 ; line_cnt < 0x10 ; line_cnt ++) {
      if ((value = getc(in_fp)) == EOF) {
        done = TRUE;
            break;
            }
```

Figure 2.5   (Continued)

```
        even_line[line_cnt]  = value;

        if (split) {
          if ((value = getc (in_fp)) = = EOF) {
            odd_line[line_cnt++]  = 0xFF;
            done = TRUE;
            break;
            }
          }
        odd_line[line_cnt]  = value;
        }

      even_checksum = line_cnt;
      even_checksum += 0xFF & (even_index )) 8);
      even_checksum += 0xFF & even_index;

      if (split) odd_checksum = even_checksum;

      fprintf (even_fp. ":%02X%04X00",line_cnt.even_index);
      if (split) fprintf (odd_fp. ":%02X%04X00",line_cnt.odd_index);

      for (index = 0 ; index ( line_cnt ; index ++) {
        fprintf (even_fp, "%02X", even_line[index]);
        even_checksum += even_line[index];
        if (split) {
          fprintf (odd_fp, "%02X", odd_line[index]);
          odd_checksum += odd_line[index];
          }
        }
      fprintf (even_fp."%02X\n", 0XFF & (0X100 - even_checksum));
      if (split)     fprintf (odd_fp,"%02X\n", 0XFF & (0X100 - odd_
      checksum));

      hex_size += line_cnt;
      even_index += line_cnt;
      if (split) odd_index += line_cnt;
      {
while (!done);
fprintf (even_fp,":0000000000\n");
if (split) fprintf (odd_fp,":0000000000\n");

if (split)
      {
        printf("\n\nEven file generated: ");
        printf("%s",evenfile."\n");
        printf("\nOdd file generated:   ");
```

Figure 2.5 (Continued)

```
printf("%s",oddfile,"\n");
        }
        else
        {
        printf("\n\nHex file generated:  ");
        printf("%s",evenfile,"\n");
        }
}
```

Figure 2.5 (Continued)

the segment start addresses and intersegment references where needed. The services of the loader are not available in an embedded system, but that is no reason to eschew the high-quality, low-cost compilers from Microsoft, Borland, and others. Third party LOCATE utilities will reformat the .EXE file to an extended OMF format (another de facto standard) in which the code is absolute.

Debugging C code requires a tremendous amount of information about the program's structure. The OMF format produced by a LOCATE includes records defining virtually everything one could wish to know about the program. Many source-level debuggers will accept the OMF format.

The LOCATEs also assist with the start-up code. This is somewhat different in an embedded system than in the normal distribution version of the compiler, since MS-DOS is not available to support program initialization.

Sixteen-bit systems still depend on 8-bit-wide ROMs that must be programmed a byte at a time. If you think of the program consisting of a number of sequential bytes, then all of the even bytes (those with address bit 0 = 0) go into one ROM, while the odd (A0 = 1) ones fit into the other. Some PROM programmers automatically split an Intel hex file into even and odd groups, burning the ROM pairs separately. The program in Figure 2.5 will split a hex file.

Unlike conventional computers that load programs into a safe initialized environment, the embedded system starts from a cold boot with all of the hardware in random states. Carefully write the code to power up in a safe and meaningful way. (See Fig. 2.6.)

Most embedded programs start with a load of the stack pointer—*before* any pushes, pops, or subroutine calls. It's a good idea to preface even this step with a disable interrupt instruction. Sure, all computers do a hardware disable on reset. But during debug you'll often skip the reset step, restarting the code from the reset vector via an emulator

Disable interrupts
Load of stack pointer
Disable critical hardware
Hardware initializations
Variable initializations
Vector initializations (if in RAM)
Multiprocessor synchronization (if any)
Enable interrupts
⟨Main routine⟩

Figure 2.6 Typical start-up sequence.

"Go" command. A disable interrupt instruction will prevent previously enabled interrupts from taking effect before the code is completely reinitialized. Similarly, always explicitly load the registers inside the peripheral chips. Counting on a default reset value will theoretically work but will make debugging much more tedious.

Some embedded systems control critical or dangerous hardware. Obviously, in a CAT scanner the first thing the code should do is disable the radiation source! We designed a device that used computer-controlled motors driving a 7-ton instrument package on railroad tracks. Forgetting to set the drive motors to "all stop" when power was applied could have been very expensive. While wringing out the code, extra limit switches were installed as well as massive welded stops. Thank God.

The PC's dynamic RAMs are refreshed by a DMA controller. RAM just doesn't function until the computer executes a dozen or so instructions to start the DMA logic. Pushes, pops, calls, and returns won't work since the stack is in RAM. This sort of situation is really not that uncommon. Sometimes the culprit is memory-management logic, which might have to be initialized to access RAM or other parts of the program. Other times a "phantom" ROM occupies the entire address space until it disables itself. As always, embedded programmers can never stray far from the hardware.

Once RAM is enabled other hardware can be programmed. In these days of complex peripherals this is no easy task. A floppy disk controller can require quite a few dozen setup parameters. Some programmable logic devices can be completely reconfigured on the fly and so resemble software more than hardware. These devices might need initialization via a serial link or some other means.

CHAPTER 3

Elegant Structures

The perfection of mathematical beauty is such that whatsoever is most beautiful and regular is also found to be most useful and excellent.—Sir D'Arcy Wentworth Thompson

Finally, after twenty years of passionate pleas from structured programming advocates, most programmers resist the temptation to start coding as soon as a rough specification is available. Programming has evolved from almost a cult phenomenon populated by the twinkie-and-pizza crowd to a professional environment with well-tried methods and techniques. Only the twinkies and pizza remain constant.

Long before the coding begins some sort of specification must be worked out along with a reasonable design to meet that spec. On the very large projects typical of those managed by the Department of Defense, the specification, design, and coding are usually handled by different people. However, it's surprising just how many embedded systems are designed by tiny groups. Often no formal specifications exist. The design team blocks out critical parameters and starts work. This approach does in fact work, but only for small groups and projects of limited size.

Coming up with a written or verbal specification requires above all an ability to listen. What is the system supposed to do? Who will be using it? No specification can be complete or can itemize every possible combination of inputs and outputs; if it were, that spec would be just as complex as the software. It's important that those involved in the design and coding understand the problem being solved in its entirety so they can make the thousands of little decisions needed to write code in a manner consistent with the system's intended use.

Specification is the bane of large projects. No one knows how to completely describe a complex system's behavior. Problems arise during development because no one is smart enough to foresee all possible consequences of their decisions when doing a top-down design of a million or more lines of code. Make sure those doing the coding understand the goals!

Listening, whether to a customer, to a specifications committee, or to management, is a skill worth developing. It's particularly hard for technology people to listen carefully and effectively to those not immersed in the computer business; we tend to want to put all of their needs into the context of the computer rather than the opposite. This is the problem with expert systems. How do you extract everything there is to know about designing kitchen cabinets from a nontechnical person who doesn't understand algorithmic processes? Yet this sort of listening will become ever more necessary as we automate more of the work of other industries.

While consulting for a large corporation some years back, I spent some time traveling with an engineer-turned-salesman. He had failed at a number of enterprises and now worked as a sort of pathetic high-tech Willy Loman, peddling engineering services to the government. It quickly became apparent that he just could not listen. When a potential customer began describing a need, my salesman friend immediately interrupted and started estimating memory needs, what sort of computer to use, etc. By never sitting still long enough to hear the customer out, he never understood the customer's problems.

Remember that customers generally do know what they want, all evidence to the contrary notwithstanding. They may have trouble expressing it; they may be completely unfocussed. It's our duty during the specification phase to somehow get a complete picture of what we are supposed to build.

Every government project seems to take life as a brilliant idea, which is then circulated to a cast of thousands. Everyone throws in yet another feature until the entire concept becomes a hopeless quagmire long before a contract is let. Projects in industry usually fare better, as the pressure to get a sellable product out the door is the prime concern. It seems that despite the efforts of an army of structured programming advocates and legions of CASE vendors, most non-DOD embedded code takes life more or less incrementally. In recent years this has become codified in the industry's new infatuation with rapid prototyping and "time to market."

Studies indicate that overspending your R&D budget by 100% typically affects the company's bottom line by a paltry 3 to 5% over the long run, but being only 6 months late on delivery can reduce market share by 30%. Certainly, the pressure is on to start coding immediately.

How will you structure the program? When designing a mainframe-based accounting system this is a valid question. Not so in the embedded world. A better question, to be addressed by the hardware and software team working together, is "how will we structure the system?"

The software cannot stand alone in any embedded system. It is almost a component, much like the microprocessor and peripherals. All of the components work together to accomplish a certain task. In these days of increasing specialization it is more and more common to see hardware and software people go about their work separately. This invariably results in a more complex product that is costly to produce.

It's instructive to reverse-engineer a variety of embedded products. Some accomplish their tasks with a minimum of hardware, with clever code supplanting dozens or hundreds of chips. Others look like they were designed by automatons. Board after board is packed into a standard card cage. While in many cases this is necessary due to the system's complexity, far too often it comes about from lazy design.

The microprocessor was invented by Intel in response to a need by Busicom for a line of calculators. It was a classic case of elegant design. Busicom, a Japanese trading company, asked Intel's designers for a custom set of 12 chips to implement a simple calculator. Intel realized they could cut the number of chips down to four and come up with a universal chip set by designing a general-purpose computer IC. Their vision transcended the customer specification; they gave the customer a much better solution by fusing software into the design.

Embedded systems are unique in their tight integration between iron and code. Strive for appropriate designs. If you are designing a simple controller that will be produced in volume, look for ways to replace hardware with the code. Software costs nothing in volume. No one solution is correct for all applications, so as designers we should always try to think broadly and creatively. Some examples follow.

A lot of embedded systems use small keypads to accept operator commands. Most are arranged as a matrix, say 16 keys in a 4×4 array. Rather than bring 16 separate sets or wires (one per key) into the computer, most use a scanning technique. The keys are wired in a 4×4 matrix, with four wires coming out orthogonally to four on the other axis. A keypad chip repeatedly drives each of four of the lines low and then looks for a closure at the other four. It sends a 4-bit code to the computer. Sometimes you can eliminate the keypad chip altogether. Have an interrupt service routine in the computer send out a 4-bit scan code and let the software read the output. More complex software saves a chip; in high-volume applications this can be an important cost savings.

Other sorts of scanning might be appropriate for software control. An interrupt service routine can update multiplexed LED or LCD displays. (I saw one application where the refresh signal to a dynamic RAM array was generated completely under control of the program, a neat trick since the memories must be updated every 2 msec to keep their data intact.)

A simple controller is the epitome of elegant embedded design. Computerless circuits require some sort of complicated state machine to sequence a number of wires. With a processor, the software assumes all of the sequencing details.

Copper is an expensive and increasingly rare natural resource. Frequently we have to transmit data over long distances, from one end of a factory to another. For example, a remote position encoder might generate 12 bits of data. A cost analysis will show that transmitting the signals over 12 pairs of wire (the conventional approach) is much more expensive than adding a simple computer to multiplex the data onto a single optical fiber and then using another computer at the receiving end to demultiplex it back to parallel.

Computerization can be taken to extremes. On a scanning monochrometer project one engineer wanted to bring a switch into the computer. The software was to detect a closure and then actuate an output bit. Why not just run the switch to the output, skipping the computer altogether?

In no other area of the software engineer's art are so many choices available. The range is as wide as your imagination. The following few pages briefly discuss the software issues around several major structural approaches.

Designs with One CPU

Most simple systems use a single processor running one main loop repeatedly. External inputs request some activity; the code branches off to service each request and then returns to the main loop. This structure is commonly referred to as "sequential organization," a name that reflects the software's flow of control.

In real life only rarely do we see embedded systems not dependent on one or more interrupt sources for sequencing activities. (Interrupts are discussed in greater detail in Chapter 8.) The advantage of interrupt-driven I/O is that it eliminates tedious polling of possibly lots of inputs and generally results in faster response to an external event. While any interrupt will asyncronously affect the program's flow of control, in general they are used just to service hardware events.

Essentially all software theory revolves around single processor architectures. As we'll see, embedded systems are particularly well adapted for using more than one computer. Still, even in situations where the work load is spread between compute units, within any one computer the organization is sequential.

Only the simplest embedded systems use a main loop that polls

I/O, looking for a command. Most employ some sort of real-time operating system (RTOS) to manage many competing activities more or less simultaneously. See Chapter 9 for a complete discussion of RTOSs.

One of the most common mistakes in the embedded world is to try and make do with a big loop. After all, using an RTOS increases the complexity of writing and debugging the code; most of us want to avoid that complexity, if at all possible. Still, it's surprising just how many systems wind up late in the game with some sort of RTOS shoehorned in. It's almost impossible to rework old code to add an operating system, so carefully analyze your needs long before starting development to see if, in the long run, an RTOS makes sense.

Whether or not an RTOS is used, be sure to isolate complex I/O services by some sort of BIOS (basic input/output system). One of the easiest ways to do this is by programming in a high-level language. For example, printing formatted floating-point numbers from assembly language is a nightmare. Formatted output is built into C.

All of us succumb to the temptation to issue IN and OUT statements in the mainline code to get to simple bits. Resist the siren call of lazy coding! Where it might not make sense to write a conventional I/O subroutine, at the very least use a well-documented macro. Give the software a level of hardware abstraction, so changes won't necessitate complete recoding.

State Machines

A variation on a sequential system is the so-called state machine. A state machine is a system whose next output is simply a function of its current condition (state) and its inputs. While this surely describes most conventional software, the state machine concept is a powerful abstraction that can greatly improve the structure of some code.

Any state machine has n possible states and x possible inputs. The next state is determined solely by its current state and inputs. In effect, a state machine is a system that works only with the present; past operations bear no impact on its decision-making process.

State machines are commonly represented by graphs showing the inputs and state transitions, such as shown in Fig. 3.1. In this picture the four states (S1 to S4) are shown as circles, with curved lines indicating transitions between them. For the system to go from S1 to S3, for example, an input I2 must occur. No other condition will get the system to S3. It remains in S3 until input I4 or I2 is detected, at which point the system flips to state S4.

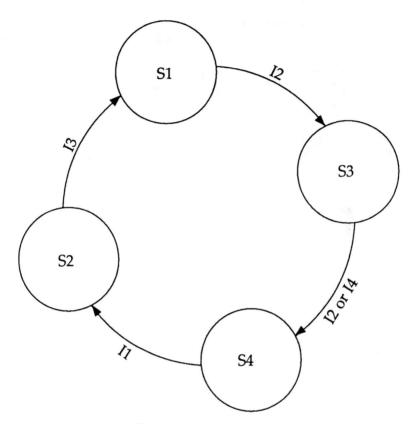

Figure 3.1 Elegant structures.

A more concrete application demonstrates a state machine in action. Fig. 3.2 is a state transition diagram of a simple microwave oven, the ubiquitous example of microprocessor technology in the home. To the chef (and to the software, the point of the exercise), the oven is always latched into one of these states until some action occurs. The program's flow of control is regulated by these actions.

Most of the time the oven rests in state S1, waiting for a keypad command. Follow the curved arrows: pressing the SET COOKING TIME key drives the oven into state S5, which acquires melt-to-scorch times from our high-tech gourmet. Pressing ENTER returns the microwave to S1. No other inputs or outputs will drive the oven through state S5, a fact illustrated very clearly in the diagram.

Of course, the purpose of the appliance is to cook dinner. If, and

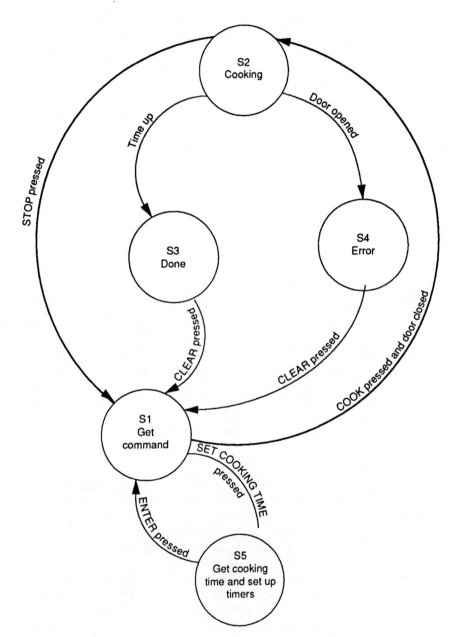

Figure 3.2 State diagram of a microwave oven.

only if, the user presses COOK with the door closed (for safety's sake) will the magnetron start spewing RF radiation throughout the oven. In this simple unit the meal will continue to cook until one of three events happens: the baking time elapses, the STOP button is pressed, or a chef who places far too much faith in the efficacy of microswitches opens the door. Each path is shown in the diagram.

State diagrams clearly show transitions between operating modes. While probably useless in conventional mainframe programming, they form a concise diagram of the operation of real-time systems. But a state diagram is far more than a pretty picture. If you can reduce a system to a number of latched states with clearly defined transitions, then consider coding the software as a state machine to simplify and speed its development.

How should we implement the oven? Again, consider Fig. 3.2. Each state is just a trivial subroutine. The transitions are equally simple— indeed, so simple that one could easily write the program as a jumble of calls and conditional comparisons. This conventional approach means that the system's structure is spread throughout the whole program, making changes and maintenance difficult.

A state machine, on the other hand, is completely described in a table of states and their transitions. An interpreter sequences between states using the table entries as rules. Tables remove the program's organization from thousands of obscure lines of C or assembly and centralizes it in one easily understood spot.

Let's organize the microwave oven into a state table. Suppose each entry corresponds to the condition needed to start a particular state and has the following elements:

Current state
Next state
Inputs needed to transition to the next state
Name of subroutine to call to start the state

Then, the oven is completely described by

S1, S5, cook time key, get__time
S1, S2, cook key AND door closed, start__cooking
S2, S4, door opened, show__error
S2, S3, time up, show__done
S2, S1, stop key, get__command
S3, S1, clear key, get__command
S4, S1, clear key, get__command

Note that the table concisely and clearly describes every possible transition. The rest of the code consists of the subroutines listed in the table, plus the interpreter.

The interpreter is like a musical conductor, leading the action with the table as its score. Its general form is

> Start at top of table.
> Compare **current___state** to the present state field in
> table.
> If same, compare inputs to table input values.
> > If same, set **current___state** = next state from table.
> > If same, invoke routine in table.
> Otherwise, check next table entry. Continue looping through table
> > until a condition is satisfied.

One critical variable is **current___state**, which maintains the name of the state the system is currently operating in.

As we all know, even the best program can crumble once users or management finally gets their anxious hands on it. "But I really wanted it this way" is the plaint of those not tasked with making things work. Sometimes the users really don't know what they want until they start using the product. Recoding (or worse, hasty patching) to implement a lot of changes is a nightmare. Since a state machine's operation is contained in a table of <next state> and <inputs to get there>, many truly fundamental modifications will just require shuffling table entries.

Assembly programmers should define the table using a specially constructed macro. Be sure to assign reasonable, readable state names and input values so you'll be able to understand the table at a glance. C programmers can use pointers to functions and structure definitions.

One stumbling block is the handling of inputs. Most real embedded systems use more than a few inputs; even the smallest will usually have at least two or three ports. Write an interpreter that reads each port and saves the data. Then set the I/O up as bit fields and compare against the bit data. For example, suppose two ports contain 16 switch values. If bit 0 is switch 0, and bit 1 switch 1, etc., then define a 16-bit word in the table, containing 1 bit per switch. The interpreter will read two 8-bit ports and compress the results into a single word. Define switch settings using mnemonics as follows:

```
switch0        equ        0000000000000001b
switch1        equ        0000000000000010b
switch2        equ        0000000000000100b
```

```
switch3        equ       0000000000001000b
etc.
```

Now the input section of the table is just the switch name.

Sometimes state transitions might be predicated on a number of switch settings. Combine them with the logical OR operator (or even with an arithmetic plus) as follows:

```
switch0 + switch11 + switch14
```

This is a case where close cooperation between hardware and software engineers will really pay off. Minimize the number of ports used; avoid unused port bits.

Many more exotic schemes are feasible. You could combine AND/OR/NOT conditions to reduce the table's size. The interpreter will be more complicated, but the ease of coding and maintenance will most likely justify some increased intricacy.

Complex I/O is a bit harder to support with a state machine but is still usually worth the trouble. How can the interpreter read from, say, an IEEE-488 port? One solution is to build some of the I/O functions into the interpreter, making it call routines to determine all values before searching the table. Another is to employ a more object-oriented approach. Instead of listing an input in the table, list the name of the function that reads it and the value needed to satisfy the comparison. In C++ this is truly elegant.

A common problem in embedded controllers is sequentially activating various processes based solely on elapsed time. (In the days before microprocessors, most industrial controllers were sequenced by rotating cams that activated switches to turn on pumps, motors, and the like at predefined intervals.) Replace the state table's input field with an elapsed time field and control all sequencing based on a timer.

Distributed Processing

Microprocessors killed the old paradigm of a computer as an expensive centralized processing center. As embedded systems architects, we can put processing power wherever it is needed, in whatever quantity is appropriate for the task at hand. This new dynamic of the industry will reshape the design of our software.

This technology has changed the economics of design. Silicon is a lot cheaper than copper. Multiconductor copper wire (especially armored for factory environments) can cost over a dollar a foot. Transmitting data over long distances on bundles of wire is almost always much more expensive than multiplexing the same data onto a single wire or fiber. The savings in copper alone will justify a one-chip micro that converts parallel signals to one serial channel. Even more money is saved by connecting all of the remote devices to the same serial cable, eliminating the headache of running a separate wire from each sensor all the way back to the central computer.

In automating one large factory we installed encoders in a dozen locations over a half-million-square-foot building. We felt the proper engineering solution was to digitize each encoder's 12 bits and transmit the data serially over an optical fiber, greatly reducing costs. Even better, the fiber would be immune from astronomical switching transients caused by the house-sized motors that ran the plant. The fiber idea was vetoed in favor of huge wire bundles. Management believed that union electricians would refuse to pull fiber optics cable, because the union had never worked with fiber and was generally resistant to change. Fear of the unknown is a terrible thing.

Computers are cheaper than wire; we can take advantage of this truism to reduce costs and improve reliability. Electronics people are often passionate about distributing computers. Putting just enough processor power exactly where it is needed is one of the philosophical joys of this business. Refer to George Gilder's very readable *Microcosm* (see the Bibliography) for a vision of where distributed processing is headed.

Long before the end of this decade most cars will be networks of dozens of CPUs. Every simple function will be assigned its own processor. The driving force behind this is not so much to improve performance or to add features but simply to save the weight of the wiring! A serial communication link uses one pair of wires to replace the rat's nest of cabling that pervades most automobiles.

Another application is in robot joints. Rather than bring dozens of motor control wires back from each joint, why not place a small processor at an arm's wrist, elbow, and each of the fingers? Then upload high-level commands in serial and let the local CPUs handle the details of motion control.

Distributed processing also fulfills an important need in a software industry swamped with complexity. It simplifies every element of the code. The main program never has to worry about I/O events; external processors take care of the details and pass completion messages in response to high-level commands. Each distributed program is responsible for its one simple activity. The potential for complex interactions and bugs is reduced by the narrow bandwidth (i.e., simple interface) between processors. Perhaps in the future we will view external I/O controllers in the same light C+ + views objects—certainly the benefits are similar.

Consider a PC's keyboard. Instead of bringing separate wires from each key to the computer's main CPU, a microcontroller takes care of all key scanning, compressing the maze of possibilities to a simple 8-bit message when a key is hit. The message is transmitted in serial, reducing wiring problems, even though the transmission distance is only a few feet. The PC's software never scans keys, never worries about switch bounce and the like. One cheap microprocessor frees millions of PC programmers from the keyboard details. This is an embedded system in the best tradition.

While large-system architects fret about partitioning huge mono-lithic programs into separate compute streams so they can allocate the processes to parallel processors, in the embedded world the picture is a lot clearer. Usually we break a system into two or more processors wherever data must be transmitted or where a complex I/O device requires service. During system design, look for complexity in your I/O. Allocate a microcontroller to any nontrivial I/O task.

Obviously, this is simply not possible in extremely cost-sensitive applications, where data is transmitted only very short distances. Still, it is surprising just how cheap a microcontroller is and just how much easier it can make writing the mainstream code.

The microprocessor industry is currently pushing forward on two fronts. Ultrahigh-performance RISC, CISC, and DSP processors wield millions of MIPs, push the technology hard, and get all of the glory. An even bigger effort in low-capability 8- and 16-bit microcontrollers is integrating ever more capability onto a single chip, driving the cost of simple embedded systems closer and closer to zero.

Any power programmer would scoff at the crude instruction sets and slow clock rates of the Z8 or 8751, but both chips offer a mature line of small CPUs, well supported by a broad base of tools, that is ideal for distributing compute power in controller environments. Both families offer parts that are packaged in tiny 18- or 24-pin chips. Think of it—a complete dime-sized computer that costs only a few bucks! These chips (and others like them) include RAM, ROM, I/O, and CPU all in one package. In any situation where signals are to be transferred over more than a few meters, it probably makes sense to compress several parallel digital signals onto a single wire or fiber, using one of these little controllers to multiplex and demultiplex the data.

"Little controllers" will be far more influential in the future than big number crunchers. Already there is talk of integrating a CPU in every switch in the home to reduce wiring, of removing 25,000 miles of wire from each 747 using a truckload of cheap CPUs, and the like.

Originally, microcontrollers were shunned in low-volume applications because their on-board ROM required mask programming. The silicon vendor had to make a special mask containing a metalization layer specifying your code. Usually a minimum purchase was 5000 programmed CPUs, a ridiculous number when so many systems are produced in quantities of tens or hundreds. (Can you imagine the cost of correcting a program bug?) Now more and more microcontrollers are available with EPROM. It is cost effective to make a system even in single lots with this technology, and bugs can be easily corrected by erasing the parts with ultraviolet light.

Still, EPROM is only a partial solution. Erasable devices need a quartz window whose temperature coefficient is compatible only with a ceramic package. They will forever be more expensive than the cheap plastic parts that the industry thrives on. Some vendors address this by selling two versions of their devices. An expensive windowed package is ideal for prototyping or small production runs where code changes are likely. An OTP (one-time programmable) part can be used in volume production. OTP units have the same silicon die used in the EPROM version but are packaged in plastic without a window. You program them just like an EPROM, but you can never erase them.

Thus, microcontrollers now come in so many configurations that one is almost certainly ideal for any application and any production level. Very cheap mask-programmed units still serve high-volume users, OTP takes care of midrange production levels, and the EPROM versions are ideal for prototype systems. Given that a cheap microcontroller will serve as part of a distributed processing network, just how should one employ these CPUs? There are an infinite number of possibilities, limited only by the designer's imagination.

In a data acquisition environment it's only natural to place CPUs at each collection or distribution node. Always remember that copper is an expensive resource that is getting ever scarcer; try to replace multiple conductors with satellite processors that multiplex data over a single wire or optical fiber.

Most remote collection systems use microcontrollers with their code irrevocably burned into the on-board ROM. An interesting option, offering more generic control capability, is to burn only a boot loader into the processor's ROM. Let the system load its operating code over the communications link, so that software changes are easier and less expensive to implement. Sometimes where many different devices are handled by different CPUs, one microcontroller board will serve for the entire system. Perhaps each one has different code downloaded to it, but a huge savings in production costs will be realized by having a single type of computer board. Harvard architectures like the 8051 have separated code and data spaces, making this impossible.

Consider using standard communications links rather than rolling your own. Special high-integration serial chips make implementing ARCNET and other protocols quite inexpensive.

Another option for very cost-sensitive applications is Signetic's I^2 C bus, a serial protocol that ties any number of peripherals together with only two wires. One carries a clock signal that sequences the timing of bits on the other (data) line. The clock indicates when each data bit is stable and is used to signal special conditions like data start and stop. This contrasts with RS-232 and other common data transmission standards, where the data is self-clocking. In RS-232, given a known baud rate, data bits follow the start bit in an exact time sequence. By adding a distinct clock line, all communications become speed independent.

The I^2 C bus doesn't force one controller to be the perpetual bus master. Any device can assume control of the bus so that multiple processors can be attached. An arbitration scheme resolves conflicts between simultaneous requests for control of the bus.

For the purpose of controller communications, probably the best advantage of I^2 C over RS-232 is its well-defined protocol. RS-232 just shoots data between two fixed devices—each had better know what proprietary protocol, if any, is being used. The I^2 C supports an addressing scheme, so when many different devices are connected to the same two wires a particular unit can be selected. Once a connection is established between a device and the current bus master, data is transferred in precisely measured blocks; after the last block another master can gain control of the bus. Thus, like IEEE-488 or SCSI, any device that understands the communication protocol can be connected to the I^2 C interface. Unlike SCSI, the communications protocol is fairly simple, so real systems are pretty easy to implement.

Since I^2 C is speed independent, ultra cheap systems can even use a processor's parallel bits and lots of code to simulate a slow version of I^2 C, although it will eat CPU time. Look at Intel's *Serial Interfacing on the 8085* application note for more information about simulating serial this way.

Any sort of serial communications scheme does pose some interesting software design problems. For example, how does one computer read the value of a remotely located switch?

One common approach is to send a request for data as needed. This keeps the software simple but does mean that the controller will often be kept waiting for a response. Another method is to let the external peripherals transmit current data at regular intervals. Perhaps remote sensor A sends it's data every 100 msec. Then the controller can consult its current memory image of sensor A's last transmitted state.

An even better approach is to program the remotes to transmit only when their data changes. In the case of switches, this will result in a dramatic reduction in transmissions. If the data changes quickly (say from a fast encoder), consider using the same technique found in a mouse or trackball: send frequent bursts of data with each transmission containing a measure of the sensor's change from the last burst.

By all means code the serial-receive routine to be interrupt driven. Polled I/O will bring the system to crawl. This does create yet another problem: when is a block completely transferred? You can't let the code work with incomplete transmissions.

If speed is not an issue, a low-level interrupt service routine can copy entire blocks, when received, to a stable buffer that (implicitly) always contains correct data. Be sure to do this with interrupts disabled! A somewhat better approach is to employ double buffers with semaphores indicating which one contains valid data; the interrupt service routine fills one and the code uses the other. Be sure to isolate the data structures from your code with a driver routine, since every data access will involve a semaphore test.

The dream of true parallel processing just doesn't exist except in special cases in the embedded world. Monolithic programs are almost never spread over multiple CPUs. Where more than one computer shares the workload, each one is generally tasked with different sets of specific responsibilities. If your system requires more than one computer just to handle the computations (i.e., not for remote data acquisition), then carefully analyze the problem. Find a division of labor between the processors that minimizes communications and shared data structures. Wherever two processors share common data, all sorts of synchronization problems arise. How does one processor know the data is not being manipulated by the other? While it's easy to resolve these issues with semaphores, the added code sometimes cripples system throughput, negating the advantage of multiple CPUs.

The most successful multiple CPU embedded systems (again, disregarding those using remote processors for data acquisition) assign a separate, distinct function to each CPU. Perhaps one is an I/O server, concentrating thousands of interrupts from external sources into data streams for the main number cruncher. Or, maybe one computer is just a number cruncher, reducing equations provided by another running mainline code.

Watchdogs

"Watchdog timer" sounds like some sort of technology-smitten canine, but it is actually a crucial part of the hardware and software of many high-reliability embedded systems. A watchdog timer is a mechanism to restart the program if it wanders off or if the hardware suffers some failure.

Watchdogs take many forms. The most common is an external timer set up to reset the processor once every few hundred milliseconds. The software can reinitialize the watchdog, restarting the timing interval without resetting the processor. The trick is to make the software restart the timer at a rate greater than its countdown time, so it never has a chance to reset the CPU. In theory, if the software stops executing correctly it will stop tickling the watchdog, which will eventually timeout and reset the CPU, restarting the code.

Generally, the code's main loop includes an I/O instruction to reset the timer. Or each subroutine can include watchdog reset code. This is a bit cumbersome, but it is far superior to the apparently elegant approach of using a separate task that does the resetting. It's not unusual to see the main loop crash while various interrupt service routines stay active.

This sort of watchdog resets the CPU, restarting the entire program. Perhaps some slightly degraded operation is acceptable. If the nonmaskable interrupt input is substituted for reset, then watchdog timeouts could theoretically be managed in a cleaner fashion. Suppose the system controls critical hardware. A watchdog timeout that dives NMI could invoke a routine to put the hardware in a safe mode.

This does assume that at least some of the code will continue to function. Some processors can actually fail in a more serious mode when using an interrupt. If the glitch that caused the watchdog timeout in the first place was related to an address violation error due to the stack pointer being corrupt, then an NMI pulse might drive the processor into a "double fault" condition: two address violations in a row. Most CPUs recover from double fault only through an external reset.

Companies making systems with high-litigation potential might be exceptionally paranoid about failures and go a step further. If a simple I/O instruction reinitializes the watchdog, then conceivably when the program fails it could wander into a loop that just happens to execute that instruction. It's pretty easy to devise fiendishly complex watchdog circuits that require the code to issue, say, three different I/O cycles to reset the timer. The odds of false triggering then diminish to practically zero. This sort of insurance is particularly important in medical instruments and other life-critical applications. No family will stand for "hardware glitch" as the cause listed on the death certificate.

What action should the system take when a watchdog timeout is detected? This depends partly on what you might suspect the problem to be from. If your main concern is software bugs, then a simple program restart might be appropriate. A watchdog tied to the processor's reset pin will do just this.

Do you report the failure to the user or just try and slide by, restarting the code without making a fuss about it? Perhaps this is an issue tied to your pessimism about the code's reliability. I'm inclined to report all software crashes. Bugs severe enough to crash the system need to be fixed. An invisible reset will cause nightmares in the test department. Worse, you'll never really know if all bugs are cured.

Perhaps the fear of crashing stems more from hardware failures than from the software. In some factories huge motors run the production line. Sometimes they throw tremendous spikes into the power lines, possibly causing an occasional computer hiccup. Resetting the CPU will cure a short glitch.

A real, honest-to-God hardware failure will probably not be cured by a reset. If the hardware is critical or controls dangerous mechanisms, make sure that the designers realize that the software will probably never restart once a chip fails. They should design things so an external circuit drives everything, including the code, to a safe state. One way is to permit only one reset—the one after power-up, which starts the code. All others permanently drive the CPU into a reset state. Then the software will be stopped, for sure, and will not run erratically.

One clever error detector monitors the address bus to detect any accesses outside the normal program space. This is rather simple to do with small programs that need only a subset of all of the addressing lines: if any unused line (say, address line 15) goes high on a read or write cycle, then toggle the watchdog. Other products include hardware that monitors all I/O cycles to look for illegal references.

One simple software-only bug detector just monitors the contents of the stack pointer to find a creeping stack, indicative of mismatched pushes and pops. This will detect some problems, but a lot of catastrophic bugs will crash the system long before the creep would be detected.

Regardless of what kind of watchdog is used, make sure it can be easily disabled for debugging. The watchdog timer is sure to timeout when the debugger is at a breakpoint.

The Software Engineering Methodology

Does your software evolve or is it carefully designed before coding starts? The last thing many embedded programmers want to hear about is design methodologies. An astonishing number are electronic engineers who handle both ends of development. Often, EEs have little formal training on the methodologies embraced by computer scientists, and they may not have the deep-seated understanding of their value. Instead, the techniques are often viewed as crutches for novices or as pain-in-the-neck documentation procedures required only by Department of Defense projects. In fact, we all use some sort of methodology, whether we recognize it or not.

A lot of approaches have been advocated; all have some value. The most important rule, regardless of formal methodology, is to adopt a planned technique that solves your company's objectives. Common sense dictates a method that promotes correctness, reducing the amount of time spent debugging. Jumping in and coding is the single biggest programming mistake, particularly in the embedded world where many projects are completely coded by one or two people. Common sense suggests top-down decomposition, well-structured code consisting of short modules, and good internal documentation (at least). Common sense also suggests that reusability be a concern. Write the code in such a way that you or others can take advantage of it again. In short, plan before starting: set your ground rules before writing any code.

Big projects will always depend on the meticulous methodologies promoted by Constantine, Boehm, and dozens of others (see the Bibliography). Some smaller systems will benefit from these teachings; others will simply evolve, being born in the basement in some technology wizard's quest for the "big score." Computer scientists are often aghast at the cavalier attitude the microprocessor industry sometimes has toward careful design. No matter what your motivations, at the very least strive toward thoughtful design before committing to coding.

Read the classic structured-programming texts. Learn more about systematic, efficient methods to design software. The subject is far too broad to address here, but certain aspects are unique to embedded projects.

Always code in such as way as to leave yourself an out—don't paint yourself into a corner. Remember that everything will change as the product evolves and matures. For example, don't use every last bit of CPU horsepower, or every last byte of memory.

Figure on problems with interfacing to complex peripherals. Segment time-critical routines together, so that if they need to be recoded in assembly language or otherwise optimized, they'll at least be grouped logically.

Try to minimize the product's time to market. As mentioned earlier, being six months late with a new product will substantially reduce its market share. As the developer, what can you do to get something together fast yet insure that it is right? One solution is incremental releases. Make version 1.0 a subset of the project; a subset designed to accomplish the system's most important functions, yet one that is designed so that adding the rest of the features will not entail a complete rewrite.

Most computer-based products include an abundance of features, some of which are included just because they can be included, others to deter potential competitors. Can you defer some of these till version 1.1? Remember that many customers might never use the more sophisticated capabilities of the system. I have yet to exploit all of the potential of my VCR—who has the time to learn how to use all variations of its functions? The same is true of most systems. It's probably better to release a robust yet limited version 1.0 rather than a buggy, error-prone 1.0 with all of the features but few of which that are really usable.

The microprocessor and semiconductor revolution has made it possible for even one-man companies to design and market a product internationally. Smaller businesses are always undercapitalized. Incremental releases provide a way to generate some cash flow without spending years in product development.

Complex products should be prototyped, much as a hardware designer prototypes chips and wires. It's a trifle naive to completely design a system and expect it to be what the customers are looking for without their having an opportunity to see it long before all the coding is done.

One particular area of concern is the user interface. Always consider some sort of prototype for operator interaction. Logic does not always rule with screen design; give the marketing people and customers an opportunity to make suggestions and alter things to their liking. Much like a great work of art, the users will know what they like when they see it . . . but maybe not until that time. A screen prototype is easy to generate using packages like Dan Brinklin's Demo. It will probably save lots of time in the long run.

Pick an overall software structure and stick to it. Changing from a linear model to one with a real-time operating system will cost a fortune in time spent rewriting and retesting modules. Don't figure on kludging patches into an overextended structure sometime in the future. The cutest programming tricks often create the ugliest problems. It's generally a good idea to consider some blue-sky projections of the product's future when you first start planning its implementation. Pick a structure that will then carry the product through its entire life cycle.

ON THE CODE

Unlike the artist or sculptor, our work is judged on what it does, not on its intrinsic beauty or design elegance. Embedded systems usually compute quietly in the background, taking care of important but scarcely noted tasks. Only a programming expert can appreciate the details of our craft, and then only after weeks of study of the source code itself.

Shoddy workmanship that more or less functions might appear to be just as good as meticulously designed and implemented code. In most cases, particularly when only one or two people write the entire project, it is up to our professional honesty to write well-structured, maintainable code. No one will reward us in the short term for this, nor will functioning spaghetti code draw recriminations. But just as a poorly built house will eventually settle and develop wall cracks, crummy code will sooner or later show up its deficiencies. How long does it take to fix a bug? Is adding every new feature a nightmare? Does changing one routine cause a dozen unrelated bugs to crop up?

Practically every system takes on a life of its own. Sometimes even prototypes designed to never see the light of the marketplace somehow get shipped and quickly evolve into a standard product. Strive to write good code that you can be proud of from the first on every project. You'll never have cause to regret it.

Start with a debuggable structure. A DMA-driven state machine will be a nightmare to make work. Make sure the tools are consistent with the structure—don't use 20 interrupts if you have no way to troubleshoot real-time problems.

Above all, aim toward small modules that permit "test-and-forget" strategies: once a routine is debugged you should never have to worry about it again. Encapsulation, as promoted by object-oriented programming enthusiasts, is a step in the right direction.

Where possible, couple small modules with a single entry and exit point. When coding in assembly language it is awfully hard to resist conditional return instructions. Yet these consistently cause lots of trouble. Invariably, one executes a conditional return forgetting that something was left pushed on the stack, causing hard-to-find program self-destruction.

Control the urge to push and pop excessively. Who can track what the stack looks like when a lot of pushes are intermixed with a number of conditional jumps?

More has been written about comments than any other part of programming, but proper commenting still remains one of the most serious and commonplace deficiencies in the industry. There is a simple solution: managers should make a habit of reading their programmers' code from time to time and simply reject that which is poorly described and structured. After a few rejects, standards will improve or the offending individual will leave—either outcome is probably an acceptable solution.

Figures 3.3 and 3.4 show the same subroutine, each written with different commenting practices. Figure 3.3 looks like the code a lot of embedded programmers write. A few token comments are carelessly tossed in to satisfy the boss but little is really described. This is unacceptably sloppy. Wouldn't you rather maintain the code shown in Fig. 3.4? The overall strategy is clearly described. Caveats are included to prevent future changes from violating assumptions essential to the code's correct operation. Every subroutine call and macro is described: This programmer is trying to make it easy for future maintenance! Also notice that the data removed from the stack with each POP is described.

Writers and programmers should share an important trait: the ability to think clearly. If you cannot understand a problem, then dissect it and convert that knowledge into another form (prose or code). I often think that as programs become more complex, writing becomes as important a skill for programmers as is coding. Given that you must document the code (at least in the comments), and given that this documentation is in more or less conventional English, then it follows that programmers should study and practice writing much as they follow the precepts of top-down decomposition. If you hate commenting and do just the minimum needed to get by, the code and the project will suffer.

If you can't write, learn how. Take technical or even creative writing courses. This is the communications age—make sure you have the ability to communicate effectively. Learn to enjoy the documentation process as much as you like crafting the control flow. Comments reflect

```
;
; read_low - called by the read routines if the read address
; is under 256k.
;
extrn   read_low_0:near
read_low:
        push    edi
        push    es
        push    esi
        mov     ax.dgroup
        mov     es.ax
        mov     dl.0
        mov     esi.offset oram_bank0
        mov     ebx.es:|esi|
        cmp     ebx.0           ; does obank0 start here?
        jnz     rd1
        mov     dl.0b0h         ; set oram bank 0 on for 0
rd1:    pop     esi
        push    esi
        mov     eax.esi
        and     eax.03f000h     ; isolate part of address for middle rams
        shr     eax.12          ; put in low order part
        add     eax.offset oram_buf
        mov     esi.eax
        mov     al.es:|esi|     ; get setting from table
        and     al.1fh          ; use bits pertinent to middle RAMS only
        or      dl.al
        mov     dh.dl


        pop     esi
        matchhi on
        matchlo off
        cmp     esi.09000h      ; see if this is under 9000h
        js      rd2
        pop     es              ; destination selector
        pop     edi
        call    read_low_0      ; access target using read_low_0
        ret


rd2:    mov     ax.alt_enbuf
        mov     es.ax
        mov     edi.offset alt_databuf
        push    ecx             ; save byte count of transaction

        mov     ebx.esi         ; address of transfer
        and     ebx.0ffff000h   ; isolate to 4k resolution
        ld_rams on
        en_rams on
        mov     |ebx|.dx
        mov     |ebx+4096|.dx   ; do two sequential 4k blocks
        en_rams off
        ld_rams off
        rep     movs  byte ptr es:|edi|.byte ptr ds:|esi|; get target data
        matchlo on
        ld_rams on
        en_rams on  .
        mov     |ebx|.dx
        mov     |ebx+4096.dx
        en_rams off
```

Figure 3.3 Common example of poor commenting practice. (*Figure continues.*)

```
ld_rams off
push      es              : selector where of temp data buffer
pop       ds
pop       ecx             : transaction byte count
pop       es
pop       edi
mov       eax.offset alt_databuf: point to temp data buffer
mov       esi.eax
rep       movs    byte ptr es: |edi|. byte ptr ds: |esi|: move temp
ret
read_phy         endp
```

Figure 3.3 (Continued)

the programmer's personal pride in his or her work. If you have none, find another career.

Over the years I've found that describing the program is more interesting than actually coding it. I like to write the header blocks to all of my functions before getting started with coding. After all, this is where the real creativity lies: designing the program's structure and inventing algorithms to implement the details. If your comments describe each function's inputs, outputs, structural relationship to the big picture, and how the algorithms work, then translating these words to C is almost trivial. It barely qualifies as creative.

Even the most well-intentioned commenter will often give up halfway through the project as management pressures you to produce lots of code fast. Incorrect comments are worse than no comments; work hard to insure their accuracy throughout the program's life cycle.

Every organization has different ideas about how routines should be commented. Certainly each function must start with a block that clearly defines the purpose and operation of the function. List all input and output parameters.

Avoid enclosing function headers in a box drawn of asterisks or other characters. It's hard to change the comments without modifying spacing to make the characters on the right side line up, and it looks so nice that one's natural inclination is to not change things.

Other details will greatly improve the odds of debugging a program in a reasonable amount of time. Variable and function names are one. Compilers and assemblers that only take 6 to 8 character names are obsolete; avoid them at all costs. Modern products usually support 32 characters or more. Use them. It seems that we all start using short names and learn through hard experience to be more descriptive.

Consider the function **getdata**. Wouldn't **get__timer__count** be easier to understand? The underscore character can really help improve readability.

```
:
:  read_low - called by the read routines if the read address
:  is under 256k.
:
:  Here we have flat seg set in DS and the offset
:  (really a 32 bit physical address) in esi.
:
:  On entry.
:      ecx is the number of bytes to transfer
:      es:edi is where to store the result
:      ds:esi is where to read the target data from
:
:  This monitor runs at addresses 00000-0ffff all of
:  the time - mostly. To make the code easy. addresses 0-3ffff (the first
:  256k) are set to NO-ENABLE; any access ) 3ffff will do an enable
:  cycle.
:
:  If we get here. we open just two 4k windows to the target
:  (i.e.. set two adjacent ENABLE-OK areas) starting at the address
:  passed. Using two lets us do a block move that crosses a 4k
:  boundary.
:
:  If the address is under 09000h. then we do the work here. This
:  area must be linked so it is at address 9000h AT LEAST. The code
:  opens up two little windows. does the memory transaction. and
:  then closes the windows. Note that since we'll be turning a hunk
:  of memory off somewhere below 8000. we might lose the place where the
:  result of the operation is to be stored (and the stack!). Therefore. we
:  do the transaction to a temporary buffer in its own descriptor
:  table entry - alt_enbuf (for alternate enable buffer). The linker
:  has this guy located above 8000 so it at least will be available
:  even when low memory is off.
:
:  If the address is )=9000. then this code calls a very similar routine
:  located at address 8000 and something - it is less than 9000. It
:  does the same thing this code does. except that it opens windows
:  that just might be on top of this code. See read_low_0. located in
:  module alten.asm (alternate enable). alten.asm is linked carefully
:  to be between 8000 and 9000.
:
:  SEE THE COMMENTS AT THE BEGINNING OF MODULE COMM.ASM FOR IMPORTANT
:  LINKING INFORMATION. If any of this gets changed. make sure you
:  change the linking information therein.
:
:  The hardware bits for setting addressing RAMs is:
:
:  Bit 7                                        bit 0
:  *****************************************************************
:  *       *       *       *       *       *       *       *       *
:  * wait0 * obank0 * obank1 * wait1 * obank2 * obank3 * bkpt * nmi *
:  *       *       *       *       *       *       *       *       *
:  *****************************************************************
:  |(---to high addr RAMs----)|(---to low addr RAMs----)|
:  |   Addresses A18-31    |    Address A12-17   | Addresses A1-11
:
:  wait0.1       If both are 1. this selects at WAIT at the given address
:
:  bkpt          If 1. then this is the address of the breakpoint vector
:  nmi           If 1. then this is the address of the NMI vector
:  obank0.1      Overlay control bits
```

Figure 3.4 Much better commenting. (*Figure continues.*)

```
;
;    Obank0  obank1  obank2  obank3  bkpt      result
;      1       0       1       x       x     oram bank 1 on
;      0       1       x       0       x     oram bank 0 on
;      0       1       x       1    not bkpt  oram bank 0 on
;      0       1       x       1     bkpt     breakpoint
;      1       1       x       1     bkpt     breakpoint
;
extrn   read_low_0:near
read_low:
        push    edi             ; address to store transaction result
        push    es              ; destination address - read
                                ; target to this selector
        push    esi             ; address to do transaction to
        mov     ax,dgroup
        mov     es,ax           ; make the oram_buf accessible so we
                                ; can get and save setting of obank 0
        mov     dl,0            ; assume no ORAM at 0000 area
        mov     esi,offset oram_bank0
        mov     ebx,es:|esi|    ; ebx= current start of bank 0
        cmp     ebx,0           ; does obank0 start here?
        jnz     rd1             ; j if obank0 does not start at 0
        mov     dl,0b0h         ; set oram bank 0 on for 0
;
; Now DX has the settings to write to the addressing RAMs, except for
; the middle addressing RAM bits. These are used to disable/enable
; sections of overlay RAM bank 1. Extract the right one from the
; oram_buf table (one byte per entry in the middle rams), and OR the
; result into the DX settings
;
rd1:    pop     esi             ; transaction address
        push    esi
        mov     eax,esi         ; eax= transaction address
        and     eax,03f000h     ; isolate part of address for middle rams
        shr     eax,12          ; put in low order part
        add     eax,offset oram_buf; point to proper entry in table
        mov     esi,eax
        mov     al,es:|esi|     ; get setting from table
        and     al,1fh          ; use bits pertinent to middle RAMs only
        or      dl,al           ; mix in with other settings
        mov     dh,dl           ; dup setting in hi and lo since data is word

        pop     esi             ; restore pointer to where we'll get the data
        matchhi on              ; upper ram set to no-enable
        matchlo off             ; lower ram set to enable
        cmp     esi,09000h      ; see if this is under 9000h
        js      rd2             ; j if target address <9000
        pop     es              ; destination selector
        pop     edi             ; destination offset
        call    read_low_0      ; access target using read_low_0
        ret


rd2:    mov     ax,alt_enbuf    ; use alt_enbuf segment as our destination
        mov     es,ax
        mov     edi,offset alt_databuf
        push    ecx             ; save byte count of transaction

        mov     ebx,esi         ; address of transfer
        and     ebx,0ffff000h   ; isolate to 4k resolution
```

Figure 3.4 (Continued)

```
 :
 :    Note: from this point on. till we redisable the addressing RAMs.
 :  do not access any memory outside of this area. Addresses from
 :  0000 to 9000 may very well cause enables. This means no stack operations!
 :

    ld_rams on
    en_rams on                  ; send writes to addressing rams
    mov     |ebx|.dx            ; enable at target addr (ds is flat_seq)
    mov     |ebx+4096|.dx       ; do two sequential 4k blocks
    en_rams off
    ld_rams off
    rep     movs   byte ptr es:|edi|.byte ptr ds:|esi|; get target data
    matchlo on                  ; both match bits on so we can redisable this
    ld_rams on
    en_rams on                  ; enable writes to addressing rams
    mov     |ebx|.dx            ; both 4k blocks
    en_rams off
    ld_rams off

 :
 :   Now it is safe to access memory again
 :

    push    es                  ; selector where of temp data buffer
    pop     ds                  ; put it in ds
    pop     ecx                 ; transaction byte count
    pop     es                  ; selector of where we really want the data
    pop     edi                 ; offset of where we really want the data
    mov     eax.offset alt_databuf; point to temp data buffer
    mov     esi.eax
    rep     movs   byte ptr es:|edi|. byte ptr ds:|esi|: move temp
    ret
read_phy        endp
```

Figure 3.4 *(Continued)*

Try to use a systematic naming convention. Use common names for common functions. For example, if the program uses a lot of queues, then make sure all of the pointers look the same:

```
input_q_end_ptr
output_q_end_ptr
analog_q_end_ptr
input_q_start
output_q_start
analog_q_start
input_q_extraction_ptr
output_q_extraction_ptr
analog_q_extraction_ptr
```

An intelligent naming strategy will save lots of time during debugging. Since it makes intuitive sense, the number of routine names to remember is greatly reduced.

When working in C, always, always use function prototypes. If your compiler doesn't support this vital ANSI feature, change to one that does. Make sure that the compiler doesn't simply accept but ignore the declaration! Function prototypes are the single most effective debugging aid built into a compiler. They'll prevent the all-too-easy-to-make mistake of passing incorrect parameters.

CHAPTER **4**

Design for Debugging

These are the times that try men's souls.—Thomas Paine

Introduction

Programmers are an optimistic lot, always counting on projects going smoother than they ever do. It's hard to plan for problems; we'd rather believe in our own perfect coding skills, assuming that perhaps a little debugging will be inevitable, but that the project won't be dominated by long problem-hunting sessions.

In fact, debugging often accounts for most of the NRE hours in any project. Some big systems never become truly bug free. One Army program with which I am familiar consists of over a million lines of code. Today, 10 years after delivery and final acceptance, a full-time staff of 15 to 20 people continue to maintain the code, adding enhancements and chasing bugs. Few commercial systems can afford this level of after-the-sale support (read: "crummy deliverables").

The pressure is on to jump in and start coding practically from the product's inception. Even in the most methodical shops where Larry Constantine and friends may be worshiped as near gods, little thought is given to debugging issues. The structured-programming revolution addresses front-end problems, assuming that correctness can be designed in from the outset. Top-down design, coupled with almost any of the methodologies that are now so well known, is vital and worthwhile. I don't believe we'll ever remove the back-end, or debugging,

63

problem. In fact, it will only get worse as we struggle to cope with new technologies and more complex applications.

Usually little or no thought goes to debugging until late in the project when things are going terribly wrong. The old 90/10 rule holds true: most of the time 90% of the work in a software project is in the last 10% of the job—the debugging. Even the best-run projects that miraculously keep to schedule all throughout development will often fall apart during this last phase. Things will be worse than you hoped. Problems will creep up, tools will fail, prototype hardware will become flaky. Accept these truisms and include provisions for them in your plan.

Chaos in debugging shouldn't exist, but it is the norm. Debugging by its nature is at the end of the project, when scheduling pressures are at the worst. Tempers are already frayed. Tools usually are selected in a panic. Sixty percent of the emulators my company sells are shipped Federal Express; other companies confirm similar buying habits. This suggests that projects are in trouble and, gasps of desperation, the managers are trying to buy their way out of their difficulty.

A little forethought can eliminate many of these problems. As with all other aspects of an embedded project, up front planning will greatly ease debugging and speed project completion. Don't try to defer tool and structural decisions till the end of the project. Plan an environment, select compatible tools, and design the project's hardware and software to make the tools work well together. Above all, avoid undebuggable code!

CODE FOR DEBUGGING

Well thought-out and organized code is the single most effective weapon in eliminating bugs before they appear. A sure sign of disaster is the programmer who doesn't seem to have a firm grasp of the program's data and control flow, or who writes spaghetti code. Sometimes what starts out as a nice structured design becomes horribly convoluted as creeping featurism takes over or as its problems are uncovered during testing. A wise sage once commented that we should do projects twice, tossing out the first version and starting over once we finally understand what we're doing. Few of us have this option and must deliver code almost as soon as written.

Comments are the second line of defense. Most programmers hate to comment their programs, thinking that it detracts from the time spent cranking out code. Embedded systems use the most obtuse of languages. C, assembly, Forth, and the like are all but impossible to read and understand. Only with sufficiently detailed (and accurate!) comments can we remember what a function does and then pass that knowledge on to our successors. Who wants to maintain the same software forever?

ALGORITHM DEVELOPMENT

Debugging starts long before you start writing embedded code. Simple controllers might not have complex algorithms, but quite a few systems are chock full of complicated iterative math like Fourier transforms, digital filters, and so forth.

Before jumping in and writing code, study the riskiest routines. Will you be developing a complicated algorithm of some sort? Think of a better environment for working out the code's details than in the embedded system itself.

An example: If the system will fit curves to input data, write the regression code in a high-level language. Run it on your PC with a file of simulated data to be sure that it works. I like to do this in an interactive language like Turbo-C or even BASIC. In the case of a regression, 30 lines of BASIC will let you experiment with the concept; this sure beats writing a thousand lines of assembly and then finding a fundamental algorithm flaw.

This approach works equally well in hardware design. Once, in a flash of inspiration I came up with a new address decoding scheme that would cut out a lot of parts from a product. It almost seemed too good to be true. Instead of prototyping the concept, I spent a week laying out a PC board and then several thousand dollars to have it manufactured. Alas, it was too good to be true. The concept was seductive in its simplicity but just didn't work. I could have made a wire-wrapped prototype or written a simple program to test the idea, but instead I wasted lots of time and money by not building a prototype. The moral? A little time invested up front in experimenting, even when your boss is screaming for final code, will almost certainly pay off.

Experiment in the friendliest possible environment. No matter how good your embedded development tools are, they just won't compare to fast, efficient, and easy-to-use mass-produced software packages for the PC.

Modern interactive compilers like Borland's Turbo C make software prototyping a breeze. You can enter and test code incrementally. While this violates almost every tenet of structured programming, it is a valuable way to prove an algorithm's correctness. By experimenting in C, you may be able to port your results directly to the final product's code. However, be wary of using your experimental code in a real product. If you end up hacking it to death to make the algorithm work, it's generally a good idea to recode first, and then port.

Debugging Tools

Software complexity and costs are spiraling. Product development cycles are often measured in man-decades or even -centuries. The dearth of competent software engineers has driven salaries up; the combination of long engineering cycles and high salaries creates an insatiable demand for software productivity tools. While experts argue the merits of CASE technology to solve the front end (software design) problem, a number of effective methods for eliminating bugs in the back end have evolved. Typically, 50% or more of the development effort is consumed by debug and test. Every improvement in debugging productivity will net large dollar and time savings.

Debugging code in an embedded system is far more tedious and challenging than on a large mainframe. An embedded system rarely has a facility for operator interaction. The program, being hard-coded in ROM, is fixed and almost inaccessible. Most embedded processors have no inherent debugging facilities.

In the past a rather casual approach to debugging was both common and adequate. Once the code was complete, the software engineer spent months isolating bugs using whatever tools were at hand. The process was often a game of wits, earning programmers reputations as practitioners of a mysterious art. Programming is now recognized as a complex activity to be managed like any other aspect of business. The day of the hacker is gone; programmers, whether working alone or as part of a large group, are now expected to carefully plan their use of resources.

Accept the fact that your programs will initially have bugs—perhaps lots of bugs. Embedded systems of a useful size often start life almost hopelessly bug-ridden. Obviously, it's important to strive for perfection during design and coding, but even a respectable 1% error rate means hundreds of problems in a typical program.

Once, the language was selected independently of the other development tools; there was relatively little interaction between them. Now it is important to consider how each component of the development environment will interact. As noted in Chapter 2, be sure that the language will interface cleanly to your debugging tools.

The modern development environment consists of the following tightly coupled components:

A host computer, typically a PC, is the platform on which all editing, compilations, and linking takes place.

A debugging engine gives you a window into the target system to see just what it is your code is doing. This component can range from a simple monitor program to an in-circuit emulator.

A source-level debugger (SLD) is the debugging engine's control software package hosted on the PC. It dynamically links the debugging engine to the program's source code.

The ubiquitous PC has become the de facto standard for development platforms. Even traditional development system vendors have unbundled their equipment to take advantage of the PC that is inevitably found on every engineer's desk. Its standardization has encouraged numerous third-party vendors to supply a wide variety of powerful software products designed to help debug embedded code. You can tailor a configuration ideally suited for your unique requirements, but you must make intelligent choices to insure compatibility between products.

Most designers have migrated from the PC-XT to AT- and 386-class platforms for the host computer. Many high-level languages require lots of compute horsepower when compiling large programs. Use a hard disk for all serious development projects; don't try to limp along with a floppy-based system. With the current low cost and wide availability of high-performance clones, it makes economic sense to acquire as much performance as possible.

THE SOURCE-LEVEL DEBUGGER

In any reasonable development environment you'll need some sort of communications package running on the PC that talks to the debugging engine. Think in terms of using the host computer's compute capability to your advantage. Avoid bare bones communications programs like PROCOMM.

One of the few really profound advances in debugging technology in the last decade is the source-level debugger (SLD). An SLD is, at its lowest level, a communications utility that links the host computer to the debugging engine. More important, it acts as a sort of intelligent assistant that gives you information about the program's state in high-level form. It eliminates the need to page through piles of listings. The SLD does this electronically, displaying the source code at the current program counter address every time the PC changes. It resolves symbolic references, so you can avoid working with raw hex addresses. It examines data items in the format you've defined them. In short, the SLD translates the debugging engine's raw, machine-level information back into the original source form you wrote your code in.

Consider debugging a program written in C or C++. How will you set a breakpoint? Using a hex address? There is little obvious correlation between C source lines and the raw machine code, so just figuring out where the program is can become a nightmare without an SLD. C supports a wide range of variable types. Quick—what does 80 33 42 9A mean in floating point? The SLD will translate each data item immediately and painlessly. C++ is an even bigger problem—how can you examine an object? Some SLDs include inspectors that break objects down into their component parts and show them just as you defined them originally.

Suppose you need to single step through the code. Working in a high-level language, the last thing you'd like to see is each step moving through the compiled code. Rather, it makes more sense to step one source line (e.g., one C line) at a time. SLDs make this easy. In short, the SLD automatically ties the debugging session to the original source code.

Most SLDs are window-based. One window shows a portion of the source at the current program counter address, so you'll always know exactly where the CPU is executing. A good debugger will draw a multiwindow screen that presents all of the most important program parameters in an easy-to-use format. The key here is efficiency; the SLD must optimize what the programmer sees while minimizing the keystrokes needed to control the emulator.

Nothing in this business is easy, and source debugging is no exception. Linkers produce symbol files that will let you debug without knowing the absolute hex address of every label; but far too few generate the detailed information needed to support a source-level debugger. Even if one does produce an SLD file, it may not make enough information to completely debug a block-structured language like C. Although OMF is often believed to be the standard object file format, there are currently at least four incompatible OMF formats supported by various companies. The moral is to carefully research your language selections and to make sure all components from the compiler, assembler, and linker on down will tie together and generate the detailed information needed by your SLD.

The debugging engine, host computer, and source-level debugger form a unified whole that acts as a single environment with the programmer. All of the debugging resources are controlled through this interface.

When working in a high-level language like C, an SLD is absolutely essential since there is no direct or obvious correlation between the disassembled code and the original C source. A source debugger is just as useful in systems coded entirely in assembly language. For now, at least until the next real improvement in debugging technology occurs, plan on using an SLD and carefully design your debugging environment around it.

DEBUGGING ENGINES

Embedded systems pose tough debugging problems. Just how do you gain access to the system's innards? How can you start and stop program execution, modify and display the program, and interactively interact with a system running from ROM with no CRT or keyboard? Over the years a number of different approaches have appeared, each offering its own set of benefits and problems.

When programmers were mostly college kids developing products in off hours, it might have made sense to skimp on tools. Now, with salaries going ever higher and "time to market" the mantra of product managers, it makes sense to invest in the right tools to get the job done efficiently.

It might seem hard to believe, but I still talk to people developing embedded code using the "burn and hope" strategy. They burn an EPROM, plug it in, and then try to guess by the system's symptoms what the bugs are. I can't think of a worse use of programmers' time or a more (ultimately) expensive way of getting a project done.

Some development tools are indeed very expensive, particularly for fast 32- and 64-bit processors. High-speed oscilloscopes cost $20,000 and up; fast emulators can run over $50,000. Companies try to skimp on tools to cut back on capital equipment costs, but this invariably creates a situation where programmers are forced to wait in line for access to the tools. With salaries what they are, cutting these capital budgets is a false economy.

An editor of one of the trade magazines told me about his previous job. Cash was short, so the engineering manager bought the worst possible set of compilers, linkers, and emulators. The products were so slow that while waiting for links and downloads the programming group became quite adept at a game of making basketballs out of masking tape. The goal was to make them stick to the ceiling on the first try. At $50,000 per year per programmer, this game cost the business a lot more than the money they saved on the cheap tools.

Some vendors do offer lower performance tools for greatly reduced prices. Sometimes 70% of the cost is in the last 5% of the unit's features—a clever performance trade-off can bring tools to each programmer's desk. Be sure, though, that the tools will really be adequate.

Embedded debugging strategies have changed a lot in recent years. When assembly language dominated the industry, you could find (somehow) a bug and then hand assemble a patch directly in the machine code to solve or work around the problem, immediately carrying onto the next bug. This is no longer true. In C or any other high-level language, your patching options are all but nonexistant. If a C statement is just simply wrong, the only viable option is to exit the debugging session, invoke the editor, compiler, and linker, and then redownload the code and start all over. If the linker takes 10 minutes to do its thing and the debugging engine requires another 20 minutes to download the code, you'll spend a lot of time making masking-tape basketballs.

Compilation times for C usually are not a big problem. Good program design results in a number of small modules, each of which can be compiled in (generally) seconds. Linking is another issue altogether. The linker makes multiple passes over every object file (whether recently recompiled or not) to resolve external references. Currently, some work is being done on incremental linkers, where the object file is basically left intact except for the handful of changed bytes. But this technology is still in its infancy.

Downloading is another issue. Whether you are using "burn and hope," an emulator, a monitor, or even an ROM emulator before resuming debugging, you'll have to transfer the linked code to the target system or debugging engine. Most use RS-232 interfaces, which even at high-baud rates tend to be slow. In the best case, when the host computer and debugging engine have no overhead, 19,200 baud is only about 1800 bytes per second, or 38 sec. for a 64k program and 10 min. for a 1-Mbyte program. Usually the real transfer rate is quite a bit slower, as internal overhead greatly slows things down. Consider other connection options like Ethernet and fiber optics. These are well worth their cost but be sure to ask the vendor what the real sustained transfer rate is. Most quote a bit rate that bears little resemblance to actually downloading a real program.

All of these speed-reducing factors contribute to lower productivity. If it takes a half hour to correct even the simplest problem, then even in the best of cases you cannot find more than 16 bugs per day. Usually finding the problem will take quite some time as well, significantly reducing this figure. While this might sound like a convincing argument to stay in assembly language (since it is patchable), C saves so much time in the coding phase that a better solution is to carefully search out efficient tools.

Tool complexity is another concern. Can you really use it? Will you spend months learning its intricacies? The oscilloscope is a powerful debugging aid, but most pure software types have a hard time getting familiar with it. Remember that you have to debug the code *now*, and you might not have a lot of time for studying manuals. Still, spend some time with unfamiliar tools. Build up your repertoire of debugging tricks. Maybe you won't use it today, but tomorrow, next year, or in a decade you'll have yet one more weapon in your troubleshooting arsenal.

Will the debugging engine operate without target hardware? In the real world of embedded systems, prototype hardware goes down with annoying frequency. If you can continue with at least some aspects of the debugging without the hardware, you'll stay productive while others repair the target. Big projects suffer from a variation on this theme. If 20 programmers are debugging on 20 prototypes, who will maintain the revision level of the hardware? Every time an engineering change is made, will someone have to run around to all 20 units adding little blue wires? All could be down at once or have different revisions, effectively stopping software development for long periods.

In real estate the cry is "Location! Location! Location!" In embedded software projects an appropriate counterpart is "Integration! Integration! Integration!" Chapter 2 discussed this in terms of languages. Be sure that the languages, debugging engine, and source debugger are all on friendly terms, and that all share a common object module format. There is no more effective way of ruining an effective development environment than by adding one incompatible piece of hardware or software.

It goes without saying that the debugging engine must offer enough features and performance to get the job done efficiently. This is a rather personal matter. Some programmers demand every last ounce of power from their tools while others are satisfied with the ability to set a single breakpoint. Cost plays an important role here, as features do drive up cost. Sometimes you can substitute careful thought for the latest whiz-bang thingamajig.

In the emulator business we find that it is important to offer complex breakpoints as a feature, even though practically no one uses them. In some units we have 131k hardware breakpoints, yet most users need only 2 or 3. Some features, however, are truly indispensable—like real-time trace. As vendors, we're forced to offer what people want, maybe not what they need.

Finally, consider costs. Will programmers have to line up to use the tools? Programmers are expensive. Pick an environment that keeps them busy.

SIMULATORS

Simulators have been around for a long time, always promising "hardwareless" debugging platforms. For years they've been a sort of industry embarrassment, promising much more than they've ever delivered. In 1988 the ex-president of a simulator company admitted that out of 1000 units sold, he knew of only two successful applications.

As the name implies, a simulator is a software model of the target hardware environment, including the target processor itself. The simulator runs on a host computer, so typically it is an MS-DOS program that emulates the functions of the embedded controller, say, an 8051. You load your program into the simulator, which then executes every instruction by invoking a subroutine that tortuously reproduces what a real 8051 would do.

The promise of simulation is to reduce programmers' dependence on notoriously unreliable prototype target hardware. Working in the environment of a stable host computer, a simulator should give a quick, interactive response with few delays and with powerful bug-isolation techniques. In fact, most modern simulators do offer all of the above.

Simulators' great failing, however, is in dealing with I/O and real-time events, the two areas that practically define embedded systems. How can an off-the-shelf simulator deal with the unique I/O of your target system? Most now include some way for you to code an I/O simulation package, so you can model your oddball processor-driven state machine (or whatever). In reality, how many of us will take the time needed to write I/O simulations for all of our peripherals?

Useful I/O simulations require much more than just emulating the particular device of interest. For example, it's easy to model a polled UART, since to the software it looks like a data register with a few status bits. The hard part comes in duplicating a realistic data stream. What will come in from the outside world? What if the input is a function of what the processor does? How can you build a model of a software-scanned keypad?

Today's simulators seem to sell especially well for single-chip controllers like the 8051, where a lot of the peripherals are integrated on-chip and are therefore well defined. The simulators generally come with drivers for these high integration devices as well as some sort of structure to emulate inputs to the devices. Generally you create a file of inputs and outputs that the simulator feeds into the model of the target system. I'm sure that soon we'll see optional libraries of drivers for common peripheral chips, like parallel I/Os, UARTs, and so forth.

Real-time, asynchronous events like interrupts and DMA are very difficult to simulate. It's not hard to spend as much time building the model as it will take to implement a real system. Simulators are just not very useful when it comes to real-time problems.

Despite this difficulty in handling real-world I/O, simulators do serve an important function in the embedded world: debugging algorithms. Many systems (particularly those other than controllers) use complex algorithms for processing input data. Do you really want to debug a fast Fourier transform in a ROMed environment? As mentioned previously, it makes sense to model the algorithms with a friendly high-level language like C or even BASIC, but at some point you'll have to transition to the actual embedded code. A simulator will be a valuable tool for working out the final software kinks.

Some simulators now share a common front end with emulators and other debugging tools. Only the low-level drivers change. The beauty of such a toolchain is the universal interface. You only need to learn one set of commands.

THE OSCILLOSCOPE

Oscilloscopes and logic analyzers are the tools of choice for our hardware counterparts. Both are designed to give a low-level view of different aspects of an electronic circuit. In some circumstances they are very effective software troubleshooting tools as well.

An oscilloscope (colloquially called "scope") shows electronic signals in a time versus voltage format. The horizontal axis represents time while the vertical one corresponds to voltage. Typical scopes can display two signals at once.

The signals in Figure 4.1 little resemble anything a traditional programmer would be concerned with. Nevertheless, in embedded systems the software controls hardware; it's not unusual for a piece of code to replace hardware components. Take a software scanned keypad: the code must assert scan signals to the keypad over and over. A scope is the perfect tool to see if these signals are coming out properly. Suppose the program sends an acknowledge pulse out whenever an interrupt occurs. With a scope you can see the signals to insure that things are indeed happening as they should.

In fact, an oscilloscope is one of the more useful debugging tools for embedded systems. It won't help you work the bugs out of a mathe-

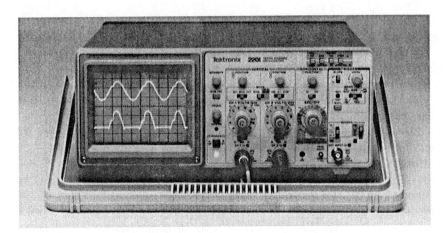

Figure 4.1 Typical oscilloscope.

matics algorithm or tune a screen format, but it will be invaluable in checking the sequence of output signals in a controller or in working with any discrete I/O device. Embedded systems are by their definition tied closely to the hardware, typically toggling bits and causing physical events to happen. The scope is the only tool that lets you see the low-level effects of your code.

A scope can even serve as a crude performance analyzer. Have your code set an output bit high when a routine is invoked and then low as it exits. The scope's display will show exactly how long the bit is asserted.

A variation on this theme checks that the code is properly synchronized to the hardware. Suppose that the code must respond to an interrupt within a certain number of microseconds. Make the service routine toggle an I/O bit. Then show the interrupt signal on one channel and the I/O bit on the other—the difference in time is the interrupt latency.

Unfortunately, programmers usually view scopes as exclusively hardware debugging aids, rather like a soldering iron and wire cutters. Worse, most scopes are an intimidating sea of knobs and dials, the total antithesis of screen-based software development tools. The scope won't be particularly useful unless you have at least some knowledge of hardware. Pure software types should make an effort to get some grounding in logic fundamentals, as this knowledge will only make it easier to debug their code.

The scope's trace is formed by a dot that rapidly scans across the screen. It redraws the screen so quickly that the trace appears as a solid line as long as the signal repeats itself. An event that occurs once (say, a bit that goes high once a minute) will trigger just one quick sweep, which will be faster than your eye can see. Successful oscilloscope use lies in making sure the signal repeats itself often. A single interrupt will be hard to capture; much better is one that repeats hundreds or millions of times per second. With the advent of inexpensive digital scopes some of this problem disappears, since a digital scope will remember even a one-time event. It's still awfully tricky setting things up to capture that event.

THE LOGIC ANALYZER

A logic analyzer is a sort of scope designed explicitly to capture single-shot events (see Fig. 4.2). It is an entirely digital machine that saves dozens of separate channels of information, compared to only two for most oscilloscopes.

In the computer world we deal with very wide address, data, and

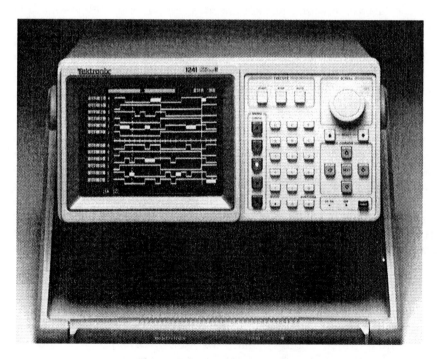

Figure 4.2 Typical logic analyzer.

control busses. It's not unusual to work with 48 or more signals simultaneously. Logic analyzers capture all of this information and show it in multiple traces. A typical analyzer will save several thousand 16- to 32-bit words.

Analyzers are used mostly for debugging microprocessor-based hardware, but a surprising number of programmers rely on them as primary debugging tools. By setting up an appropriate trigger condition, the analyzer's data capture will start or stop on an explicit condition—somewhat like a breakpoint. Unlike conventional emulator or debugger breakpoints, the code continues to run past the trigger; the break condition only affects the analyzer.

Suitably set up, any analyzer will save address and data busses from a run of the program. Some will disassemble the acquired data, so you get a pretty good view of just what the code was doing at the trigger point. Registers will not be visible, but all memory and I/O transactions are saved and displayed.

Logic analyzers, however, won't help much when working in a high-level language unless you care to manually correlate the disassembled data with the original source files. Prefetching processors, discussed later, will horribly corrupt the disassembled display.

Some programs drive very complex patterns through the I/O ports. The logic analyzer is the ideal tool for capturing this data flow, so you can see just what the program did. The capture buffer is very wide (16 or more bits); lots of port information can be included.

ROM EMULATORS

The scope and logic analyzer, while immensely valuable for debugging embedded hardware and software, are both limited to nonintrusively monitoring the operation of a system. Neither can start and stop the program; neither can alter or display specific memory or I/O addresses. Embedded debugging should be as interactive as debugging conventional PC-based code. It's been a long time since we relied on seeding code with lots of print statements. Now various sorts of debuggers give you an interactive window into the code.

The vast majority of all embedded systems have no display or keyboard, no way to interactively get access to the internals of the system. Your dual-processor toaster might have a "toast-insertion lever" as its only human interface. Interactive debugging is only possible if external hardware is added to the system. This need spawned ROM emulators and in-circuit emulators, both of which form a link between the embedded system and an external computer or terminal, and both of which include debugging facilities.

A ROM emulator is a rather simple device that plugs into your system's ROM socket. Its internal RAM maps in place of the ROM. A serial interface connects to a host computer. It breaks the EPROM burn, test, and hope cycle by letting you download code from the host computer to its internal RAM. When you find a bug, you simply download fixed code, saving quite a bit of debugging time. Some of the more sophisticated units support simple breakpoints by clipping probes onto the microprocessor.

ROM emulators are cheap, ranging in price from under $200 to about $700. Even better, since they plug into the ROM socket, a single unit will support practically any microprocessor. For organizations with no capital equipment budget, a ROM emulator, software monitor (described later) and logic analyzer form about the cheapest development environment possible. For very small projects coded in assembly language this can be fairly efficient. Larger programs, or those written in a high-level language, need more debugging horsepower.

THE IN-CIRCUIT EMULATOR

Intel invented the in-circuit emulator (colloquially known as an "emulator") right on the heels of the introduction of the first microprocessor. Now almost all embedded projects of any size are debugged with this tool.

An emulator is a hardware device that replaces the CPU in your system. Its pod plugs into the microprocessor's socket and cables all of the signals back to the emulator proper. As its name suggests, the unit emulates all of a processor's functions down to the last detail. In its simplest operating mode the emulator is just a very expensive microprocessor.

The tool's powers lies in its ability to stop execution of the target program in a controlled manner, change things (registers, memory, and the like), and resume execution. This gives you just the sort of debugging environment you'd expect while working on nonembedded code using CodeView or Turbo-Debugger. The difference is that a rather complex piece of hardware is needed to gain access to the target system.

An emulator brings a number of different resources to debugging. These include

Breakpoints: What is the state of the CPU at a particular point in the program? A breakpoint is a controlled event that lets you stop execution and examine or modify any aspect of the computer's operation. Suppose you'd like to see what value a function returns; set a breakpoint at the return address and examine the parameter. If wrong, the emulator lets you make a change and carry on so you can try experiments with different kinds of data.

All emulators support simple address-only breakpoints, where the code stops running when a specific address is fetched. Ninety-eight percent of all debugging relies on these address-only conditions. More sophisticated units permit some amount of qualification of the break condition, using data values and cycle types as well as the address. For example, suppose a function fails only if the input data is 1234—set a breakpoint on the function's address qualified by a data break. Some emulators let you set truly astonishingly complex breaks, holding off the break until a number of conditions are satisfied. While not always needed, sometimes this level of control will save weeks of searching through code.

Real-time trace: A breakpoint won't tell you how the code got to a particular point or where it goes after execution starts. Real-time trace, a part of almost all emulators, captures the execution stream without slowing the code down. Suppose the code wanders off after leaving function **get_value.** Stop at the function's return point, arm the trace mechanism, and let it rip! The trace buffer will show several thousand instructions of execution history.

Trace always has some limited depth, typically 1000 to 8000 machine cycles. Any instruction will use at least one and possibly quite a few machine cycles, so the average useful trace depth in instructions is quite a bit less than the advertised number.

Trace systems often use the emulator's breakpoint mechanism to trigger the start and stop of collection. Complex problems such as those found in troubleshooting interrupt-related difficulties demand this sort of sophisticated triggering.

Overlay RAM: Most embedded systems execute their code from ROM. Reburning the system's ROMs with each code patch is tedious and slow. You can replace the target system's ROMs with RAM and use the emulator to download code to this RAM for test. Or, you can use overlay RAM, memory located within the emulator itself, in place of the ROM. While the overlay RAM is physically not in your system, logic in the emulator makes all references to it appear just as if it were a part of the target.

Performance analysis: Any given processor has only so much horsepower. Poor code can overwhelm even the mightiest 32-bit wonder. What do you do when the code simply can't keep up with external events? An old adage holds that 90% of the time is spent in just 10% of the code. If you can identify this 10%, then a little recoding will yield much faster code. A performance analyzer captures the code's execution and measures how much time is spent in each routine. It eliminates the guessing game of trying to determine where the bottlenecks really are. There's nothing worse than spending days optimizing the wrong routine!

A good performance analysis capability is essential to the long-term health of any software group. During the original design did you figure on using 70% of the CPU's time? How close was that prediction? Without the feedback afforded by this sort of feature you'll never know just how well you're doing during conceptual design.

The emulator (coupled with a good source-level debugger) is the ideal debugging tool for embedded systems. No other piece of equipment gets you as close to your code.

The downside to emulation, however, is the cost, which ranges from thousands to tens of thousands of dollars. Worse, either the entire unit or a substantial part of it must be replaced when changing processors. Costs are relative and should be analyzed dispassionately. Spending $10,000 to $20,000 to keep a $50,000 (perhaps more like $100,000 with overhead added in) programmer productive is certainly worthwhile. Nevertheless, costs remain the single biggest objection to use of emulators.

EMULATOR PERILS

Emulators are extremely complex devices. By their very nature they are intrusive (after all, breakpoints stop execution, and other commands alter registers, memory, and I/O). A scope or logic analyzer just measures signals presented to probes, while the emulator must exactly simulate the processor's actions. Consider the emulator's constraints before starting hardware or software design to ensure that your system will be debuggable. In situations where separate hardware and software teams work together, make sure both groups consider the tools' effects on the system.

Timing Shifts

As processor speeds creep up, physical aspects of the emulator become more important. Electrons move at the speed of light. We just can't push them any faster. Every emulator will have an effect on the system's timing.

All of an emulator's electronics, including the emulation processor (i.e., the CPU that runs your code), is isolated from your target system by bus driver chips and an emulation cable. These ICs and the cable will shift the timing of signals applied to your system.

Electrons flow at 2 nsec/ft, so even a 24-in. cable induces a 4-nsec timing shift. If a signal must propagate up the cable and then back down (say, an interrupt request and acknowledge pair), then the shift is more like 8 nsec.

The bus driver chips will toss in more delay. The fastest parts available add about 5 nsec. With the cable's 4 to 8 nsec, this starts to be a lot of time. Suppose your 386 emulator added a 10-nsec shift to the signals. At 33 MHz, 10 nsec is a third of the entire machine cycle!

Some emulators get around this problem by eliminating the cable and bus drivers. This is a reasonable way of making the emulator more transparent, but it does impose severe restrictions on the mechanical and electrical design of the target system. Vendors do a pretty good job of documenting these trade-offs, but all the documentation in the world is worthless if you don't follow the advice when first starting the design.

Even at 10 MHz, timing can be a problem. Zilog's Z280 uses a multiplexed address/data bus with rather tight timing requirements on the address strobe signal. If the design uses marginal speed components, the emulator's 6 to 10 nsec added delay might eat up all of the margin and then some.

The moral of the story is to design lots of timing margin into your target system. Otherwise, it may function but be literally undebuggable.

I visited a customer in New York whose emulator just didn't function with his system. With the processor chip inserted in place of the emulator it ran properly—most of the time. The emulator could never communicate with a serial communications controller. Intel, the manufacturer of the microprocessor, noted in their extensive data sheet that those using this serial part with the CPU were bound to have troubles without adding a PAL to adjust the timing a bit. The customer had not done this, and when we alerted them to the application note their response was "So what, it's only timing"! *Timing is the basis of all digital electronics and can never be neglected.*

Timing is important. Rarely, we see a system with a hardware state machine that tracks the CPU's execution state without using many control signals. If the ICE injects a wait state (say, when not emulating, when waits don't affect the target), some of these systems get confused. Typically DRAM timing suffers. Give the emulator a break and use reasonable design practices.

Noise

Ever-increasing CPU speeds are driving designers to extremely fast logic devices to minimize circuit propagation delays. Old-fashioned logic devices forgave poor PC layouts. Now designers use exotic logic like FCT and ACT with blindingly fast rise and fall times. These rapid edges, however, generate noise spikes on signals, power, and ground lines. No longer can we view a printed circuit trace as a perfect wire. Any track longer than a few inches will look like a transmission line.

Minimizing noise is crucial in every fast design. Fast means a design using FCT or ACT logic at any clock speed (since the edges are independent of clock), or one with a CPU speed over 10 MHz.

An emulator only makes the noise problems worse. Again, consider the ICE's design: an emulation processor, separated from the target by bus drivers and cable. Electrically, especially since we're now talking transmission lines and not wire, this configuration little resembles an NMOS or CMOS CPU's output. Multiplexed busses cause the biggest problems. The 80186 outputs an address and then the data on shared wires. When the address is valid an ALE signal is asserted so the target system logic can latch addresses. If the ALE line has any noise, expect erratic addresses latching.

Some power will flow between the emulator and target, even if only in the signal lines. If the target's power distribution tracks on the PC board are poorly designed the emulator can induce even more noise. Make sure your design group uses multilayer PC boards to ensure good clean power routing to the chips and ultimately to the emulator. Two-layer boards will simply not be reliable in fast systems.

Clocks

Noisy or otherwise inadequate clock circuits account for around 70% of all emulation problems. Microprocessors are very sensitive to the clock's voltage level, duty cycle, and noise.

Clock inputs on microprocessors are rarely TTL levels. Most other inputs are considered a ONE when the input exceeds 2.4 V. Not so the clock. Typically, the clock's minimum voltage for a ONE is about 4.5 V.

Clock shape is important as well. Some processors (like the 8088) require a particular duty cycle. Most CPUs demand certain minimum rise and fall times. The emulator will simply not work if these specifications are not met. Take nothing for granted; check the processor's specifications and compare against your design.

Logic Families

Digital designers are now faced with an abundance of logic families to chose from. Low-power designs might use 74HCT logic. Fast units could use the 74F series. Dozens of possibilities exist; no one family is the solution for all applications.

As noted previously, emulators alter timing, capacitive drive, and other electrical characteristics of a CPU. One subtle effect is caused by the reactance of the emulation cable. For those not familiar with things electrical, reactance is a characteristic of wires that make them look like capacitors and inductors at high speeds.

Emulators buffer the CPU chip from your target system with several interface chips. Most vendors use very fast ICs to minimize delays. The downside of this is that fast edges, when propagated over the emulation cable, will sometimes cause overshoots and undershoots to appear on signals in your target. Vendors minimize this by putting the emulation processor as close to the target system as possible. In some cases these voltage transients are literally enough to destroy chips in the target! CMOS devices will self-destruct if any input pin exceeds the 5-V supply by some small amount.

The solution is to avoid pure CMOS logic, especially in the prototype. 74HC, CD4000, and some other CMOS devices are the worst offenders. (CMOS in all of its various guises now dominates the electronics industry. Most CMOS families tolerate spikes fairly well, but beware of 74HC.)

A related problem occurs when you select a family that is not well matched to the processor. Most CPUs are guaranteed to produce at least 2.4 V when outputting a logic-one state. This is more than adequate for any conventional TTL logic family, but it is simply not enough for 74HC and some other devices. In truth, the CPU will usually produce an almost 5-V swing. Don't depend on it, as an emulator will likely exacerbate problems. Be sure your designers match the worst-case specifications of all devices in the system.

Interrupts

Few embedded systems don't use interrupts. Be sure your design is compatible with the restrictions imposed by the emulator vendor. Some emulators take control of one interrupt (typically NMI, the crucial non-maskable one) for their internal operations.

Even those emulators that don't steal an interrupt often work poorly if these external events are not sequenced in some fashion. It's common to see problems with interrupts that remain asserted for long periods of time. Figure 4.3 shows NMI, an edge-sensitive input, left low (asserted) even when it isn't used. The emulator masks off the input so spurious NMIs won't crash the tool whenever a breakpoint is encountered. By ORing a logic one, the emulator has essentially created the very condition it wishes to avoid!

This is a problem only with edge-sensitive interrupts and only on some emulators. Don't leave one of these inputs asserted when not

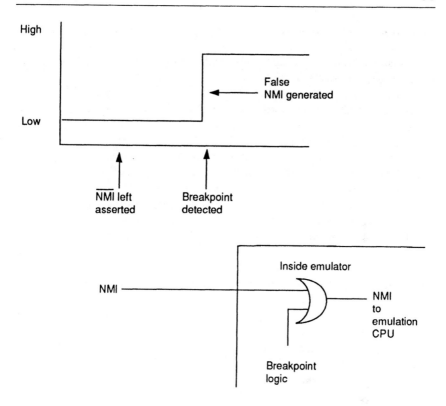

Figure 4.3 Possible NMI problem.

needed. Drive it to the deasserted state once it is acknowledged. Since the input is edge sensitive, it does seem perfectly reasonable to leave it asserted, but be kind to your tools.

What if your software controls mechanical motion? Suppose the code starts some action and an interrupt stops it. If you hit a breakpoint after starting the motion, the "stop" interrupt won't get serviced.

One developer uses a Z80 to run a punched-card reader. A constantly running motor feeds cards all day long through the reader. A short interrupt service routine dumps cards into one of two bins. Most emulators are useless to this individual, as the breakpoint condition stops interrupt service and spews cards all over the room.

A few emulators support limited interrupt and DMA servicing even while at a breakpoint. All impose severe restrictions: obviously, the interrupt service routines must be well debugged before starting such an activity.

Prefetch

Most 16- and 32-bit CPUs are really a combination of two tightly integrated processors. The execution unit runs the code. A bus interface unit manages the processor's pins, always trying to fill a small pipeline (or instruction queue, or prefetcher) with the next instruction to execute. Memory is slow; if the instruction is already on-chip, quite a bit of time will be saved.

Prefetchers cause two sorts of emulation problems. They often hopelessly confuse the real-time trace data, and they sometimes cause incorrect breakpoint operation. Both conditions are correctly handled by some emulators; others will cause lots of grief. Don't be surprised by tool deficiencies! Check with your vendor early in the game.

The CPU's bus interface unit is fairly unintelligent. It constantly issues requests for the next sequential instruction until a jump or other program transfer invalidates the prefetched, but not executed, data. The real-time trace in some emulators cannot deal with these erratic and sometimes incomplete instruction fetches. When the processor prefetches an instruction, a jump that is pending in the internal prefetch queue could stop the fetch even before the entire instruction is read. If the trace system doesn't model the processor's internal operations the displayed data will be meaningless.

Since the bus interface unit fetches ahead, regardless of what instruction is actually being executed, it may fetch an instruction that is never or only rarely executed. Consider the following loop:

```
label:
      <loop code>
      jnz label                ; jump if not zero to label
      <more code>
```

If you place a breakpoint on the first instruction after the conditional jump, every loop iteration might cause a breakpoint—even if the jump is taken. The emulator only sees the address fetch and can't distinguish a fetch that will be executed from one that will not be.

If the emulator's breakpoint circuits work by inserting a special instruction in the execution stream and then monitoring bus cycles to see if it is executed (the preferred method), then the breakpoint will occur only if <more code> is really executed.

Check with your emulator vendor to see what the restrictions will be. If the unit will exhibit this problem, you can pad every loop with enough NOP instructions to fill the prefetcher and then set the breakpoint after the last of the NOPs.

Running without the Emulator

It's a mistake to wait until the night before delivering the product to make the transition from developing with an ICE to plugging in a ROM and CPU for the first time. Often nothing works.

The emulator can sometimes mask real problems. It always makes sense to try your system stand-alone every once in a while to insure that unrealized problems don't lie dormant till delivery time.

Usually these problems come from a bug in the initialization code. Perhaps the emulator comes up with memory zeroed and the code relies on this. Or perhaps during debug the program was started in its middle, skipping a long self-test that has some unsuspected impact on the main routines.

Occasionally the culprit is a hardware problem. Usually the emulator alters or bypasses the target system's reset signal. Marginal resets will prevent reliable self-starting. Like the clock, a CPU usually requires reset to go to above 4.5 V. On some processors reset must be synchronous, so a simple resistor-capacitor circuit is out of the question.

The emulator can usually drive a lot of capacitive load—generally far more than the processor. Be sure that your circuit obeys the microprocessor's ac and dc loading guidelines.

Downgradable Code

Plan for the worst. Sometimes your wire-wrapped prototype just won't operate at the design goal of 10 MHz. Or if you're using leading-edge components, the very fast memories or peripherals you need might not be available until long after debugging is slated to begin.

Speed, timing, and noise are the curses of new projects and emulators. When you design your code don't assume it will run at the advertised speed, for you may find that until production boards are finally available you'll have to slip a slower clock into the prototype. Come up with a way to slow things down and still have enough of the system functional to do useful debugging. Count on spending many sleepless nights at the office if your code really won't run at all unless the clock is running full bore at 33 MHz.

Some processors have integrated cache memories, burst-mode DMA controllers, and other speed-enhancing features. Try to come up with a software architecture that can take advantage of these features, but one that you can debug even when they are disabled.

For example, the 486 and 68030 have on-board caches that can greatly increase software throughput. Unfortunately, cache is a nightmare to handle with an emulator. If your program is executing a loop in cache, no external bus cycles are generated. How can the emulator trace instruction execution? One solution is to use a bond-out chip, a special version of the CPU provided by the vendor that brings internal busses out to extra pins so the emulator can monitor the actual instruction execution stream.

Bond-outs are no panacea, however. Some foundries refuse to sell them since they are in the ICE business themselves and don't care to help the competition. Others don't bother to make bond-outs at all.

Motorola has a cache disable pin on the 68030. This is suggestive: presumably some ICEs run the chip with the cache off when you wish to breakpoint or collect trace data. If you can operate with cache disabled, your code is that much more debuggable.

At the other end of the processor spectrum, low-performance single-chip microcontrollers can be a source of emulation grief because of their on-chip ROM. Some emulators use bond-outs and so nonintrusively monitor all CPU operations. In cases where no bond-out is available some use the chip in an expanded mode and simulate the internal ROM with external RAM. A lot of microcontrollers run slower in external bus mode: NEC's K-Series runs about a third as fast as with internal ROM. Hitachi's H8 adds an extra cycle to external bus accesses, reducing throughput by 33%. There are good reasons for these longer cycles, but if your emulator runs one-third slower, be sure that the code will still work properly.

Adding Debugging Code

Hardware tools are an important but incomplete part of debugging. Even with the best tools it pays to add some amount of code just for debugging purposes. Simpler systems can sometimes dispense entirely with external tools. Perhaps the system's development will be a bit slower, but in cases where capital is lacking (i.e., a lone innovator working at night in a basement), the debugging code could make a new product possible.

One caveat, though: debugging code works best in systems coded in assembly language. C or other high-level languages, while greatly decreasing coding time, do demand the use of more sophisticated source-level debuggers and the like. Electing to make do with simple software tools, while possible, is mind-numbingly tedious.

While everyone occasionally adds short routines just "to try something," debugging code generally comes in four flavors: snapshot dumps, exception handlers, logging queues, and monitors. All rely on some sort of serial port, LCD display, or other output device to convey information. With the exception of a monitor, all are particularly useful with an emulator. Write the result of the debugging routine to a predefined area of memory so the emulator can then pick off these bytes.

A snapshot dump records the current status of the CPU and program. Typically it will print all of the machine's registers, status flags, and important memory locations. Snapshot dump is really just a glorified name for the print statements we liberally sprinkle throughout the code to track bugs down.

Consider writing a generic snapshot-dump routine that you can invoke anywhere in the code. Program it to perform the most frequently used logging tasks like saving registers. You'll certainly use it a lot throughout any one project, so the hour or so spent coding a useful routine will pay for itself many times over.

Exception handlers are rather new to embedded systems. The proliferation of processors with hardware-exception conditions (e.g., divide by zero and illegal instruction traps) creates new problems and opportunities. Few of us care to write handlers for conditions such as these, especially when our code should never produce such a problem. In fact, even the best-intentioned software will exhibit some pretty strange characteristics during debugging. It pays to write exception handlers early in the game to at least aid the development process.

A few lines of code will suffice to at least log the exception address and type. When using an emulator set a breakpoint on the handler so any unexpected interrupt will flag your attention. Or just put a snapshot-dump routine there.

Often a single exception handler can be used for all critical error conditions. Put a jump to it at all important unused addresses. Candidates include the NMI vector, all unused interrupt vectors, and of course traditional exception vectors.

This point was brought home with a vengeance while debugging a product based on the 386 processor. My tools were primitive, to say the least. Once in a while the code just ran wild. After lots of head scratching I wrote an exception handler and discovered the processor sometimes executed an illegal instruction. Looking at the exception address I was surprised to find that my code was writing over itself. This product still has the handler installed to trap possible future problems brought on by upgrades and fixes.

Logging queues save important data into a circular buffer. Suppose a serial link transfers commands to your embedded processor: write a short queue manager to save each command in a circular buffer. While debugging, you'll always be able to look at the last few (depending on the queue size) commands.

Most systems have one or more critical communications ports that are well served by a logging queue. Wherever the system transfers data externally, a logging queue is a good idea. I usually leave logging queues latent in the code, running all of the time or at least whenever a compile time switch is set.

Monitors are the final weapon in a software debugging arsenal. A monitor is essentially a minidebugger that communicates with you over some serial link or other keyboard/display interface. Every monitor will dump and alter the memory and I/O; some will set breakpoints and more.

Some embedded developers use a monitor as their prime debugging tool. Sometimes this makes sense. Several companies sell very powerful monitors that even support source level debugging via a powerful program running on a host computer connected to the embedded system over a serial link.

A monitor is a software version of the emulator, with some restrictions imposed. First, the embedded system needs an extra serial port for monitor communications with a host computer. Second, the monitor requires extra RAM and ROM. Sometimes it is linked into the target code itself; otherwise it runs as a stand-alone program in the target's ROM. No monitor can capture real-time trace data, do performance analysis, or execute complex breakpoints in real time. However, in simple systems this might not be needed.

A monitor is worth using even when you have high-quality tools. As one who has been called into the field a number of times to fix problems without the benefit of my electronic assistants, I find a permanently resident monitor a great aid. Most of the products my company produces have a secret command that invokes a debugging monitor that we can use for test/repair and for diagnoses of software problems. Given a bit of extra ROM space and a spare serial port, an embedded monitor is worthwhile.

The previously mentioned exception handlers and snapshot dumps could be included as part of the monitor. Other possibilities include a stack checker that runs as a background task to flag problems if the stack grows too large, or a software watchdog timer that indicates if various impossible conditions occur.

A simple monitor written in C follows. Breakpoints are so processor-specific that they are not included. Within any given architecture, though, breakpoints are fairly simple to implement. Replace the instruction at the breakpoint address with a single byte CALL to a given location (say, an RST 7 on a Z80 or INT 3 on the 80x88, or an illegal opcode on a 680x0 machine). Put a routine at that address that pops the return address from the stack. Print the return address minus 1 (the breakpoint address), replace the 1-byte CALL with the original instruction, and reset the program counter to the break address.

```
/*   Copyright 1990 Computer Design Solutions Inc.
     This code may be used by anyone in any way.
     CDS Inc. grants full rights to code to all users.

     Computer Design Solutions Inc.
     P.O. Box 127
     Statesville, NC 28677
     704-876-2346   Fax 704-876-2348
*/

#define TRUE    1
#define FALSE   0
#define CR      0x0d

/*   Flag definitions   */
#define OK      0
#define NODATA  1      /* Rets from get_v when no data
found */

static unsigned int start,end,value,last;
static unsigned char temp[16];
static unsigned char cin,flag;
static unsigned char *p;

main()
    {

/*   Sign on and say hello*/
     crlf();
     print("CDS Small Monitor Version 1.0");
     start=end=value=last=0; /* init vars   */

/*   Loop forever or until control C*/
     while(1)
        {
```

```
/*    Get Command*/
      crlf();
      putchar('>');
      cin=toupper(getchar());

      switch(cin)
      {
      case 'F':              /* Fill Memory */
            f_mem();
            break;
      case 'D':              /* Dump Memory */
            d_mem();
            break;
      case 'E':              /* Examine Memory */
            e_mem();
            break;
      case 3:                /* Ctl C Exit */
            exit_mon();
      default:
            break;

      }
      }
      }

/*    Examine memory */
e_mem()
      {
      print("xamine ");

/*    Get address*/
      start=get_v();
      cin=' ';
      p=start;
      flag=OK;

/*    Loop till CR*/
      while(flag==OK)
            {
            crlf();

/*    Print address*/
            phex(p,4,2);
            print("= ");
```

```
/*    Print contents*/
          phex(*p,2,2);

/*    Get new value*/
          value=get_v();
          *p=value;

/*    Next address*/
          p++;
          }
      }

/*    Fill memory    */
f_mem()
      {
      print("ill ");

/*    Get start, end, and data pattern*/
        start=get_v();
        if(flag==NODATA)
            fer();
        end=get_v();
        if(flag==NODATA)
            fer();
        value=get_v();
        rcheck();
        fill(start,end,value);
        }

fer()
      {
      error("Fill needs more data");
      }

/*    Dump memory    */
d_mem()
      {
      clear();
      print("ump ");
```

```
/*    Get Start and end*/
      start=get_v();
      if(cin!=CR)
      end=get_v();
      crlf();
      rcheck();
      dump(start,end);
      }


/*    Error processing     */

error(s)
      char *s;
      {
      crlf();
      bell();
      print(s);
      crlf();
      main();
      }

/*    Ring the bell        */
bell()
      {
      putchar(7);
      }

/*    Range check start to end */
rcheck()
      {
      if(end<=start)
          end=start16;
      }

/*    Clear start,end,value,cin*/
clear()
      {
      start=end=value=0;
      cin=0;
      }

/* get a hexadecimal value from the keyboard */
```

```
get_v()
      {
      unsigned int val;
      unsigned char cnt;
      cnt=cin=0;
      while((cin!=CR) && (cin!=','))
      {
      cin=getchar();
      if(cnt==0) flag=NODATA; else flag=OK;
      temp[cnt++]=cin;
      if(cnt>5)
            {
            bell();
            cnt-;
            }

      /*    Back space occurred   */
      if(cin=='\b')
            {
            if(cnt>0) cnt--; else bell();
            print("\b");
            }

      }
      temp[--cnt]=0;
      upcase(temp);
      val=htob(temp,16);
      if(flag==NODATA) return(last);
      last=val;
      return(val);
      }

/*    Fill from ad1 to ad2 with data*/

fill(start,end,data)
      unsigned int start,end;
      unsigned char data;
      {
      char *p;
      for(p=start;p<end;)
            *p++=data;
      }
```

```
/*    Hex dump with address on left and ASCII on right    */
/*    Start is the begin address and end is the end */
dump (start, end)
      int start, end;

      {
      int c_cnt;
      crlf ();
      for (p=start; p<end; )
      {
                              /* Print the address */
      phex (p, 4, 4);
      for (c_cnt=0; c_cnt<16; c_cnt++)
      {
      phex (*p++, 2, 1);
      }
      p-=16;                        /* reset */
                              /* Print the ASCII   */
      for (c_cnt=0; c_cnt<16; c_cnt++)
      {
      pascii (*p++, '.', 0);
      }
      crlf ();
      }
      }


      /*    Print a new line sequence */

crlf ()
      {
      print ("\n\r");
      }


/*    rept will print char. s n times       */

rept (s, n)
      char s, n;
      {
      if (n==0) return;
      while (n--)
            putchar (s);
      }
```

```
/* pascii(char,fill,spc)
     print ascii or fill and spc traiing spaces */

pascii(chr,fill,spc)
     unsigned char chr,fill,spc;
     {
     if(chr<' ' || chr>'}')
     putchar(fill);
     else
     putchar(chr);
     space(spc);
     }

/*    phex(n,len,spc)
      print(len) digits of (n) in hex. Zero fill with (spc)
      zeros. E.g., phex(100,4,2) will print 0064. */

phex(n,lgth,spc)
     unsigned int n;
     unsigned char lgth,spc;

     itob(n,temp,16);
     rept('0',(lgth-len(temp)));   /* 0 fill */
     print(temp);
     space(spc):                    /* print sep.   */
                          /* Print the 16 hex digits */
     }

/* String Print    */
print(s)
     char *s;
     {
     while(*s)
     putchar(*s++);
     }

/*    space(x)    will print x spaces   */
space(x)
     char x;
     {
     if(x==0) return;
     while (x--)
     putchar(' ');
     }
```

```
/* This is where you put your char. out
   code. The CDS Z-80/Z-280 compiler passes
   the char in L. */
putchar(s)
     char s;
     {

#asm
     push bc
     push ix
     ld   e,l
     ld   c,2
     call 5
     pop  ix
     pop  bc
     #endasm


         }
     /* get a character from the keyboard    */
     getchar()
         {
     #asm
     push bc
     push ix
     ld   c,1
     call 5
;    and  a,5fh              ; force upper case
     ld   l,a
     pop  ix
     ld   h,0
     pop  bc
#endasm
     }


/* len returns the length of a string */
len(s)
     char *s;
     {
     char i;
     i=0;
     while(*s++)
     i++;
     return i;
     }
```

```
/* Convert a string to upper case */
upcase(str)
   char *str;
{
   char *start;
   start = str;
   while (*str) {
      if (islower(*str))
         *str = toupper(*str);
      str++; }
   return(start);
}


/* itob-convert an integer to a string in any base (2-36)
   where
      n is the number to convert
      s is a temp. string
      base is the number base */

itob(n, s, base)
char *s;
   {
   unsigned int u;
   char *p, *q;
   int negative, c;

   if (n < 0 && base == -10) {
      negative = TRUE;
      u = -n;
      }
   else {
      negative = FALSE;
      u = n;
      }
   if (base == -10)        /* signals signed conversion*/
      base = 10;
   p = q = s;
   do {            /* generate digits in reverse order*/
      if ((*p = u % base + '0') > '9')
         *p += ('A'-('9' + 1));
      ++p;
      } while ((u /= base) > 0);
   if (negative)
      *p++ = '-';
   *p = '\0';                /* terminate the string */
```

```
    while (q <-p) {          /* reverse the digits */
        c = *q;
        *q++ = *p;
        *p = c;
        }
    return s;


    }


/* Convert string to integer */
int htob(str,radix)
    char *str;
    unsigned int radix;
{
    unsigned int digit, number;
    number=0;
    while (*str) {
        if (isdigit(*str)) digit = *str-'0';
        else if (islower(digit)) digit = *str-'a' + 10;
        else digit = *str-'A' + 10;
        number = number * radix + digit;
        str++; }
    return(number) ;
}
```

Common Debugging Problems

Speed kills. If the system must run blazingly fast, design in all of the speed you can but try to win through the use of fast algorithms rather than painfully tuned code. Where every last microsecond counts try to come up with an intermediate approach that may not be fast enough but lets you experiment with the approach. Tune for speed only after you are sure the techniques are correct.

Use decent tools to find speed problems and then optimize only where absolutely necessary. Use a performance analyzer or profiling software. Without the right tools, you'll be like a blind man hunting for a contact lens.

Part of the challenge of debugging embedded systems is in out-thinking the program and devising new means of getting useful information out of the limited I/O found in the system. Be creative.

Use spare I/O ports for software debugging purposes. An extra serial port, frequently found on microcontrollers and other high integration processors, is a godsend. Either have the hardware designers add RS-232 drivers to the product so you can connect the port to a computer or build up a prototype version with drivers glued on. Then write low-level serial drivers (usually needing only a handful of lines of code) so you can easily send data (like snapshot dumps) out the port.

A spare parallel port is helpful as well. Don't hesitate to write codes to it indicating the system's mode, particular output data, or the like. Use a scope or logic analyzer to capture the information.

UNUSED BITS

Microprocessors and their peripherals usually include dozens of registers needed to configure the chip's operations. Frequently, many of the bits in any register are unassigned. Religiously obey the vendor's rules about setting these bits to ones or zeroes; never assume that you can set an unused bit to any convenient value. Sometimes violating this stricture will cause the chip to enter a manufacturing test mode! Future revisions of the silicon might include new features that will be invoked via currently unused bits.

Along similar lines, never, never use undocumented instructions. Years ago the 8085 and other processors included quite a few undocumented opcodes that, through experimentation, programmers found did useful things. New mask changes and parts from second sources almost never support these "features."

DEALING WITH PREFETCHERS

In an effort to minimize bus delays, some microprocessors prefetch instructions that might be needed by the program. This has subtle effects on embedded systems.

Be particularly careful when using memory-mapped I/O with prefetching processors. If the code is at an address near the I/O space, the prefetcher may occasionally execute reads from the peripherals. Suppose the code runs from 00000 to 7FFFF and I/O starts at 80000. If the processor executes from addresses near the end of its space (near 7FFFF), then sometimes the prefetcher will read from the first few addresses above 80000.

Some prefetching processors include an on-board memory management unit (MMU). Generally, the code can program the MMU to invalidate a page. Any read from an invalid page will cause some sort of exception. If the code executes near the end of one page that is adjacent to an invalid one, spurious address violation exceptions will occur as the prefetcher reads ahead into the invalid region.

Make sure that your tools will properly distinguish an actual instruction breakpoint from a prefetch read that never executes. Oddly, the cheapest tool of all, a software monitor, will never have a problem with prefetched breakpoints; the INT 3, RST 7, or whatever will have an effect only after it is executed.

Common Sense

The most important debugging tool is a healthy dose of common sense, a sometimes rare commodity in the frenzy of debugging. Some programmers spend more time chasing ghosts than real problems. Are you sure there is a bug? Maybe the system really is supposed to work this way!

Common sense suggests that if a bug appears just after you changed a module, no matter how remote that module is from the problem, then the change is suspect. Common sense suggests that if the ROM is almost full and you've added a few lines of code, you should check to be sure that the program didn't overflow the ROM. Common sense suggests that if you can't outthink a bug in a few minutes, instrument the code via snapshot dumps or by using other tools to get more information about what is going on.

Don't immediately question the hardware or the tools when a bug appears, as most problems are indeed real bugs. But be aware of the potential for failures, for miscompilations, and other troubles.

Be wary of your assumptions. Document them in the comments. Is the maximum input value to **square__root** 1000? Better make a note of it in the comments before it causes troubles in the future. Does some characteristic of the system require a peculiar link sequence? Document it.

Finally, live up to the specification document (if any). Don't expect your boss or users to check the system against the original concept. Regularly reread the specifications to be sure what you are doing fits the customer's needs. Run short acceptance tests yourself, without waiting for that embarrassing moment when someone else finds your mistakes.

CHAPTER 5

Design for Test

You can have no test which is not fanciful save by trial.—Sophocles

For some inexplicable reason most programmers seldom worry about making a product manufacturable. The product has to more than function correctly—it must be producible. While our hardware brethren tune their designs to meet cost, manufacturing, and performance goals, as software people we tend to concern ourselves only with satisfying a functional specification.

In a typical manufacturing operation, boards are stuffed, assembled into units, tested, and perhaps repaired. While the code doesn't impact board stuffing and assembly operations, it can strongly influence product test and repair. Smart designers will produce a product that easily fits into the company's manufacturing operation; software engineers can contribute by writing code that speeds the daily grind of production test.

All employees are hopefully working toward common corporate goals, yet each has a different vision of the company's needs and problems. To a programmer the word "testing" conjures images of correctness proofs, exhaustive software trials, and code-coverage analysis. A production person probably has never heard of any of these concepts; he looks at testing as the daily routine of ensuring that each and every unit works correctly before being shipped.

Conventional software test is a one-time event. Once the product is complete it is truly over. Product test goes on every day. Very complex products are tested and repaired by technicians with little formal computer training. The best are usually culled and assigned to work in engineering support, leaving production with workers who may be skilled but who lack much depth in computer matters. As software engineers it is our responsibility to give the techs the tools they need to ship product. As software managers, it is our responsibility to convince management that this is an important and desirable goal.

Internal Diagnostics

Quite a few embedded systems include diagnostics as part of the product's ROM to give a sort of go/no-go indication without using other test equipment. The unit's own display or status lamps show test results.

Internal diagnostics are worthwhile because they do give the test technician some ability to track down problems. They're also an effective marketing tool, giving the customer a (possibly false) feeling of confidence in the integrity of the product each time it is turned on. Though internal diagnostics are often viewed as a universal solution to finding system problems, their value lies more in giving a crude test of limited system functions. Not that this isn't worthwhile. Internal diagnostics can test quite a bit of the unit's I/O and some of the "kernal," or the CPU, RAM, and ROM areas.

The computer's kernal frequently defies stand-alone testing, since so much of it must be functional for the diagnostics to run at all. Most systems couple at least the main ROM and RAM closely to the processor. The result: a single address-, data-, or control-line short prevents the program from running at all.

It's easy to waste a lot of time coding internal diagnostics that will never provide useful information. They may satisfy vague marketing promises of self-testing capability, but why write dishonest code? Realize that internal diagnostics have intrinsic limitations, but if carefully designed they can yield some valuable information. Apply your engineering expertise to the diagnostic problem; carefully analyze the trade-offs and identify reasonable ways to find at least some of the common hardware failures. The first step is to separate the tests into kernal (CPU, RAM, ROM, and decoders) and beyond-kernal tests. Then consider the most likely failure modes; try to design tests that will first survive the failure and second will identify and report it. Yes, the kernal tests will never be very robust since lots of hardware glitches will prevent the program from running at all. But if carefully designed, they'll really help the production department.

What portions of the kernal should be tested? Some programmers have a tendency to check the CPU chip itself, running through a sequence of instructions guaranteed to prove that this essential chip is operating properly. Witness the PC's BIOS CPU tests. I wonder just how often failures are detected. On the PC an instruction test failure makes the code execute a HALT, causing the CPU to look just as dead as if it never started. More extensive error reporting with a defective CPU is a fool's dream. Instruction tests stem from minicomputer days, where hundreds of discrete ICs were needed to implement the CPU; a single chip failure might only shut down a small portion of the processor. Today's highly integrated parts tend to either work or not; partial failures are pretty rare.

Similarly, memory tests rely on operating memory to run—a high-tech oxymoron that makes one question their value. Obviously, if the ROM is not functioning, then the program won't start and the diagnostic will not be invoked. Or if the diagnostic is coded with subroutine calls, a RAM (read: "stack") failure will prematurely crash the test without providing any useful information. The moral is to design diagnostics to ensure that each test uses as few unproven components as possible.

Check at least a portion of the RAM first so later diagnostics can use the stack and other temporaries. Since a ROM failure is usually catastrophic it might seem more logical to test ROM first. However, without using RAM the diagnostics will be ugly and unmaintainable—we want to minimize convoluted code.

The RAM test should be small, using only a tiny amount of the as yet unverified ROM space. In a multi-ROM system, store it (and all the diagnostics) in the boot ROM near the reset address. The low-order address lines must operate to run even a trivial program, and enough of the upper ones must work to select the boot ROM. Try to write RAM and ROM test routines that rely on a minimal number of working address lines. Fully decoded systems, more common now with cheap, huge, bytewide memories, generally run quite a number of lines to each memory chip; any single failure on an address or data line will thus crash the diagnostic.

RAM tests commonly write out a pattern of alternating ones and zeroes, read the data back, and repeat the test using data that is the complement of the first. This amateurish approach reflects poor analysis of the problem. Put on your hardware hat (or get some help from another member of the design team) before you write the code. Consider the most likely failure modes. Tailor the test to identify all or most of these problems. A typical list includes

Address-/data-line shorts: Nine times out of ten these problems will crash the diagnostic. Sometimes RAM is isolated from the kernal by buffers; in this case post-buffer problems can be found.

No chip select: One or more signals may be needed to turn each device on. The chip-select complexity can range from a simple undecoded address line to a nightmare of PALs and logic. Regardless, every RAM must receive a proper chip select to function.

Pin not inserted: Socketed RAM devices may not be properly seated. Sometimes a pin bends under the device.

Bad device: The semiconductor vendors do a wonderful job of delivering functioning chips. Rarely, though, a bad one may slip through (or, through mishandling, one may "toggle to the bad state"). Device geometry is now so small that it is unusual to see the pattern sensitivity that once plagued DRAMs. Usually the entire chip is just plain bad, making it a lot easier to identify problems.

Multiple addressing: This is a variant of the chip-select problem. If more than one memory device is used, several can sometimes be turned on at once.

Refresh: Dynamic RAMs need periodic accesses to keep the memory alive. This refresh signal is generated by external logic or by the CPU itself. Sometimes the refresh circuitry fails. The entire memory array must be refreshed every few milliseconds to stay within the chips' specifications, but it's surprising just how long DRAMs can remember their data after loosing refresh. One to two seconds seems to be the extreme limit.

With the above in mind we can design a routine to test RAMs. The first criteria is that the test itself certainly cannot make use of RAM.

Several of the failure modes manifest themselves by an inability to store data. Data-bus problems, a bad device, chip-select failures, or an incorrectly inserted pin will usually exhibit a simple read/write error. The traditional write and read of a 55 and an AA will find these problems quickly.

Writing a pattern of 55s and AAs tests the ability of the devices to hold data, but it doesn't insure that the RAMs are being addressed correctly. Examples of failures that could pass this simple test are a post-buffer address short, an open address line (say, from a pin not being inserted properly), or chip-select failures causing multiple addressing. It's important to run a second routine that isolates these not-uncommon problems.

An addressing test works by writing a unique data value to each location and then reading the memory to see that that value is still stored. An easy-to-compute pattern is the low-order address of the location: at 100 store 00, at 101 store a 01, etc. This isn't really unique, since an 8-bit location can only store 256 different values. If we repeat the test using the locations' high-order address bytes as the data pattern (for memory sizes to 64k), after two passes the entire array will be tested uniquely. The first test insures that address lines A0 to A7 function correctly; the second checks lines A8 to A15 and also the chip-select logic.

What is the purpose of the 55–AA test? Consider any individual address. At location 0, the addressing diagnostic will write 0 (the low address) and later another 0 (the high address). While addressability will be confirmed, some doubt remains about its ability to store data. The 55–AA check tests every bit.

The peril of these diagnostics is that the address lines cycle throughout all of memory as the test proceeds. If the refresh circuit has failed, most likely the test itself will keep DRAMs alive. This is the worst possible situation; the process of testing camouflages failures. A simple solution is to add a long delay after writing a pattern and before doing the readback. This delay should be on the order of several seconds. It is also important to constrain the test code to a small area, so the CPU's instruction fetches don't create artificial refreshes. Write the code in a small, tight loop to minimize address-line cycling.

Don't succumb to the temptation to write a byte and then compare it immediately to the correct value. This eliminates the virtues of the address test. Write all locations first, and only then check the results. With the RAMs removed from their sockets, sometimes residual bus capacitance will cause the value just written to be read back. This is yet another reason to write the entire pattern first and only then to check it.

In the bad old days small DRAMs manufacturing defects and alpha particles caused some memories to exhibit pattern sensitivity problems; selected cells would not hold a particular byte if a nearby cell held another specific byte. Elaborate tests were devised to isolate these problems. The walking ones test, in particular, burned an enormous amount of computer time and could find really complex pattern failures. Fortunately these sorts of problems just don't show up anymore.

Figure 5.1 is a complete RAM test. It is coded in 8088 assembly language and uses no RAM at all. More structured code with CALLs and RETs just will not be dependable, since it would rely on the very RAM we're testing.

While it is easy to see some justification for testing the product's RAM, ROM tests are perhaps not as valuable. How can a failed ROM test itself? A completely dead kernal that doesn't even boot cannot run

```
      title       Ram test code
code segment public
      assume      cs:code,ds:data
;
;   This routine performs a RAM test on an 80x88 type machine.
;
;   This test is sequenced through the following phases:
;
;       55 written to all addresses and read back
;       AA written to all addresses and read back
;       Low-order address written and read
;       High-order address written and read
;
;   Note that this code makes no use of RAM, so some of its
;   structure may seem arbitrarily cumbersome.
;
;   The test is not coded as a traditional subroutine with a
;   "return" instruction. Your code must flow into it—it
;   leaves at exit point ram_done.
;
;   On entry, the address to test is contained in register
;   DS:BX. The length of the test is in CX. It does not
;   support overflows into the segment register; be sure
;   that BX+CX is no more than FFFF.
;
;   On exit, if the test fails AX will be set nonzero,
;   and DS:BX will have the address of the first failed byte.
;   AX will be set to 55 if the 55 test failed,
;   or to AA if the AA test
;   failed, 1 if the low address test failed, and 2 if the
;   high test failed. Register CX will contain the number of
;   contiguous bytes that are bad; note that only one
;   contiguous block is tagged.
;
;   If the RAM passes the test, then AX will be 0.
;
ram_test:
      mov   si,bx         ; save start address in si
      mov   bp,cx         ; save length in bp
      mov   ax,55h
```

Figure 5.1   RAM text code. *(Figure continues.)*

```
ram_55_load:
      mov   [bx],al            ; load memory with 55s first
      inc   bx
      loop  ram_55_load
      mov   bx,si              ; restore start of test address
      mov   cx,bp              ; restore length of test
      dec   bx
ram_55_check:
      inc   bx
      cmp   [bx],al            ; see if we still have 55s
      loope ram_55_check       ; loop as long we get 55s back
      test  cx,cx              ; if zero, test passed
      jz    ram_aa_test        ; br if test passed
      mov   dx,0               ; dx will be # bad bytes found
      mov   si,bx              ; set first bad address
ram_55_bad:                    ; failure found—find length of
                               ; bad block
      inc   si
      inc   dx                 ; inc # bad bytes found
      dec   cx                 ; dec total # to test
      jz    ram_bad1           ; end of test
      cmp   [si],al            ; see if this location is also bad
      jnz   ram_55_bad
ram_bad1:
      jmp   ram_bad            ; end of the bad block found
;
; Run the AA test
;
ram_aa_test:
      mov   bx,si              ; start address of test
      mov   cx,bp              ; length of test
      mov   ax,0aah
ram_aa_load:
      mov   [bx],al            ; load memory with AAs first
      inc   bx
      loop  ram_aa_load
      mov   bx,si              ; restore start of test address
      mov   cx,bp              ; restore length of test
      dec   bx
ram_aa_check:
      inc   bx
      cmp   [bx],al            ; see if we still have AAs
      loope ram_aa_check       ; loop as long we get AAs back
      test  cx,cx              ; if zero, test passed
      jz    ram_low_test       ; br if test passed
      mov   dx,0               ; dx will be # bad bytes found
      mov   si,bx              ; set first bad address
```

Figure 5.1 (Continued)

```
ram_aa_bad:                    ; failure found–find length
      inc   si
      inc   dx                 ; inc # bad bytes found
      dec   cx                 ; dec total # to test
      jz    ram_bad            ; end of test
      cmp   [si],al            ; see if this location is also bad
      jnz   ram_aa_bad         ; end of the bad block found
      jmp   ram_bad
;
; Run the low address test
;
ram_low_test:
      mov   bx,si              ; start address of test
      mov   cx,bp              ; length of test
ram_low_load:
      mov   [bx],bl            ; load memory with low address
      inc   bx
      loop  ram_low_load
;
; Add in a delay of about 2-3 seconds to let DRAMs "forget"
; if refresh is not active.
;
      mov   bx,si              ; restore start of test address
      mov   cx,bp              ; restore length of test
      dec   bx
ram_low_check:
      inc   bx
      cmp   [bx],bl            ; see if we still have low address
      loope ram_low_check      ; loop as long as data ok
      test  cx,cx              ; if zero, test passed
      jz    ram_hi_test        ; br if test passed
      mov   dx,0               ; dx will be # bad bytes found
      mov   si,bx              ; set first bad address
ram_low_bad:                   ; failure found–find length
      inc   si
      inc   dx                 ; inc # bad bytes found
      dec   cx                 ; dec total # to test
      jz    ram_bad            ; end of test
      mov   ax,si              ; get address we stored
      cmp   [si],al            ; see if this location is also bad
      jnz   ram_low_bad
      mov   ax,1               ; 1 indicates low address failure
      jmp   ram_bad            ; end of the bad block found
;
; Run the high address test
;
```

Figure 5.1 (Continued)

```
ram_hi_test:
      mov   bx, si          ; start address of test
      mov   cx, bp          ; length of test
      mov   ax, 0           ; assume test will pass
ram_hi_load:
      mov   [bx], bh        ; load memory with high address
      inc   bx
      loop  ram_hi_load
;
; Add in a delay of about 2-33 seconds to let DRAMs "forget"
; if refresh is not active.
;
      mov   bx, si          ; restore start of test address
      mov   cx, bp          ; restore length of test
      dec   bx
ram_hi_check:
      inc   bx
      cmp   [bx], bh        ; see if we still have high address
      loope ram_hi_check    ; loop as long we get good data
      test  cx, cx          ; if zero, test passed
      jz    ram_done        ; br if test passed
      mov   dx, 0
      mov   si, bx          ; set first bad address
ram_hi_bad:                 ; failure found–find length
      inc   si
      inc   dx              ; inc # bad bytes found
      dec   cx              ; dec total # to test
      jz    ram_bad         ; end of test
      mov   ax, si          ; get address we stored
      cmp   [si], ah        ; see if this location is also bad
      jnz   ram_hi_bad
      mov   ax, 2           ; 2 indicates high address failure
      jmp   ram_bad         ; end of the bad block found
;
;
;
ram_bad:
      mov   cx, dx          ; cx=# bad bytes
                            ; ax=test number
                            ; bx=start of bad address
ram_done:                   ; exit point

code ends

data segment public
data ends

      end
```

Figure 5.1 (Continued)

diagnostics. If the boot ROM does at least partially work, then some testing is valuable.

In the boot ROM itself we can realistically expect to detect only a simple failure, like a partially programmed device, although with some luck it might be possible to find a shorted or open high-order address line. Luck proves helpful because if the line floats or is tied to the wrong level the diagnostic code will not start.

It's tedious to burn code into a ROM—sometimes technicians will unknowingly, in their impatience, remove the chip before the programmer is completely done. If you do elect to include a ROM test be sure to locate it early in the code so it stands a chance of executing even if the ROM is not entirely programmed. It's easier to make an argument for ROM testing in multiple ROM systems. If the boot ROM starts, then diagnostics located in it can test all of the others.

Probably the most common failure is a misinserted pin. If you've spent time troubleshooting electronics you'll know that it can be awfully hard to tell if all pins are in the sockets. Other problems cover the usual range of broken circuit board tracks (i.e., address, data, control lines), misprogrammed devices, and nonfunctioning chip-select lines.

One way to test ROMs is to read the devices and compare each byte to a known value. Such redundancy is impractical, so most programmers simply compute an 8- or 16-bit sum of the data in the ROMs and compare it to a previously saved checksum. Usually this is adequate, but a number of pathological cases will report incorrect results. For example, a long string of zeroes always checksums to zero, regardless of the number of items summed.

A much better approach than a simple checksum is the cyclic redundancy check (CRC). The CRC is a polynomial that is seeded, typically with FFFF, and then divided into the input data (in this case the ROM data) a byte at a time, using the dividend at each step as the new seed. While mathematically complicated, the CRC is pretty easy to implement. Its great virtue is that each byte of repeated strings (say, zeroes) will yield a different CRC. The CRC is a bit harder to code than a simple checksum, but the code listed in Fig. 5.2 is a cookbook solution. It is written in 8088 assembly language to insure that it uses the minimal number of as-yet-untested CPU resources.

A CRC or checksum test is easy to code and yields useful information, but it is sometimes a nuisance to implement because the correct value must be computed and stored in ROM. No assembler or compiler has a built-in function to build this automatically. Generally you'll run the program under an emulator, record the CRC or checksum the routine computes, and then manually patch the resulting value into an

```
      title       CRC program
code segment      public
      assume      cs: code, ds: data
;
;  this routine will compute a CRC of a block of
;  data starting at the address in DS:BX with the
;  length in CX. Don't try to exceed a 64k segment (keep
;  BX+CX <= FFFF).
;
;  The CRC will be computed into register DX and compared to
;  a value saved in ROM.
;
rom_test:
      mov    dx, 0ffffh      ; initialize CRC to -1
rom_loop:
      mov    al, [bx]        ; get a character to CRC
      inc    bx              ; pt to next value
      xor    al, dl          ; compute crc
      mov    ah, al          ; save temp result
      shr    al, 1           ; shift right 4
      shr    al, 1
      shr    al, 1
      shr    al, 1
      xor    al, ah          ; xor temp with partial product
      mov    ah, al          ; new temp
      shl    al, 1           ; shift left 4
      shl    al, 1
      shl    al, 1
      shl    al, 1
      mor    al, dh          ; combine with high crc
      mov    dl, al          ; save low result
      mov    al, ah
      shr    al, 1           ; shift right 3
      shr    al, 1
      shr    al, 1
      xor    al, dl
      mov    dl, al
      mov    al, ah          ; get temp back
      shl    al, 1           ; shift left 5
      shl    al, 1
      shl    al, 1
      shl    al, 1
      shl    al, 1
      xor    al, ah
      mov    dh, al          ; high crc result
```

Figure 5.2 ROM CRC test. (*Figure continues.*)

```
        dec   cx              ; dec data byte count
        jnz   rom_loop        ; loop till all CRCed
        cmp   dx,word ptr cs:crc; crc match?
        jnz   rom_error       ; error if no match
        jmp   rom_ok          ; jmp if ok
crc: dw 0                     ; save crc here
rom_error:                    ; error location-flag an error
rom_ok:                       ; rom crc compare ok

code ends

data segment   public

data ends
        end
```

Figure 5.2 (Continued)

absolute location in ROM. The only way to automate this is to write a short program that CRCs the linker output file and patches the result into the ROM file.

It's easy to extend the CRC idea to testing RAM memories. The RAM algorithm shown in Fig. 5.1 takes a long time to test large memory spaces. If a crude functional test will suffice (rather than the exhaustive test of all locations and bits), then use the CRC to test memory in small chunks.

The principle is simple: devise a short pattern of numbers with a known CRC, write this pattern to the entire memory array, and then CRC each section of memory, comparing the computed CRC to the known value. It's speedy, as only one write/read pass is needed. If you pick a clever pattern, the test will detect most common problems. Figure 5.3 shows the algorithm.

If the pattern is a prime number of bytes long, addressing errors will be detected. 257 bytes is a particularly good number; it covers just over

If the pattern's length is pattern_length, and the memory's size is memory_size, then
Write pattern (memory_size/pattern_length) times.
For index = 0 to memory_size:
    compute memory CRC from index to index + pattern_length.
    index = index + pattern_length.
    if (CRC is not the same as precomputed one) ERROR.

Figure 5.3 RAM test using a CRC.

one page (so will find page-sensitive addressing errors) yet is reasonably short.

What is a good pattern? In fact, practically any more-or-less random collection of data will do. It's a good idea to make sure the pathological cases are tested, such as all ones (FF), all zeroes, and the like. One easy method is to write a random number generator in BASIC or C, edit the output to include FF, 00, AA, and 55, and then cut and paste these values into the source code.

The algorithm depends on a known good CRC. The program that generated the pattern in the first place could also output a CRC that is stored in the system's ROMs, but this makes changing the pattern difficult. It's much easier to compute the CRC on the fly when the values are stored into RAM during the test.

ANALOG CONSIDERATIONS

Most embedded systems interface to mechanical and electronic sensors and actuators. Certainly the mechanical portions are prone to failure; just as certainly analog I/O is subject to drift, noise, and other effects that we digital people hate to acknowledge. Give the test technician and end user a back door into a diagnostics suite.

Consider the system's analog circuits. Potentiometers (pots) tune offsets and gains resulting from the slightly different characteristics of these components. Sometimes, lots of pots are used. It's interesting to watch a test group calibrate these sorts of instruments; frequently, special test equipment monitors the voltages during pot twiddling. Without this equipment these adjustments simply cannot be made in the field.

In most cases a bit of clever software can take advantage of a panel display to replace the test gear. Write a short routine to show raw voltage, or whatever is being monitored, on the system's own output device. Certainly you've already written low-level routines to get the data (for use in the main program); spend an afternoon writing a simple diagnostic that calls this subroutine and formats the output.

Looping tests for analog circuits will find drifty electronics. If your system measures low-level signals where drift and offset are potential problems, consider writing code that will run long-term evaluations of the input data. Then the technicians can start overnight checks on their touchy analog electronics. The code will require little more than a routine to call the A/D routine and compare against user-specified limits. If the input value moves out of some allowable range, flash an LED or print a warning.

Is analog noise a problem? Some embedded systems acquire signals whose value is measured in microvolts. Tiny amounts of noise could be devastating. A long-term averaging routine that reports excessive noise will greatly simplify production test.

Pots are a continuous source of frustration to users. Think: can you come up with a better, self-calibrating design? Try writing code that removes offset, gain, and other errors mathematically. Chapter 10 discusses this in more detail.

THE SCOPE

When you design diagnostics for field or in-house use, be sure to bear in mind the sorts of tools users will have available. Most test and repair technicians rely on the scope almost exclusively. Logic analyzers, emulators, and the other tools used in engineering are not nearly so ubiquitous in the test environment. Remember this when writing diagnostic code.

While the scope is the universally accepted troubleshooting tool, computer-based systems are not really well suited to scope diagnosis. Digital events tend to be wide (requiring many channels—like for addresses and data) or very intermittent (a 1-μsec event once per second). Even the most sophisticated scope can't capture these signals without some help from the code. The solution? Write diagnostics that run in repetitive loops and be sure to toggle a bit (say, an I/O port) at the start of each loop. The technician can trigger the scope's sweep (i.e., start the trace at the left side of the screen) each time the bit is asserted. This scope trigger point gives an essential reference to the sequencing of events, making the scope as useful as a logic analyzer.

High-integration microcontrollers are an extreme example of unfixable systems. The processor's operations are all concealed inside a single package. How will the technician tell what the processor is doing? If you dedicate a bit or two to scope trigger points, perhaps toggling one up and down whenever a critical event takes place, at least the technician will get some insight into its operation. You might want to cycle a bit when the program is idle—the subsequent scope activity will clearly indicate when the CPU is off servicing an interrupt or other activity and when it is at the program's root node.

REPORTING FAILURES

I've always hated the annoying beep my Macintosh makes on reset. Until recently, that is, when the computer died with a dramatic belch of smoke. Where, exactly, was the failure? The screen went blank—was the CPU dead? Could the power supply have failed? But wait—on reset the computer still beeps! Power must be OK and the CPU is probably working. Indeed, it turned out that the problem was localized to the video circuits, and a $100 mail-order board brought the computer back to life. The once annoying beep saved an expensive trip to the Mac man.

Years ago Computer Automation installed go/no-go LEDs on every board in their Naked Mini computers. Like the Mac's beep, these simple indicators save users a lot of grief. Nothing this simple is foolproof, but even an 80% success rate is impressive.

Certainly systems with CRTs or other alphanumeric displays can easily show lots of useful error information. Working in C makes formatting output especially easy. Use these resources but don't depend on them. An awful lot of hardware and software must work before even a single character can be displayed on a CRT; self-test routines should depend on the absolute minimum of functioning hardware.

Learn from the automotive companies. Cars have a lot of sensors, all wired to an under-hood computer. Dozens of potential failure nodes exist. Ford, GM, and others let the mechanic put the computer into a self-test mode, flagging errors by toggling 1 bit very slowly. The engineers cleverly realized that a voltmeter is about all you can count on a mechanic having and understanding, so their software drives the bit up and down so slowly that even a meter needle can show the transitions. Error 51 might mean "failed PCV valve," which is indicated by five needle deflections, a pause, followed by one more. What could be simpler?

An LED is just as effective and even easier to use. If the product is too cost sensitive to include even a ten-cent LED, provide a place to clip one on.

If you use an LED rather than a voltmeter, the flashes can be quite a bit faster. A subroutine to show one digit of a code is simple and typically takes the following form:

```
            Set COUNT = # flashes wanted
LOOP:       turn LED ON
            delay for 1/4 second
            turn LED off
            delay for 1/2 second
            COUNT = COUNT - 1
            Go to LOOP as long as COUNT is nonzero
```

Avoid using zeroes as part of an error code. While zero might correspond to "no flash," it is visually very confusing.

Putting error codes on a single LED is arguably better than showing the complete code in a conventional seven-segment or ASCII display. The single-bit approach is more robust; not much hardware support is needed. If the system has a number of LEDs, consider sending the same pattern to all of them. A single LED (or port) failure will then be obvious, and the remaining LEDs will still show the error code.

INTERNAL DIAGNOSTICS TRICKS

A nice way of finding bus shorts, memory failures, and the like is to execute a looping program, letting the technician examine each address and data line with a scope to find the source of the trouble. Of course, if the memories don't work, or if the address bus is shorted, how can we run a program?

On the Z80 and 8085 family the RST 7 instruction is a 1-byte CALL to location 38. Was Intel clairvoyant or was it just luck that caused them to use opcode FF for this instruction? If you add pullup resistors to the bus, then simply removing all memory chips will make the processor execute CALLs to 38 all day long. The stack pointer will decrement through the processor's entire address space, so the technician can look at address lines and check that they cycle properly. The data bus will show return addresses after each RST 7 executes; since the stack pointer decrements, these addresses will change as well. This trivial test gives the repetitive signals needed to effectively use a scope to check out the hardest parts of the system.

On the 8088 family the INT 3 instruction is a similar 1-byte opcode. A 1-byte PUSH might even be better. Since these instructions are not FF opcodes, pull up the bus and add a jumper field so the technician can set the proper opcode.

As a vendor of microprocessor development tools, our success lies in helping customers make their systems work. Sometimes we forget to solve our own problems. For instance, our emulators come with real-time trace that captures the user's program as it executes. It was only until several years after first introducing this feature that we realized it could help our production crew as well. Now the emulators have a special mode that lets our technicians trace the code executed by the emulator rather than that executed by the user's code. For no additional cost, they can use the feature we installed for our customers as a sort of logic analyzer to solve production problems. The moral: think creatively and broadly. Use the resources in your system in many ways.

OK, so you say this is a one-off unit that will never be reproduced and has a design life of only a few weeks—why spend time writing diagnostics? This is a valid point, but even in these extreme cases be sure that the system has at least an "easy mode." That is, be sure that on power up (or by installing a jumper or setting a switch) a dramatic event occurs—say, a lamp lights. This way you can tell in a second if the computer is running and power is applied. You don't want to spend time chasing timing problems in a complex system when the computer hasn't even started.

It always seems that just before a demo everything falls apart. After a late night of removing the final bugs from microcontroller-based design, I unplugged the emulator and installed the computer chip. On power up the unit did nothing—it was completely dead. Fortunately the code had a simple test routine that blinked an LED before any other initialization took place. Since the LED didn't blink, I knew immediately that the code was not starting and indeed found that a floating DMA request line was keeping the processor idle. The emulator's slightly different dc characteristics masked the problem during weeks of code development.

ROM MONITORS

Let's not forget the sophisticated troubleshooter. We've all had the unpleasant experience of being called in to find and fix design flaws. Build in tools to make this sort of work easier for you and your associates.

If the embedded system includes some sort of terminal interface, then including a monitor is a nice way to give the high-end user access to the system's internals. A ROM monitor may not be as powerful as an emulator or logic analyzer, but it is easy to invoke. A built-in monitor is like a sleeping giant, dormant, waiting to be called into action by entering a secret command. But be careful—I once failed to check for keyboard overflow in a product, and a user called to complain about the weird mode (the monitor) that the product entered when his cat sat on the keyboard.

A simple monitor lets you change and examine memory and I/O. Giving the hardware troubleshooter access to I/O can save that person hours of work—entering an input command to see what a port does is much simpler than trying to capture the event on a logic analyzer. If you feel really generous with your time, display the status of all system I/O in a table, converting cryptic hex statuses to meaningful keywords. "Data ready" is a lot easier to understand than "02."

A disassembler, assembler, and simple breakpoints are a lot more work to add, but if you go through the trouble you can then patch small test routines into the product's RAM. At the very least have a GO command that starts a program at any address. Then you can patch in instruction hex codes and start simple test loops that perhaps cycle a particular port. The scope-happy technicians will love you for it. Is a port very occasionally intermittent? A few bytes of code can monitor this much more effectively than any other means.

A monitor can serve as a diagnostics platform. It is an easy way to invoke complex test routines, and it forms the backbone of a nice interface for communicating test results. A monitor is a sort of software bus to hang diagnostics and other utilities from.

External Diagnostics

Ask yourself "what tools will the production test and service people use?" They'll certainly have at least a scope. Perhaps, depending on the product's complexity and production quantities, it will make sense to have them invest in equipment better suited to the tests they'll need to run.

The trend is certainly toward emulators or emulator-like devices. Cost is an important consideration—a $40,000 development system like the one you use to write the code is just too expensive and too complex for test technicians. Other options do exist. Look for inexpensive emulators or even special troubleshooting tools designed for the microprocessor world. Many are available, some specifically targeted toward test. The following discussion refers to conventional emulators or emulator-like devices such as Fluke's Microsystem Troubleshooter, which is specifically designed to help test micro-based products.

Any single failure (sometimes lasting only microseconds) can make self-diagnostic routines unusable and can throw the processor into a mode where conventional test techniques are useless. Yet in the development lab engineers routinely bring up haphazardly assembled prototypes. While this is often attributed to superior electronic skills, it is really more a result of clever use of the sophisticated tools at an engineer's disposal.

Where the system's program, sans emulator, might just run away due to an address-line short, an emulator provides resources for identifying that short. By comparison, a scope or a logic analyzer can only show what the system is doing—neither affects its operation. An incorrect read from an I/O port may crash the program—no scope can see such a single-shot event. A logic analyzer overwhelms the user with data; finding a single bad read is unacceptably tedious. An emulator lets the user easily access the port manually and display the resulting data.

Suppose a technician is presented with a target system that does nothing—the internal self-tests are dead, the processor is either halted or running wild, and there are no good diagnostic symptoms available. With a scope he might probe almost at random, hoping by some serendipitous magic to find an abnormal signal that just might be related to the problem. Since the CPU can enter a tri-state at any time, conventional wisdom that says a floating signal is unconnected is not valid. Finding the problem inevitably requires a certain amount of luck and much more time than is reasonable.

Contrast that situation to using even a simple emulator. Since the unit is dead, you replace the processor with the emulator's pod. Issuing a checksum command determines in a matter of seconds if the ROMs have correct data. A bad checksum (compared to that obtained from a known-good unit) indicates a bus problem, ROM problem, or ROM decoder failure. If the ROM test passes, you know immediately that all of these areas are intact. Then check the DUT's read/write memory with the emulator's built-in test RAM command. A quick but exhaustive test tells you if the RAMs work. These elementary tests are impossible with any other sort of tool.

Some I/O devices are truly devilish to test. Often dozens of internal registers must be programmed before any meaningful data transfers can take place. Again, an emulator can help find these faults. The software engineer who originally wrote the system's code can port the I/O initialization routines to the test department. Technicians can download these small diagnostic routines to the overlay RAM and run them. Complex I/O can thus be easily checked using the same code that runs in the system.

If RAM, ROM, and the busses function properly, the next logical item to examine is the DUT's I/O. These tests can be as simple or as complex as needed. It's generally quite easy to read A/D values, read/set parallel bits, and check more complex devices like UARTs and DMA channels.

In the care of a competent technician, an emulator will quickly find most problems. Unfortunately, not all test personnel are as computer-literate as might be required by today's complex products. Some problems will require an intimate knowledge of the system's operation—possibly more than can reasonably be expected of the average technician.

Several of the debuggers currently on the market include simplified C-like programming languages. Using the features of these languages, an engineer can write a remarkably simple program that issues the

ROM, RAM, and I/O test commands. Any emulator command can generally be included in the program. A simple construct might resemble the following:

```
if (checksum(0,1fff) != 123) printf("Error in ROM test")
```

An error could invoke an error-logging routine or even initiate more complex fault isolation.

The concept of emulator programming really shines when testing I/O. The complicated setup of a device can be included in the test code. Data returned from, say, a UART is usually a bit mask; the emulator code can isolate each bit and make decisions about the bit's correctness. Even better, a simple emulator-control program can translate confusing bit patterns into an English description. Instead of reporting bit pattern 01100001, it could report "DATA READY."

The development team should spend a week in the production plant testing existing products. It's one of the best ways to understand the need for diagnostics.

CHAPTER 6

Memory Management

The researches of many commentators have already thrown much darkness on this subject, and it is probable that, if they continue, we shall soon know nothing at all about it.—Mark Twain.

No matter how carefully we plan, sometimes it seems our programs always grow bigger than whatever amount of memory we have. Is the definition of a mature product one whose ROM has only three empty bytes? Trying to compress and recode working software to fix bugs or add features takes an inordinate amount of time.

Memory is an important resource we must manage carefully. Chapter 2 discusses estimating your memory needs, but sloppy coding will quickly eat up any number of megabytes allocated to the code. Remember that you should deliver a product with plenty of spare address space, since creeping featurism is sure to demand substantial additional amounts of memory over the product's maintenance cycle.

Yesterday's 8048 microcontroller included a paltry 1k of on-board ROM. Some cleverly coded control applications fit in this device, but this processor's descendants now pack 32k or more. Even this is often not enough, so we can be sure that single-chip microcontrollers will include ever more bytes of RAM and ROM as time goes on.

Various surveys indicate that by 1990 the average embedded program ran around 30,000 lines, up from 17,000 in 1987. While the microprocessor will always have lots of minimal applications (very simple controllers, greeting card buzzers, and the like), most systems will continue to evolve toward complexity. The minimum stakes for entering any market spiral upward with time—in a few years no PC program that comes without an elaborate graphics user interface will be competitive. This is a sort of Darwinian evolution toward complexity and product survival.

There's a yin and yang to program sizes measured in number of lines. Switching to C reduces the line count, while ever-increasing complexity (i.e., more features and capability) drives it up. The savings in NRE from a high-level language creates more opportunity to use the saved time to add functionality, requiring yet more memory.

Programs are getting big! Part of the shift toward 16- and 32-bit processors comes from the need for correspondingly huge address spaces, since conventional wisdom holds that a 512-kbyte program just cannot fit in the 64k address space of an 8-bit CPU.

Programs are not the only consumers of memory. Big local data buffers can dwarf ROM requirements. Video circuits, high-speed transmission devices, and other applications often need staggering amounts of RAM for temporary data storage.

Everyone knows that programs keep growing, and concerns are tempered with the sure knowledge that at least memory is cheap. Dynamic RAMs offer a particularly attractive cost per bit; even better, their density doubles every two years. Static RAMs and EPROMs need four times as many transistors per bit—they follow the same evolutionarily path but lag by several years.

With the start of the 1990s, Motorola announced plans for a 256-million-bit DRAM by 1999. Other vendors concurred. We're fortunate that the path of at least this aspect of computer technology is so clear, and even more fortunate that plans are afoot to assimilate this technology. Standardization committees work far in advance of today's capabilities to define future memory pinouts. These JEDEC memory configurations make it easy to design tomorrow's parts into a system.

For example, the 32-pin JEDEC ROM and static RAM standard permit upgrade from a 32- to 256-kbyte device with no circuit changes. If your system will need 20k of EPROM, don't even consider designing for a 28-pin 32-kbyte 27256. Look ahead just a little, remember that the code will surely grow, and modify the design ever so slightly for 32-pin EPROMs. No extra production costs will be incurred—you can still use the 27256 until the code grows beyond 32k. You'll be a hero when, three years hence, a simple chip substitution solves a crucial memory space problem.

How Memory Mappers Work

Thirty-two-bit microcomputers have huge linear address spaces. Need more RAM? Just glue additional chips into the circuit. This isn't so easy in the 8- and 16-bit world, where the processor's address space might be smaller than that required by the application. *Address space* is the amount of memory directly accessible by the processor, which might be substantially less than what is needed. The 68000, a 16-bit CPU with 24 address bits, can only issue addresses in the range of 0 to 16 mbytes. More memory than 16 mbytes requires external mapping hardware or a 32-bit processor.

In the minicomputer days, programmers faced the same sort of problems. It's hard to believe that a 64k machine like the venerable PDP-11 could support dozens of users quite well. Even though minicomputer memory was large, slow, and expensive, multiuser applications demanded what was then considered huge amounts (typically 256 to 512 kbytes).

The PDP-11 and other minicomputers employed memory-management schemes to map the computer's limited 64k address space into a larger amount of physical memory.

In a sense, memory management came back into favor with the introduction of Intel's 8088 family of processors. In an effort to maintain some sort of compatibility with their 8-bit 8080, Intel gave the 8088 a 20-bit physical-address bus but limited program addresses to 16 bits. In 1978, 64k seemed like a lot of memory; 1 mbyte (the 20-bit physical limit) was close to infinity.

Instead of adopting a conventional memory management unit (MMU), Intel added the now famous 16-bit segment registers. CS, the code segment register, modifies all accesses to the program. Data references work through DS, the stack uses SS, and ES, the extra segment register, handles string manipulation.

Every memory access is modified by the contents of one of the registers. The CPU shifts the segment register left four bits and adds the program-generated address. For example, if DS is 1000h and the program generates a load from address 234h, the effective physical address on the bus is 10234h.

These computers are really limited to 128k address spaces. A program just can't use more than 64k of code and 64k of data without issuing explicit instructions to change a segment register (or by using long jumps and calls). Compilers must be designed to generate intersegment transfers—witness the multitude of memory models provided by both Microsoft's and Borland's Cs.

The 8088 family is so ubiquitous that an investment in careful compiler design has paid off handsomely for the vendors. Unfortunately this is not quite so true in the 8-bit world. Even though some 8-bit architectures are sold in huge volume, there is no standard memory-management interface, making it all but impossible to implement a general compiler or assembler-based mapping mechanism.

Thankfully, later members of the family like the 80386 are true 32-bit CPUs that can directly issue 32-bit addresses. Unfortunately, as I write this, almost all 80386 machines run in 8088 compatibility mode; hopefully soon the 386 will become the new base standard for the PC with a plethora of native software supporting it.

Intel's main competitor in the 16- and 32-bit wars has always been Motorola's 68000 family. Pin count and die size limitations restricted the original 68000's address bus to 24 bits. Some applications demand more than the 16 mbytes available from 24 bits, so Motorola designed an external memory management chip to translate addresses.

However, nowhere is memory management needed so much as with 8-bit computers. I think it's safe to say that no 8-bit CPU can directly use an address bigger than 64k. For an increasing number of applications this is just not enough memory, yet the cost of migrating to a real 16- or 32-bit architecture is simply too high. Memory managers are a cost effective solution.

LOGICAL AND PHYSICAL ADDRESSES

The problem of memory management is easy to define: We need some (hopefully simple) way of connecting large amounts of memory to a processor that just cannot handle or address it. For example, we might want to put 512 kbytes on a Z80. Since the Z80 only generates 16-bit addresses it can only directly address 64k of RAM. Through memory management we can expand this capability.

For now let's assume that hardware gives us more address lines. Perhaps it is as simple as an I/O port loaded by the CPU with an extra upper 8 (A16 to A23), giving a potential address space of 24 mbytes. Or it can be hideously complex, providing some ability to access different sections of memory space in wild and wonderful ways. In any event, with an external address translation mechanism the programmer suddenly must contend with two very different sorts of address spaces.

Physical memory is that which is actually connected to the hardware. For example, the 512 kbytes we attach to the sadly overloaded

Z80 is physical memory. Its address ranges from 00000 to 80000 hex in a nice linear fashion.

Logical memory is the memory currently located in the processor's address space. Obviously, if the computer can only issue addresses in the range of 0000 to FFFF (0 to 64k), then some of the physical memory is visible and some is not. As the code changes the memory manager's settings, different memory becomes visible. That which is addressable at any time is the logical memory. Thus, addresses generated by the program are always logical addresses—they get translated by some as yet undefined hardware into real physical addresses.

At one time address 1000 logical might be translated into 28000 physical. Later 1000 could correspond to 80000 physical. The old one-to-one mapping of addresses we're all familiar with is gone.

In summary, logical addresses are those used by the code; physical ones are those applied to the memory array. Between these two the MMU falls.

While we don't think of the 8088 as having an MMU, it is instructive to consider its segmented architecture in these terms. After all, an 8088 program does issue 16-bit addresses (logical) that are translated into a 1-mbyte space (physical).

In the 8088 the translation takes place on board the CPU chip (Fig. 6.1). The program issues logical addresses, but a logic analyzer connected to its pins shows only physicals. With the 8088 many different combinations of a segment and offset can give the same physical address—there is no way that a piece of equipment monitoring the processor's pins can reconstruct what logical address was issued. This is generally true of memory management schemes.

BANKING

Once upon a time there was only one way to handle memory spaces larger than 64k with an 8-bit computer. Banking is a technique of expanding an address space by adding simple external hardware that enables and disables sections of memory under program control. While traditional banking is indeed a form of memory management, banking is characterized and differentiated from modern MMUs by its simplicity.

Banked memory was once moderately common, especially in the CP/M world. The most common use was in the computer's boot ROM. Sometimes complex disk setups could eat up a lot of memory, even when they were really only needed once to load in the CP/M operating system. With a 64k total address space, using 8k for the boot ROM

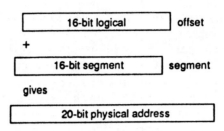

Figure 6.1 8088 address translation.

would be a terrible waste. Phantom ROMs were the solution. The hardware brought a ROM into view in place of RAM when the reset button was pressed. After booting, an I/O instruction disabled the ROM, removing it from view and parking it in the background.

Phantom ROMs showed the microcomputer world one of the biggest perils of any sort of memory management. Once an I/O instruction disabled the ROM suddenly an entirely new address space appeared—at the program counter's address! Some programs preset RAM underneath the ROM to good code, say, a jump, so the sudden change of context was safe. Other systems jumped to RAM outside of the ROM's address range and then issued the I/O instruction. A lot of people got burned trying to debug code that suddenly disappeared.

Other CP/M computers employed more sophisticated banking during the execution of application programs. Usually the code programmed a simple latch with the high-order address lines. While this did open the Z80's address space to handle lots of RAM, each design was unique, so banking was virtually unsupported by standard software packages.

Some embedded designs continue to use banking schemes. In general you can view the banking hardware as a memory management unit. The same techniques discussed below apply to the banking software.

Memory Management Units

Hardware makes the translation from logical to physical addresses on the fly. Whether located on the processor itself as part of its silicon or as an external peripheral chip, the memory management unit is located between the CPU core and the memory array. In the case of an 8-bit processor, 16 address lines go in and 20 to 24 come out.

The most important point that can be made about MMUs is that they do not provide the linear address space we all crave. After all, 8- and some 16-bit processors generally use 16-bit address operands and 16-bit register pointers—there is no way to directly address a number larger than 64k. A jump instruction will always have an argument that is 16 bits long—the logical destination address. The MMU translates this logical address to a possibly large physical number, but the software still operates in a 64k space.

This has a subtle implication: logical address space is a valuable commodity that must be conserved. Wasting physical memory is one of the deadly sins of embedded programming, but wasting logical address space is fatal. More on this later.

Until very recently, software support of banking and memory management has been minimal. Now standard MMU architectures included on high integration chips has encouraged some compiler and assembler vendors to build MMU support into their products.

STANDARD ARCHITECTURES

In the mid 1980s Hitachi introduced the 64180, a high-integration version of the venerable Z80. It is interesting that while other vendors were trying to push new proprietary architectures, Hitachi took what might seem a step backwards toward the Z80. I think they realized an important fact of the industry—customers had a fortune invested in Z80 code and were unwilling to switch to an incompatible instruction set. The 64180 is one of a family of CPUs supported by at both Hitachi and Zilog.

The 64180 is really a Z80 at heart. The designers resisted the temptation to add fancy new instructions and addressing modes that could have made it incompatible with the Z80. Rather, they integrated timers, serial ports, and DMA controllers onto the chip. Even better, they added a memory management unit to translate 64k logical addresses into a 1-mbyte physical address space (Fig. 6.2).

The 64180's MMU uses three internal control registers (Fig. 6.3). In keeping with the chip's design philosophy, on reset the MMU gives a straight logical to physical mapping, simulating the Z80 and limiting the address space to 64k.

You can divide the 64180's logical address space into one, two, or three areas. The logical space itself is unaltered; even when divided it is still a contiguous 64k. This process defines how each of the (up to three) areas exists in physical memory.

Common-base address register (CBAR) is an 8-bit I/O port that can

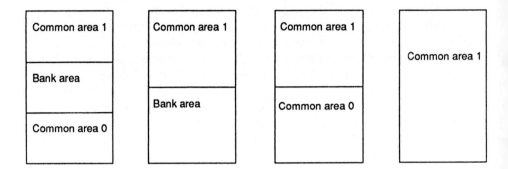

Figure 6.2   64180 memory space.

be accessed by the processor's OUT and IN instructions. The lower 4 bits specify the starting address of the bank area, and the upper 4 give the start of common 1. These bits determine the upper four bits of the address. If CBAR were A8, then the base area starts at 8000 logical and common 1 starts at A000. Common 0, if it exists, always starts at logical 0000 and runs up to the bank area. The bank area then runs to the start of common 1. You can always understand the logical address space by examining the contents of CBAR by itself.

The logical address is only part of the problem. How does logical

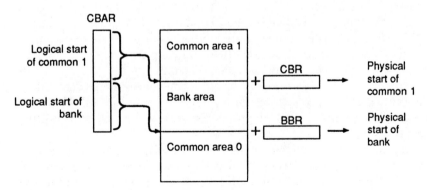

Figure 6.3   64180 MMU registers.

space get mapped to physical? Two other ports provide the rest of the answer.

The base area bank register (BBR) specifies the starting physical address of the base area (remember, the logical start was given in CBAR). Common bank register (CBR) gives the same information for common 1. Both of these specify the upper 8 bits of the 20-bit physical address.

A simple formula gives the translation from logical to physical address for the bank area:

$$Physical = Logical + (BBR \cdot 4096)$$

The same formula gives common 1:

$$Physical = Logical + (CBR \cdot 4096)$$

BBR and CBR give the upper 8 address bits only—hence the 4096 multiplier. The lower 12 bits come from the logical address. Thus, the translation only really affects the upper 8 bits; the lower 12 physical bits are always identical to the lower 12 logical.

On reset, the 64180 sets CBAR to F0, and CBR = BBR = 0. This maps logical to physical exactly, with no translation; the bank area starts at logical 0 and common 1 at F000 (since CBAR = F0), the bank area physically starts at 0000 (BBR = 0) as does common 1 (CBR = 0). If logical address 1000 is generated, the MMU allocates this to the bank area (CBAR = F0; 1000 is less than the start of common 1 at F000) and adds the physical base of the bank to it (0), giving a translated address of 01000. Similarly, logical F800 is in common 1 and is translated by adding CBR (0), yielding 0F800.

Here are some more examples:

CBAR	CBR	BBR	Common 0	Bank	Common 1
F0	00	00		00000–0EFFF	0F000–0FFFF
F0	01	00		00000–0EFFF	10000–10FFF
10	20	00		00000–00FFF	21000–30000
21	10	0F	00000–01FFF	10000–11FFF	12000–1DFFF
C6	10	00	00000–05FFF	06000–0BFFF	1C000–1FFFF

With only three distinct regions allowed in logical address space, not too many different arrangements are feasible. The most common and useful organization is to use all three banks (commons 0 and 1 and bank) partitioned as in Fig. 6.4. Common 0 and bank are never re-mapped once the initial configuration is established. Common 1 is a

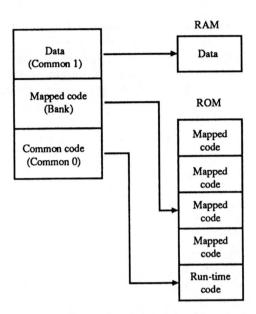

Figure 6.4 Large code model.

window into the data and probably does not get remapped. Bank points to your code. Remapping routines switch this section in and out as needed to get to various subroutines. Common 0 is usually small and consists of interrupt service routines (which should never be remapped) and small subroutines shared by much of the code. Definitely put the remapping routines in this region.

Figure 6.5 diagrams a layout for large data array with a small program. It assumes the code is small enough to fit entirely in the common 0 region. This example is the logical inverse of the first one. Common 1 is a small window to global variables (like the stack) that never get remapped. Common 0 points to your code in one homogeneous chunk. The bank area is a window into the huge arrays. Code remaps the BBR register as needed to access the proper section of data.

But what if your program and data are both huge? You can design a dynamic mapping scheme to handle both, but the result will be slow, cumbersome code that has trouble dealing with interrupts. A three bank architecture is just not ideal for this sort of application. Consider using a more powerful MMU such as the one found on the Z280.

With only three banks, the 64180 is rather simple memory manager. The other extreme in complexity is Zilog's Z280, again a high-integra-

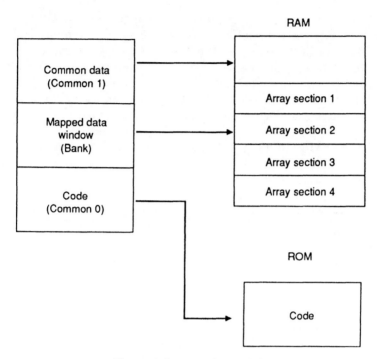

Figure 6.5 Large data model.

tion Z80-like part with an on-board MMU. The Z280 was announced with much fanfare in 1978 as the Z800—and again in 1983, 1985, and finally, for real, in 1988. The part was just too ambitious for the times, and it wasn't until the late 1980s that the design finally worked.

Like the 64180, the Z280 is a high-integration device based on the Z80. Unlike the 64180, the Z280's processor core greatly expands the number of instructions, addressing modes, and the like. It is truly a 16-bit CPU yet maintains Z80 object code compatibility. A prefetcher grabs data before the CPU needs it and an on-board cache greatly speeds loop execution.

The Z280's physical address space is 16 million bytes, or 24 bits. The 64k of logical space is supported via conventional and extended Z80 instructions. The chip can use two different address spaces: system and user. The operating system (or your code if user mode is not enabled) runs in system space. Multitasking programs usually run in user mode, which restricts access to certain dangerous instructions (like HALT). Each mode has its own 64k address space.

The memory manager segments logical space into 16 4k segments (compared with only three for the 64180). Instead of the fairly obtuse CBR, BBR, and CBAR registers, the Z280 has a page descriptor register (PDR) that describes the logical to physical mapping for each segment (or page). The chip has one PDR per page—16 for system mode and an additional 16 for user mode. Figure 6.6 shows the translation mechanism for system mode. User mode simply translates with a different set of PDRs.

Like the 64180, the mapping resolution is 4k. In other words, the lower 12 bits of the logical address are passed through the MMU unmodified. The Z280's MMU forms a physical address by using the logical's upper 4 bits as a pointer to a PDR (4 bits yield 16 PDRs) and then using the PDR's page frame address as bits 23 to 12 of the physical address.

Suppose the program issues logical address 24AB. The MMU uses the upper nibble, in this case 2, to select PDR number 2. If PDR 2 has a

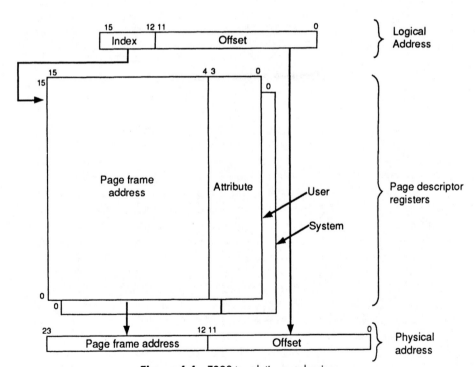

Figure 6.6 Z280 translation mechanism.

page frame address of 123, then the MMU forms a final physical address of 1234AB. The most significant 4 bits of logical address only select a PDR; they are not part of the address. The PDRs are 16-bit registers. Twelve bits provide translation addresses, the other four control the operation of that page.

Thirty-two PDRs completely describe the configuration of user and system address space. This is a lot of registers! In even the smallest system-mode-only mapped program, at least 16 of them must be set (correctly) before using the MMU. While tedious, the structure is very regular and easy to manage.

The 64180's limit of three address regions greatly limits the organization of memory. It's very difficult to map big code and data in the same program. With 16 pages, the Z280 gets around this problem. Figure 6.7 shows an example. A common area of code (interrupt vectors, frequently invoked subroutines, and the like) is in the lower part of the address space. It is constant and never remapped. The mapped code is directly above. These routines switch in and out of memory as needed, letting a huge program run in the limited logical space. A fixed section of RAM at the top of memory contains the stack and variables global to the entire program. A 4k window into a big array lies immediately below. Careful remapping of this window gives the program access to possibly megabytes of data.

A lot of variations are possible. If the program manages several huge

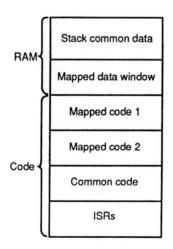

Figure 6.7 Z280 typical logical map.

data arrays, it might make sense to allocate a 4k page to each one to cut down on remapping overhead.

Other MMUs will certainly be forthcoming as vendors try to breathe more life into successful 8-bit processor families. While the details will vary, programming algorithms and design approaches will remain the same as described for these chips.

Practical Memory Management

One of the biggest attractions of memory managers is the promise of using large programs. Yes, it is possible to write huge monolithic programs that crudely simulate a more or less linear address space via the MMU. However, this is not advisable unless using a high-level language that can automatically manage the details involved.

Every experienced programmer divides a complex program into many small functions. This top-down decomposition can be combined with careful grouping of the functions into modules that share identical logical addresses to minimize the amount of remapping needed.

On the 64180, the three space memory model is the best for handling big programs. Common 0, located at physical address 0, is never remapped. It contains the interrupt service routines and all other commonly invoked code. The system's main loop typically also resides here.

Common 1, which occupies the end of the logical address space, is mapped to the system's RAM memory. It holds all of the program's variables. Remap it only at great peril, since the stack will certainly be lost.

The base area, sandwiched between the two common blocks, is where most of the remapping activity takes place. Perhaps the bank area is only 4k long; functions can be grouped together until 4k worth has been accumulated. Each group is compiled at this same address and then loaded into different physical segments of memory. (Assembly programmers might use the PHASE and DEPHASE pseudo-ops to create these virtual overlays.)

A driver routine in common 0 is used to invoke each function; no calls are made between functions without going through the driver. The driver remaps the MMU as needed every time a function call is made and then branches to the proper routine.

This approach has a profound benefit. Select a new map by reloading just the BBR register. Obviously, this is faster than resetting a complete, complex new map. Even better, the MMU is always in a good state; a partial map is never loaded and interrupts can be left on while remapping. A BBR value can be associated with each function, as well as a starting address within the bank area, making function invocation fairly easy.

A logical extension of this idea is to use a real-time operating system (RTOS) to drive the memory manager. Face it—manually manipulating the MMU is a lot of work and can be a nightmare to debug. An RTOS will institutionalize this process, hiding the details and limiting the chances for bugs. See Chapter 9 for an example.

A task is a logically complete section of code. Since only one task can be active at a time, just the active task needs to be mapped into the current space. All of the others can be mapped out till needed.

Assign each task to a separate map. The operating system can automatically reset the MMU after every context switch, bringing the proper code into view.

MAPPING DATA

Suppose you're designing a remote data collection device that gets one 16-bit A/D reading every second. This doesn't sound like much data, but after only a day the system will have acquired 86,400 words (172,800 bytes)—far more than the logical address space of 64k.

Managing a 64180's memory in this sort of application demands careful analysis of both the logical and physical address space needs. 173k will never fit within the 64k logical space, so the program will have to remap the MMU to get to the array.

This problem requires sequential access to the data—the current data point is appended immediately after the last. It is a special case of the more general array accessing situation, where a program might need any arbitrary data point in no particular order. Random array access is analogous to that employed by disk drives, while sequential is typical of tapes.

Byte-oriented data (like strings) is easy to work with. Element I is the Ith address in the string; in other words, the address of **DATA(8)** is the start address of the array plus 8 (assuming **DATA(0)** is a valid element). This is called a vector—it has only one dimension, that which is given by the subscript.

Of course, in real applications we often work with data that is 16 or more bits long. Integers are usually 2 bytes; floating-point values typically are 4 or even 8 bytes. Array element I of a vector is found from

$$\text{base} + I \cdot \text{element size}$$

where **base** is the start address of the array.

Again, this assumes element 0 is valid. Element 0 is at the first address of the array, followed sequentially by each other element.

Multidimensional arrays use an extension of this formula. In most systems these arrays are stored in row major order: given **A(row,column)**, all column elements of row 0 are stored first, then the column elements of row 1, and so forth. We can get to any element $A(I,J)$ using the formula:

$$address = base + I \cdot (J_{max} \cdot E_{size}) + J \cdot E_{size}$$

where J_{max} is the number of columns in the array and E_{size} the number of bytes per element of the array.

This is a computationally expensive way to get to an array. Multiplications are slow. Generally you can count on the quantity $J_{max} \cdot E_{size}$ to be a constant; for speed critical applications it may be wise to set this to a convenient value (a power of two), even if some memory is wasted. Similarly, aim for an element size that is 1, 2, 4, or 8 and substitute shifts for multiplies.

Any number of dimensions can be accommodated by extending the formula. Higher dimension arrays require even more math to access, so try to stay within one or two dimensions.

In real-time applications it's nice to support two forms of data access. A perfectly general form is useful for offline data reduction; your application program can request any array element in any sequence. However, during data acquisition you might need a shortcut to avoid the computational overhead of computing an array index. If data is gathered in some sequential form it's easy to visualize the data as a one dimensional vector (instead of a multidimensional array) and store each value sequentially.

If a lot of data is being handled, we'll quickly run into trouble. Limited memory space will force some sort of memory management scheme. After all, **ARRAY(100,1000)** just will not fit into a 64k space.

Using huge arrays forces you into a three-bank memory model on the 64180. One bank points to the ROMed program; in most cases this logical-to-physical mapping will never change. Another bank accesses an area of RAM for program variables and transients. (In all but extreme cases this will never be remapped because the stack will reside here.) Finally, one bank points to the huge array(s).

With the map in Fig. 6.5, a 4k section of the system's address space is a window into the huge array. This is much like a disk buffer used in operating systems—data is written to the buffer and then flushed to disk when full. Its size is a result of the mapping resolution of the

MMU. The minimum amount we can allocate is 4k. You can always make this larger, which will cut down on MMU remapping, but you'll sacrifice either variable or program area.

The window is for storage of huge arrays. Never, never store the stack or other variables here, since remapping will invalidate the data. The idea behind using this window is to compute the physical address of the proper array element and then to position the window to bring the data into view. Earlier we saw how to compute an index into any array. Now this windowing step is also introduced. The algorithm is not complex, but a wise programmer will insulate the code from the machinations of array element lookup by hiding the details in subroutines.

Routine **PUT1D** stores a byte to a huge one-dimensional array. The code to get a byte from the array is nearly identical and so is not shown. **PUT1D** accepts an array index in HL that can range all the way up to 64k. Thus, the one 4k window in logical address space gives the routine access to a 65k hunk of data. Note that it supports random accesses—it stores the data in register B into the array at the index in HL. HL can be 3 on one invocation and 40000 on the next.

PUT1D locates the array in physical memory at address 0F000 + **BASE_CBR** · 4096. Thus, if **BASE_CBR** is 1, then the array runs from 10000 to 1FFFF. This implies that the memory manager's CBAR register must be set to Fx (where "x" defines the logical start of the base area) so that logical addresses from F000 to FFFF (our window) are translated into common area 1.

For the sake of simplicity the code stores a 1-byte value. A word version would require the index to be multiplied by two before it is used in the computations. Use a shift to do the multiply but be wary of overflows.

Multiple-dimension arrays can be programmed just as easily, but you must compute the address using the formula previously discussed. Multiplies are slow and should be avoided; try to pick values of J_{max} that are powers of two and then use a series of shifts. Fast access will require some thought to optimize the computations.

One easy speed trick is shown in **NEXT1D**. Especially when gathering data, we often just put one value in the next location—random array accesses are not needed. This means we can skip all of the multiplications needed to compute the address; we just increment the last address. **PUT1D** saves the current CBR and logical addresses in **SAVE_CBR** and **SAVE_LOG** for **NEXT1D**. After one call to **PUT1D** to set things up, all further sequential accesses can use the faster

```
;
;   Put an element in a huge 1 dimensional array.
;   Here we assume:
;
;       The "window" is from F000 to FFFF.
;       BASE_CBR is the first (lowest) CBR value
;       Register B has the data to store
;       Register HL has the array index
;
;   cbr = base_cbr + (index AND ff000) / 4096
;   logical address= f000 + (index AND 0fff)
;
put1d:
        ld      a,h             ; get high order index value
        and     a,0f0h          ; mask off upper 4 bits (cbr bits)
        rra                     ; shift right 4 bits
        rra                     ; (since we ignore lower 8 bits, this
        rra                     ; a 12 bit shift)
        rra                     ; a= (index AND ff000)/4096
        add     a,base_cbr
        out0    (cbr),a         ; set new cbr value
        ld      (save_cbr),a    ; save cbr for next1d
        ld      a,h             ; high part of index
        or      a,0f0h          ; mask off high nibble and or in f0
        ld      h,a             ; hl is now right logical addr in window
        ld      (hl),b          ; save data
        ld      (save_log),hl;  save logical addr for next1d
        ret

;
; put register B in the huge dimensional array at the next
; open location. This assumes that put1d was once called to
; index a specific value.
;
;       On entry, B is the data to store
;       save_cbr was set by put1d or next1d
;       save_log was set by put1d or next1d
;
next1d:
        ld      hl,(save_log) ; last logical address used
        ld      a,(save_cbr)  ; last cbr used
        inc     hl            ; skip to next element
        jr      nz,ne1        ; jp if not exceeded the window
        ld      hl,0f000h     ; re-init to start of the window
        inc     a             ; next cbr value
        ld      (save_cbr),a  ; save current cbr
ne1:    ld      (save_log),hl ; save current logical address
        out0    (cbr),a       ; set cbr
        ld      (hl),b        ; save data
        ret
```

Figure 6.8 Huge array code.

NEXT1D. With the single indexes shown, the speed difference is not important; with a two- or three-dimensional array a tremendous time saving will result.

What if your program uses a number of big arrays? You can't assign more windows since the 64180 limits mapping to three sections. Probably the easiest solution is to write a PUT and GET routine for each array, using a different **BASE_CBR** for each (Fig. 6.8). Avoid using sequential accesses unless you can be really sure that accesses will be restricted to one array at a time.

Tips and Techniques

Any MMU is guaranteed to cause a lot of problems if a few rules are not followed. Unfortunately, it seems that most programmers acquire this knowledge through bitter experience.

As always, plan, plan, plan! Once you enable the MMU some sections of code will be inaccessible until mapped in. Think through the system's structure to come up with a memory segmentation scheme that keeps commonly used code and data (like the stack) always in the logical space and remaps as infrequently as possible. Once you pick a memory structure, it very likely can never be changed without completely rethinking the program.

Remember that logical address space is valuable. Conserve it. Both the Z280 and 64180 map with 4k granularity, which is quite coarse when spread over only 64k. If you assign a 4k map to a 1k routine, a lot of logical space is wasted.

Take a hint from the lessons of object-oriented coding. Isolate the memory manager from your code by small driver routines. It is usually a good idea to keep a small kernal mapped in low memory all of the time. Remap the MMU by calling this driver. Otherwise, your program might accidently map itself out—the routine doing the remap could get lost when the MMU I/O load instruction is executed! While in certain rare instances this can be useful, avoid it when using MMUs with prefetchers or caches.

If you call a routine in the kernal to do a remap, be sure the return address remains mapped in. This certainly applies to the stack as well! Specifically, make sure the stack is in an area of memory common to all routines. On the 64180 this is a problem; with only three banks, mapping both data and code will almost certainly mean losing the stack. It's best to plan the project carefully so you can alternate between code and data maps, using the bank area for mapping and keeping a kernal in common 0 always visible, as well as the stack in common 1.

Carefully plan each and every load of the MMU registers. On the 64180 three registers are needed to define the complete memory configuration, so the order in which the mapping registers are loaded is important. You might map your code out when simply trying to change data access areas. Load the MMU control registers in an order that ensures that the program won't ever put itself into an illegal map; critically examine the code to insure that at each step of the mapping process the program does not get mapped out.

A related and common problem is setting the MMU registers with data loaded from RAM. If each value is read from memory and then output to the memory manager, you'll frequently map out the RAM in one of the intermediate mapping steps. Make debugging easier on yourself—load all mapping values into registers or common RAM before setting MMU registers.

Carefully design interrupt driven systems so the stack is always available and the interrupt service routines are always mapped in. An interrupt that comes when the MMU is partially set up is a disaster. Usually it is a good idea to disable interrupts before changing the MMU parameters. If you can get away with a simple bank-only map (where only one MMU value changes), interrupts will not be much of a problem.

Language Support

No language can offer generic support for such vastly different MMU organizations. The 64180 and Z280 were the first de facto standards for memory management. Now, with a standard (or two) of sorts, some vendors sell language products with built-in MMU support.

Just what features are important in a 64180 or Z280 assembler and C compiler? Certainly we expect it to be fast and efficient, but more than anything else the language should provide some way of handling the MMU.

There are two related but different aspects to MMU management. The first is to provide a mechanism to control the MMU with as little programmer intervention as is needed. An ideal solution would be a smart compiler that simulates a nearly linear huge address space. The second is to provide output files that contain compiled code and debugging records in some form compatible with 8-bit tools (like the PROM programmer) despite the large address space.

Taking these two criteria separately, we'd really like some method of compiling an ordinary C program in multiple banks. Sure, you might have to tell the compiler or linker about your memory configuration, but ideally the tools should segment and package functions into memory banks as needed. Even better, we want it to automatically re-map the MMU to get to functions. We would like to be able to invoke a function through a conventional function call without worrying about its location in memory.

The second requirement is not quite so obvious. How will you burn ROMs for the final project? If the compiled/assembled code exceeds 64k, there may be a problem with using standard Intel hex records for output. Every PROM programmer in the world takes Intel hex input, but the format really only supports 16-bit addresses.

One solution is to manually divide the source program into many separately compiled chunks and burn each one individually. This is especially hard in C, since the linker will not be able to resolve calls between pieces. A better approach is to insure that the compiler or assembler can produce type 2 Intel records. Whenever the code crosses a 64k bank the linker should output a type 2 record to specify a new segment address (physical address shifted right 4 bits). This does imply that the linker can handle large physical addresses and the PROM programmer can accept type 2 records. The standard Intel hex format, with the type 2 extension, is documented in Appendix B.

Decent debugging files are just as important as useful PROM files. You can't use an emulator, simulator, or monitor to debug the code if the debug records are inadequate. Suppose you wish to display the value of a variable—the debugger must know the physical address of that quantity, since only the physical address is constant. Its logical address changes as the MMU is remapped, and at times no logical address might correspond to the variable.

This implies that the software packages must maintain both logical and physical addresses for all lines and symbols. Logicals are needed to compile, say, jumps. All jumps and calls take logical addresses as arguments. Physical addresses are needed in the debugging records so that debuggers can unambiguously resolve the location of symbols, functions, and line numbers, all of whose logical addresses change with the current MMU setting.

Most current 64180 programs written in assembly language control the memory manager by tediously issuing numerous MMU control instructions. The programmer must first decide exactly what configuration logical memory will assume and then come up with CBAR, BBR, and CBR values for every possible combination of banks. Then, wherever a new map is needed, the code must send out new bank values. Needless to say, a lot of work is involved.

Normally I don't discuss specific products, but several companies offer assemblers and compilers that provide specific solutions to memory management and illustrate innovative and important techniques.

Softools (Columbia, Maryland) came up with an interesting approach that eliminates most of the work. Their SASM assembler and linker will automatically drop in all of the code needed to bank a program. In effect, this means you can write code as if the 64180 had a 1-mbyte linear address space.

Like most good assemblers, SASM supports lots of named segments—up to 256. Most of the time we assembly programmers just need a CODE, DATA, and ASEG segment, but SASM's segmentation lets us break a program into mapped and unmapped sections. When using SASM on large programs, you can assign any segment or segments to have a mapped attribute, identifying those that require some MMU manipulation to bring them into the address space.

Segments are the key to SASM's mapping scheme. The linker identifies how much data the program uses and how much address space is needed for the unmapped code (that which must never be mapped out). It computes CBAR to define the characteristics of the run-time logical address space: common 0 being just big enough to hold all of the unmapped code, common 1 containing the data, and the rest, the bank area, being allocated to mapped routines.

The linker groups all mapped segments together and starts to assign both logical and physical addresses to each routine. Whenever a routine will exceed the size of the bank area, it is moved to the start of a new bank area. BBR values are computed for each routine.

The linker converts all jumps and calls between banked areas to transfers to **bank_call,** a routine that manages the MMU and is stored in common 0. The destination logical address and BBR value are passed as arguments, so **bank_call** can properly remap the MMU and transfer control as needed.

When finally linked, the program has three parts: a common 0 non-mapped (i.e., always in the address space) area that typically contains startup code, frequently used routines, and SASM's banking code. Common 1 is usually your data area and is also unbanked (though you can map this in and out manually, but you have to be very careful about not destroying your stack!). The bank area contains most of the program code. Calls between these banked routines will cause remapping to bring in ones that are not currently visible in the address space.

For example, suppose the program is organized as follows:

Routine	Length	Characteristics
main	3700h	not banked
vectors	80h	not banked
sub1	4000h	banked
sub2	38f0h	banked
sub3	1200h	banked
sub4	6f00h	banked
sub5	800h	banked
data	3200h	not banked

On a 64180 the reset jump is at 0, so it makes sense to put the unbanked code (vectors and main) at 0. The data area cannot be banked and is traditionally in high memory. Suppose the code that starts at physical location 0 is to go into ROM, and the data that starts at physical 40000h is assigned to RAM. The linker will first divide up the logical address space based on the unmapped memory requirements: main and vectors need 3780h bytes starting at location 0, and 3200h of data is needed at the end of the logical space. Bearing in mind that the mapping resolution of the 64180 is 4k, memory thus looks like the following:

Logical	Physical	Area
0000	00000	Unbanked (main and vectors)
4000	04000	Start of banked routines
c000	40000	Start of RAM data

All of the logical address space from 4000 to bfff is available to routines that can be banked. If the sum of all of the banked sizes is less than the bank logical area, then no mapping need take place. In our example, however, banked routines need some 64k, much more than the available logical space. If CBAR is C4 (common 1 at c000 and bank at 4000), SASM will assign addresses as follows:

Logical	Physical	Routine	Length	BBR
0000	00000	main	3700	—
3780	03780	vectors	80	—
4000	04000	sub1	4000	00
4000	08000	sub2	38f0	00
4000	0c000	sub3	1200	08
4000	0e000	sub4	6f00	0a
af00	14f00	sub5	800	0a
c000	40000	data	3200	—

This does look complicated! With a little thought it will be clear exactly how SASM allocated addresses to each routine. Since **main** and **vectors** were unbanked, they're assigned to common 0 and placed contiguously starting at location 0 (both physical and logical, since in common 0 all logical addresses are identical to physical addresses). By the same token, the data area is placed at the end of the processor's logical address space. Since we told the linker RAM was at 40000, SASM set CBAR and CBR so that the RAM is in common 1.

The bank area contains all of the mapped code—that code that does not always have to be resident. In this example, the bank starts at logical address 4000, since the size of **main + vectors** is 3780 and the MMU has a 12-bit (4k or 1000h) mapping resolution.

For **sub1** SASM assigned a logical and physical address of 4000— reasonable, since this is the first free spot after common 0. **sub1** is in bank, so a BBR value is required. BBR = 0 will map 4000 to 04000. **sub2** is placed right after **sub1**, again with BBR = 0. So far, no surprises.

sub2 ends at b8f0, practically right before the logical start of data (c000). There is no way **sub3** can fit, since **sub3** is 1200 bytes long. SASM therefore put sub3 at logical address 4000 (the same as **sub1**). The last-used physical address is rounded up to the next 4k boundary (due to the MMU's 12-bit resolution), and **sub3** is placed in physical memory at 0c000. BBR is set to 08. **sub1** and **sub3** occupy the same place in logical address space (4000) but with different physical addresses. To get to **sub3**, BBR must be set to 08 and a logical address of 4000 issued.

While **sub3** is very short, leaving plenty of room for code in the same bank map, **sub4** is not. **sub3** and **sub4** will not both fit into bank together, so SASM once again reset the logical address to 4000. **sub4** is placed in physical memory after **sub3**, rounded up 4k, and a BBR of 0a is assigned. (Remember the math: BBR · 4096 + logical = physical, so 0a · 4096 + 4000 = e000.) **sub5** fits into the space between the end of **sub4** and common 1 and is so assigned.

SASM's linker generates addresses as we've just seen, but how are calls and jumps between subroutines handled? Obviously, if **sub1**, **sub3**, and **sub4** all reside at logical address 4000, a simple CALL 4000 will not always resolve properly. As mentioned earlier, SASM's linker converts all interbank calls and jumps to a transfer through a table into **bank_call**, a utility provided by Softools that is usually linked into common 0. In particular, if **sub4** were to call **sub1**, the following will be automatically substituted for the call instruction in **sub4**:

```
call bank_table+x    ; invoke MMU handler
```

The function **bank_table** is constructed as follows, with one entry per mapped function:

```
bank_table+x:   call  bank_call      ; invoke MMU handler
                db    BBR            ; BBR of sub1
                DW    sub1           ; routine to call
```

The function **bank_call** stores the current BBR value and return address on a local stack, remaps the MMU by outputting the indicated BBR, and then transfers to the logical address supplied as a parameter. Returns operate in a reverse procedure, being vectored to another Softools-supplied routine to reverse the mapping.

SASM will assemble a simple call or jump if the caller and callee are both in the same bank, cutting down on mapping overhead.

A lot of work is involved in handling big programs. What might not be entirely obvious is that SASM does it all. Once you tell SASM's linker where ROM and RAM are (which has to be done for any linker) the allocation of logical and physical addresses is performed automatically. The linker also replaces the calls and jumps with a vector through **bank_call**. SASM does offer options to control memory allocation and the like, but in most cases these are not needed.

This means that you can write large programs without ever considering the MMU. There's an interesting subtle implication: You can link a 256k program to take up only 8k or so of logical space! Assign 4k for common 0 and 56k for data. SASM will bravely partition the 256k code into 50 or more sections, each of which gets remapped through the 4k bank area. The mapping overhead might get pretty high, but logical address space will be conserved.

Since SASM partitions the program during the link phase, the addresses of all symbols, line numbers and other parameters are correctly computed and passed to a debug file. Symbols' physical addresses are stored in the debug file, so that regardless of how the MMU is mapped true addresses are maintained. If the debugger (emulator or monitor) can handle physical addresses, then you can access any routine, variable, or source line number at any time, without manually remapping to bring the desired value into logical address space.

MAPPING IN C

We all know that there is a great shift from assembly language to C in embedded systems. Results of different surveys vary, but it seems at least half of all embedded code is now written mostly in C.

C code for the 64180 family needs built-in MMU support even more than assembly does. Compilers are not as efficient as good assembly programmers, generating even more code that must be stored. Often, management really buys into the increased programming efficiency brought about by C, so they request even more product features that require even more address space.

Archimedes' (San Francisco) approach to memory management is much like that used by SASM. As you write your C code you do not need to be especially concerned with the MMU. There are no special procedures to use or functions to invoke. All of the MMU details are handled at link time.

Before linking the compiled code, a number of parameters must be passed to the linker in its indirect command file. The first and foremost are values for CBAR and CBR. It is the programmer's responsibility to determine exactly what memory configuration is needed and to compute these simple values.

In addition to the MMU register settings, the programmer gives linker a table of module names (i.e., file of source code, each of which may contain a number of functions) and a bank number for each module. If the module is not to be banked, that must be indicated as well. In effect, this means that the user manually determines both logical and physical addresses for every module.

The memory model supported by the compiler puts all nonbanked functions into common 0, the banked code into bank, and data areas into common 1.

This technique works well but does require a lot of help from the programmer. When modules are first compiled, it may take a bit of effort to discover how to place each one in physical memory. If one module grows during development, it could bump into the next one, requiring manual recomputation of all of the physical addresses.

The linker generates a table (**FLIST**) of data about every mapped function in the program. For each function, **FLIST** gives an encrypted BBR value, logical start address, and bank number. **FLIST** is a sort of global cheat sheet, located in common 0 so it is never mapped out, that describes every function's logical and physical address.

The linker replaces all mapped function calls with

```
ld   hl,FLIST entry for the function
call remap_code
```

The **remap_code** extracts pertinent data from the **FLIST** entry and remaps the MMU as needed before branching to the function's logical address.

The beauty of using an **FLIST** table is that pointers to functions will work—the pointer becomes an **FLIST** pointer. Since **FLIST** is always mapped in, indirect function invocations work even to mapped functions.

The Archimedes compiler does produce a good debugging file, which contains useful information about the physical address of every function. The information is stored in **FLIST**.

Whitesmiths (Cambridge, Massachusetts) took a somewhat different approach to using the MMU. When writing C code for this compiler, all calls to mapped functions must be specified as FAR calls. This directs the compiler to generate code to bring the function into the map and execute it.

The called function needs no special handling, since it can be called as either a FAR or as a NEAR. For example, if a function in one module invokes another in the same module, it can use a conventional call structure. Only if a different function, possibly located outside of this bank, calls the same function does the extra call overhead have to be inserted.

A typical call sequence looks like the following:

```
far int sub();

main()
{
sub1();
}
```

The function is typed to be FAR in the definitions, and then all references to it within that module generate banked calls.

All banked calls do produce overhead, both in code size and speed. The Whitesmiths approach eliminates the overhead in cases where it is not needed. Archimedes, on the other hand, vectors all banked function calls through **FLIST,** even if both the caller and callee are coresident in bank.

Whitesmiths uses the indirect linker command file to indicate the location of every banked function. Both the logical and physical addresses of each of these functions are provided by the programmer. Again, the peril here is having to go through iterative modifications of these parameters during development. To date, no compiler is smart enough to automatically set banked addresses. Perhaps soon this will change.

The Whitesmiths compiler generates a call to library routine **c.libc,** which performs the bank switching. Space is allocated on the stack for the return address and return BBR. Routine **c.libc** is passed a far pointer to the function so it can reset BBR and the logical address.

In the embedded world, generating code is only a small part of the development battle. Somehow it must be tested and debugged. Be sure that the development tools can handle physical addresses, since only physical ones never change. While this seems fairly obvious it can be difficult to implement. Emulators use the target CPU for all target memory accesses to keep machine cycles identical to those expected with a processor in the socket. To translate from the desired physical address back to logical, CBAR, CBR, and BBR must be manipulated, since the code can only issue logical addresses.

In other words, if memory at physical address 20000 is to be displayed, then some routine has to figure out a logical address and settings for all three MMU registers. Not a trivial task.

As programmers we really don't care what the tools do or how they work. All we're really concerned with is the debugging interface—the source-level debugger (SLD) that runs on a PC. If we type DISPLAY SYMBOL **FOO**, then **FOO** should appear no matter where it is or how the MMU is set up. The SLD must therefore know about **FOO**'s physical address.

Fortunately, all three products (SASM, Archimedes C180, and Whitesmiths' C) generate physical symbol addresses in the debugging files. The SLD can send these values down to the emulator and let it deal with coming up with the proper address.

This does mean that the SLD/debugging engine interface is completely linear, rather like the 68000. You can randomly access any location in the target's memory just by typing in the right address.

What if you wish to see a logical address? Is this important? Herein lies a source of confusion. Physical addresses are needed to unambiguously identify each public symbol and line number. Your program works through logical addresses—the two are not the same or even similar. Looking at disassembled code, you might see an LD A,(1000). The 1000 is logical—its physical equivalent depends on the current MMU mapping.

The tools should provide a way to access logical or physical addresses. Of course, an emulator would use the current MMU setting to access the memory, so if the MMU is not set up as it would be when executing that instruction, the data may not be correct. Normally this is not a problem: you debug in your execution context rather than randomly hunting through code.

Most 8-bit CPUs have registers no longer than 16 bits. When used as pointers, they form logical addresses, creating the same sort of problem just mentioned. Again, when displaying the contents of a register pointer, that will be logical. If you ask for a dump of memory at the address in HL, what will result? The correct solution is to always use indirect register references as logical, since this is really what the programmer desires.

In C, an automatic pointer is stored as a 16-bit value on the stack. Suppose you wish to dump *ptr? (In other words, display the data pointed to by **ptr**, which is presumably on the stack.) Again, only one correct solution exists: get the stack pointer, convert it to physical using the current MMU, extract the 16-bit value of **ptr,** make that physical, and then access the destination address.

CHAPTER 7

Approximations

"Truth lies within a little and certain compass, but error is immense."—Henry St. John

Sooner or later our programs transform raw input data into something more useful; only the simplest controllers just sequence output bits. Instruments, data acquisition equipment, motion controllers and even games of chance all apply intricate mathematical functions to the raw data.

If speed and memory are not limitations, then by all means use the compiler's math libraries to implement trig functions and the like. You'll be spared the agony of writing transcendental code. In assembly programs, with no math library, we have to write all of the transformations—a tedious and expensive process.

Packaged libraries are no panacea. All involve trade-offs. The vendor selects some speed versus precision mix to satisfy 90% of the customers, giving a mix that might not be right for your particular application. Worse, the libraries that come with some well-known C compilers are not reentrant, so you cannot use these functions in interrupt or multitasking routines. Even in C ROM space is sometimes a problem; if you only need a cosine routine, why link in an entire trig module?

This chapter includes specific algorithms for a number of common math functions. In some cases the C examples might seem awkward, as they're coded more for clarity than conciseness. As we'll see, some of the messy C operations are trivial in assembly language.

Errors

Trigonometric functions, square roots, logarithms, and so on yield irrational results. There is no exact solution to any of these functions, except at certain round numbers (like $\pi/2$ for trig or perfect squares for square roots). All computers use algorithms that approximate the desired results. Given the correct algorithm and enough computer time, any desired level of precision is possible.

Just how accurate is a particular algorithm? Most accuracy measurements (or, better, precision—accuracy is really a measure of repeatability, but in most computer literature the two words are used interchangeably) use one of two methods to answer this question.

Absolute accuracy tells us how much an approximation is in error at any point. Mathematically it is

$$|f(x) - a(x)|$$

In English, this is the absolute value of the correct answer $f(x)$ minus the one given by the approximation $a(x)$. In one sense this is just what we're looking for. However, what if the function's value is very close to 0? An absolute accuracy of 0.00001 sounds great, but it is a 50% error if $f(x)$ is 0.00002.

Relative accuracy is normalized to $f(x)$. It is expressed as

$$|f(x) - a(x)| / |f(x)|$$

and closely resembles percentage error. A relative accuracy of 0.01 is only an absolute error of 0.001 if $f(x)$ is 10, but it is 0.0002 if the function's value is 0.02.

Select an algorithm based on its relative accuracy if your code requires extremely precise answers over a wide range of inputs. Be aware that most functions behave oddly near certain points. The sine, for example, changes very slowly in the vicinity of 0 but accelerates rapidly near $\pi/4$. The result: If you need ultra high precision for angles near $\pi/4$, be sure the approximation's accuracy is listed in relative terms.

Don't be lulled into a quest for the best possible accuracy. High precision carries a correspondingly high computational cost. Know what the project needs and then select the appropriate algorithm.

No algorithm will behave as expected if the floating-point package (add, subtract, divide, and multiply) loses much precision. Computing a log to eight decimal points is a waste of time if the addition loses bits at six places. Every addition, multiplication, division, and subtraction in even the best package will reduce the answer's precision by some small amount. Never make assumptions about your floating-point libraries, whether written by your company, supplied by a compiler vendor, or implemented in a coprocessor chip.

The computer world seems to be standardizing on the IEEE floating-point format as supported by the 80x87 coprocessors and others. Most compilers have software emulations of this format. A single-precision IEEE floating-point number is a 32-bit word that carries 24 bits of precision. That is, IEEE single-precision is accurate to about seven decimal places. Most cheap calculators do better than this! Double precision IEEE uses a 53-bit mantissa, giving about 16 decimal digits of accuracy, certainly more than enough for any reasonable application.

This chapter lists several algorithms for each function so you can make a speed-versus-accuracy trade-off. Refer to the Bibliography for references to algorithms with much higher precision than those listed.

Square Roots

It is surprisingly hard to compute square roots for any arbitrary real number. Most general computer approximations use either a modified series expansion or a Newton–Raphson iterative solution. Both methods require a fair number of floating point operations. Both yield similar accuracies.

The series expansion uses either a polynomial or the ratio of two polynomials to approximate the answer. Like all polynomial solutions, the result is valid only over a small range. In the case of the square root, a singularity at 0 (i.e., the square root of a negative number is undefined) limits the useful polynomial range quite a bit.

Figure 7.1 is a C function that computes the square root of any positive number. The ratio of two polynomials (formed by the P and Q coefficients) is valid only over the range of $x = 0.5$ to 1. Most of the function's code is devoted to transforming the input value x to this range.

Range reduction is the hardest part of any polynomial approximation. Most of the standard texts neglect this little detail, completely obfuscating the algorithms. The details of the derivation of range reductions are listed here, giving (hopefully) all of the information you'll need to write variations on these approximations.

```
double sqroot(double x)
{
double p0,p1,p2,p3,q0,q1,q2,q3,y,expa,exp2a,t,sqr2;
int a,a2;

p0= 0.2973027887;
p1= 8.9403076206;
p2=21.12522405698;
p3= 5.93049445914;
q0= 2.493471825316;
q1=17.764133828054;
q2=15.03572331299;
q3=1.0;
sqr2=1.4142135623731;

if(x==0.0) return(0.0);   /* avoid divide by zero errors */

if (x<.5)
    {
    for(a=0, expa=1.0; x<expa ; expa=expa/2.0, a--);
    a++;
    expa=expa*2.0;
    }
    else
    {
    for(a=0, expa=1.0; x>expa; expa=2.0 * expa, a++);
    };

if(a==((a/2)*2))      /* Do this if a even */
    {
    y=x/expa;         /* compute fractional part */
    t=   p0 + (p1*y) + (p2*y*y) + (p3*y*y*y);
    t=t/(q0 + (q1*y) + (q2*y*y) + (q3*y*y*y));
    if(a>0)
        {
        for(a2=a/2, expa=1.0; a2>0; a2--, expa=expa*2.0);
        }
        else
        {
        for(a2=a/2, expa=1.0; a2<0; a2++, expa=expa/2.0);
        };
    t=t * expa;
    };
```

Figure 7.1 Function to compute the square root of x. (*Figure continues.*)

```
if (a!=((a/2)*2))      /* do this if a is odd */
    {
    y=x/expa;          /* compute fractional part */
    t= p0    + (p1*y) + (p2*y*y) + (p3*y*y*y);
    t=t/(q0 + (q1*y) + (q2*y*y) + (q3*y*y*y));
    if (a>0)
        {
        for(a2=(a-1)/2, expa=1.0; a2>0; a2--, expa=expa*2.0);
        }
    else
        {
        for(a2=(a-1)/2, expa=1.0; a2<0; a2++, expa=expa/2.0);
        };
    t=t * expa * sqr2;
    };

return(t);

};
```

Figure 7.1 (Continued)

Given that we want the square root of x, find values k and f such that

$$x = 2^{2k}f$$

Then,

$$\sqrt{x} = \sqrt{2^{2k}f}$$
$$= \sqrt{f}\sqrt{2^{2k}}$$
$$= 2^{k}\sqrt{f}$$

Why go to all this trouble? If we chose k cleverly, then f will be between 0.5 to 1, a nice range to solve with a polynomial approximation. The value of 2^k is easy to figure with a computer by multiplying 2 by itself k times. An even easier way to compute 2^k will be given in a few paragraphs.

Nothing is as easy as it seems, however. We cannot always find a k that will reduce the range to 0.5 to 1. With a little thought you'll see that an integer k will reduce the range to [.25,1]. Unfortunately we have no reasonable polynomial approximation that is accurate over this range.

In some cases the value 2k must be odd to put f in the desired [.5,1] range. This is clearly impossible (i.e., $2k$ is by definition even), so we'll add another case for when an odd $2k$ is needed.

Pick k and f such that:

$$x = 2^{(2k+1)}f$$

($2k + 1$ must be odd). Then

$$\sqrt{x} = \sqrt{2^{(2k+1)}f}$$
$$= \sqrt{f}\,\sqrt{2^{(2k+1)}}$$
$$= \sqrt{f}\,\sqrt{2^{2k}2^{1}}$$
$$= \sqrt{f}\,\sqrt{2^{2k}}\sqrt{2}$$
$$= 2^{k}\sqrt{f}\,\sqrt{2}$$

The value of f will be between 0.5 and 1, so a polynomial will solve for its square root. $\sqrt{2}$ is a constant; $2k$ is, as mentioned, easily figured.

Figure 7.1 uses a value a that represents $2k$ or $2k + 1$. Then, after a short loop computes both a and **expa** (which is just 2^{a}), decision logic selects between solving an odd and even case.

The routine uses a special case for $x < 0.5$, since a must be negative. That is, the smallest nonnegative value of a is 0 for small values of x, which is too large to scale very small numbers up to the 0.5 to 1 range.

The function **expa** scales the input value x to the 0.5 to 1 range and sets y equal to the scaled result. Then, two statements solve the polynomial using y as input, setting t equal to the result.

In this square root algorithm,

$$t = p(y)/q(y)$$

where $p(y)$ and $q(y)$ are polynomials in y. That is,

$$p(y) = p_0 + p_1y + p_2y^2 + p_3y^3$$

and $q(y)$ has the same form. The p and q coefficients are derived from series expansions. While by no means magic numbers, their derivation is not relevant to this discussion. See the Bibliography for references.

Some of the code computes 2 raised to various powers. The initial loop solves for **expa** (i.e., 2^{a}). Other loops compute $\sqrt{2^{2k}}$ by iteratively multiplying 2 by itself. This is very slow, using a lot of floating-point multiplies.

Most coprocessors and floating-point packages represent real numbers as a characteristic (i.e., an exponent) and a mantissa (a scaled value ranging from 0 or 0.5 to 1). The characteristic is implicitly an exponent of 2, so to convert the number to decimal, one combines the mantissa and characteristic as follows:

$$\text{mantissa} \cdot 2^{(\text{characteristic} - \text{offset})}$$

The offset is a constant that biases the characteristic, so both positive and negative exponents are possible. For example, if the offset is 127 (a common number), then a mantissa of 0.75 and a characteristic of (2 + 127) yields a floating-point number equal to 3.0.

Given this form, we can double the number just by incrementing the characteristic field. Adding 2 quadruples the number. Avoid using multiplies to scale numbers by powers of 2; increment the characteristic the appropriate number of times to save code and time.

It makes sense to add **increment_characteristic** and **decrement_characteristic** routines to the floating-point library. Protect your data structures!

The square root of a negative number is undefined in the real plane. Some algorithms just take the absolute value of the input before proceeding. It's better just to signal an error, except that very small inputs might be slightly negative due to accumulated rounding errors in your code. The square root of a small number is a bigger one (i.e., $\sqrt{0.01} = 0.1$), so consider just setting all small negative numbers to 0.

The following function is accurate to 8.95 decimal digits, assuming all calculations are made in double-precision floating point. The accuracy is relative; no answer should be in error more than 0.0000001%. A lot of other polynomial approximations will give reasonable solutions for the square root. Some run faster (i.e., use a simpler polynomial); others are more accurate. The following coefficients are for polynomial pairs (p and q) over the same [.5,1] range as described. Just change the coefficients in Fig. 7.1 to use them. Where a coefficient is zero you should remove the term from the code, reducing the number of multiplies and adds.

Range: [.5,1]   Relative accuracy: 6.22 decimal digits

```
p0=  0.420448222
p1=  6.013201545
p2=  4.236065453
p3=  0.0
q0=  2.518779641
q1=  7.150942011
q2=  1.0
q3=  0.0
```

Range: [.5,1]   Relative accuracy: 4.85 decimal digits

      p0= 0.1475426162
      p1= 1.26450988
      p2= 0.2950851223
      p3= 0.0
      q0= 0.7071069137
      q1= 1.0
      q2= 0.0
      q3= 0.0

Range: [.5,1]   Relative accuracy: 6.04 decimal digits

      p0= 0.07363371823
      p1= 0.9466075346
      p2= 0.4440017327
      p3= -0.04103428394
      q0= 0.4232099882
      q1= 1.0

The following approximations have the indicated accuracy over different ranges. Don't use these coefficients without adjusting the range reduction code in Fig. 7.1. The first approximation is a simpler form than shown so far: the q polynomial is set to 1.0, greatly speeding computations. The wider range and simpler form is reflected in its greatly reduced accuracy.

Range: [.25,1]   Relative accuracy: 2.30 decimal digits

      p0= 0.2592768763
      p1= 1.052021187
      p2= -0.3163221431

This next approximation once again uses the two equation form $p(x)/q(x)$. Its range is quite narrow, but it exhibits very high accuracy.

Range: [.758,1]   Relative accuracy: 11.73 decimal digits

      p0=   0.615575021777584
      p1= 14.87903478543191
      p2= 28.49723938001582
      p3=   6.53908086927307
      q0=   4.62384353303268
      q1= 26.58888188856576
      q2= 18.3182046349945
      q3=   1.0

Iterative algorithms are an alternative to polynomial approximations. Square root solutions converge quickly. A very simple algorithm to compute the square root of x is

$$x_2 = \frac{(x_1 + x/x_1)}{2}$$

where x_1 is a guess of the square root of x. The value of x_2 will then be a better guess. Feed x_2 back into the equation in place of x_1 and try again. Each value of x_2 will be closer to the actual square root of x.

How fast does it converge? If the initial guess of x_1 is in error by 15%, then after two iterations x_2 will be within 0.008% of the correct square root of x. More iterations will improve the result.

An algorithm of this sort is an interesting choice when floating-point math is not an option. You'll have to deal with divisions and additions, maintaining more than integer levels of precision. In a computer with 32-bit math, consider scaling the integer number by some factor (say, 65,536—one-half of the precision of a 32-bit integer word), so that pseudofloating binary points will work.

Higher Order Roots

Higher order roots are less commonly used than the square root. Few compiler libraries contain built-in functions for any but the second root.

Where accurate roots are needed it makes sense to use logarithms and exponentials. If the yth root of x is needed, use the following equation:

$$y_{th} \text{ root} = e^{y \ln(x)}$$

The symbol ln is the natural log, or the log base e. Note that y can be integer or real, positive or negative.

The preceding equation has two transcendental functions, both of which will require a polynomial approximation. The accuracy of the result will be degraded by errors accumulated in solving each approximation. There's no reason not to use a single specially constructed approximation for taking an integer root, especially where accuracy and/or speed is a problem.

The following coefficients are for polynomials of the form $p(x)/q(x)$, and solve for the cube root of x. All cover the range [.5 to 1].

Range: [.5,1]   Relative accuracy: 6.31 decimal digits
      p0=   0.4454493777
      p1=   4.4539802456
      p2=   2.5069924737
      q0=   1.4070019956
      q1=   4.9994237596
      q2=   1.0

Range: [.5,1]   Relative accuracy: 11.75 decimal digits
      p0=   0.222724717461818
      p1=   8.292328023860137
      p2= 35.357641932978439
      p3= 29.095751763308076
      p4=   3.703512298992019
      q0=   1.039263150119302
      q1= 16.329439632480167
      q2= 39.687610666299525
      q3= 18.615645287836842
      q4=   1.0

An iterative way to find any root of any number is given by the equation

$$x_2 = \frac{x_1(n - 1) + \dfrac{x}{x_1^{(n-1)}}}{n}$$

where n is the root desired (e.g., 3 for cube root) and x_1 is a guess of the root of x. The value of x_2 will then be a better guess. Feed x_2 back into the equation in place of x_1 and try again. Each value of x_2 will be closer to the actual root of x.

The November 1986 issue of *Byte* magazine contains an intriguing algorithm for extracting any integer root of any integer. It's worth looking into where floating point solutions are not possible.

Logarithms

With the proliferation of cheap calculators few people depend on logs for day-to-day computations. Still, a lot of physical phenomena are best described with some sort of log. They are particularly useful for compressing the range of data supplied to an A/D converter to narrow the input range.

In the computer world the most common bases for logarithm work are base 2 (used mostly for information theory calculations), base 10 (the common logarithm), and base e, where e is the irrational number 2.71828. A fundamental identity makes it easy to convert between bases:

$$\log_a x = \frac{\log_b x}{\log_b a}$$

(Note: $e = 2.718281828459045$.) We can approximate the log with a polynomial over a limited range.

Figure 7.2 shows a function to compute the natural (base e) log of any positive number, accurate to about 8.5 decimal digits.

The ratio of the two polynomials, defined by the p and q coefficients, is accurate only over the range 0.5 to 1. Reducing the range to [.5,1] is simpler than it is for square roots. If

$$x = 2^a y$$

then

$$\begin{aligned}\log(x) &= \log(2^a y)\\ &= \log(y) + \log(2^a)\\ &= \log(y) + a\log(2)\end{aligned}$$

So, since the polynomial is accurate over [.5,1], we must find a value such that 2^a is just a bit bigger than x. Then, $y = x/(2^a)$. For example, solving for the log of 1000, 2^a will be 1024 (2^{10}), so $\log(1000) = \log((1000/1024)2^{10})$. 1000/1024 is between 0.5 and 1.

Two "for" expressions, one for $x > 0.5$ and one for the complementary case, iteratively compute an exponent of 2 that is greater than x. Much of the computational overhead is tied up in this loop. As discussed earlier under Square Roots, increment or decrement the floating-point number's characteristic directly to eliminate the multiplies.

An even faster solution uses a table listing all of the floating-point powers of two for all expected x values. Use a smart lookup to go directly from x to 2^a. If x will primarily be within some reasonable range (say 1 to 2^{20}), then you can put these 20 numbers in the table and resort

```
double logarithme(double x)
{
double p0,p1,p2,p3,q0,q1,q2,q3,y,expa,ln2,t;
int a;

ln2=0.693147180559945;
p0=-1.424186626;
p1=-6.143128113;
p2= 4.232254592;
p3= 3.335060106;
q0= 0.3535534746;
q1= 4.545171302;
q2= 6.427842391;
q3= 1.0;

if (x<.5)
    {
    for(a=0, expa=1.0; x<expa ; expa=expa/2.0, a--);
    a++;
    expa=expa*2.0;
    }
    else
    {
    for(a=0, expa=1.0; x>expa; expa=2.0 * expa, a++);
    };
y=x/expa;
t=   p0 + (p1*y) + (p2*y*y) + (p3*y*y*y);
t=t/(q0 + (q1*y) + (q2*y*y) + (q3*y*y*y));
t=t+ ((double) a) * ln2;
return(t);

};
```

Figure 7.2 Function to compute log base e.

to the algorithm as shown for values outside of the range, saving table space.

No matter what the value of x, the code in Fig. 7.2 computes a value 2^a a little bit greater than x. If x is less than 0.5, the algorithm reverses gears, decrementing a instead of increasing it with each iteration. This just generates the series 0.25, 0.125, 0.0625, etc., so a will be just a bit bigger than x no matter how small x is.

Variations include

Range: [.5, 1]   Relative accuracy: 3.1 decimal digits

    p0= -1.669856
    p1= 1.668387
    q0= 0.7071062
    q1= 1.0

Range: [.5, 1]   Relative accuracy: 5.76 decimal digits

    p0= -1.680596308
    p1= -0.9877464896
    p2= 2.668335341
    q0= 0.4999388118
    q1= 2.849528934
    q2= 1.0

To compute the common log (base 10) over the same range, use

Range: [.5, 1]   Relative accuracy: 8.84 decimal digits

    p0= -0.6185163887322
    p1= -2.667926630744
    p2= 1.838044802047
    p3= 1.4483981998
    q0= 0.353553472021
    q1= 4.545171276941
    q2= 6.427842372081
    q3= 1.0

Exponentials

Exponentials are the opposite of logarithms. Indeed, these two operations are related by

$$\text{If } x = a^y, \text{ then } y = \log_a x$$

All embedded programmers live and die with the (to us) most common of exponentiation functions: 2^x. If x is an integer value, most software gurus can easily tick the first 20 or so powers off from memory. Non-integer values of x are rarely used in this business.

The next two most common exponentials are the powers of 10 and e. Both are related. Given an exponential routine, the following formula raises any number to any power:

$$x^y = y^{[(x/\ln(y)]}$$

Figure 7.3 is a function that computes e^x for any x greater or equal to 0. It has a relative accuracy of 7.1 decimal digits. The routine makes use of this formula, using y set to 2. The equation $x_1 = x/\ln(2)$ just converts the base from e to 2.

The polynomial approximation computes 2^x over the range [0,1]. Scaling is rather simple, using the transformation

$$2^x = 2^{(y-a)}2^a$$

Variable a is the integer part of x; y is the fractional part. For example, if x were 3.14, then y would be 0.14 and a 3. Thus y is always in the range [0,1], perfect for the polynomial.

Although the routine uses a loop to compute the integer quantity 2^a, real code should increment the floating point number's characteristic as already discussed.

Modify the code slightly if x is negative. Convert x to $-x$, flow through the routine, and then modify the result by setting $t = 1/t$ (the definition of a negative exponent) just before returning.

Be wary of one error condition. Exponential results get very big very fast. You might want to signal an error if e^x will overflow your floating point package's maximum limit.

Add more terms to the polynomial to get greater accuracy. For example, with eight terms, this next set of coefficients carries 10.39 digits of precision for 2^x:

```
Range:  [0, 1]     Relative accuracy:  10.39 decimal digits


    p0= 0.9999999995978898922
    p1= 0.69314718608388907626
    p2= 0.240226384617999502
    p3= 0.05550512685955710087
    p4= 0.00961401701187433994
    p5= 0.00134226348241558779
    p6= 0.00014352314035598943
    p7= 0.00002149876369739293
```

```
double expe(double x)
{
double p0,p1,p2,p3,p4,p5,y,ln2,t,exp2,x1;
int a;

ln2=0.693147180559945;

p0= 0.9999999250635449;
p1= 0.6931530732007278;
p2= 0.240153617040129;
p3= 0.0558263180623292;
p4= 0.0089893400833312;
p5= 0.0018775766770276;

x1=x/ln2;             /* e**x = 2**(x/ln2) */
y= x1-(int) x1;       /* fractional part of x */
a= (int) x1;          /* integer part of x */

t=p0 + (p1*y) + (p2*y*y) + (p3*y*y*y) + (p4*y*y*y*y) +
(p5*y*y*y*y*y);

for(exp2=1; a>0; exp2=exp2*2, a--);

t=t*exp2;

return(t);

};
```

Figure 7.3 Function to compute e^x.

With a smarter range reduction formula, a smaller polynomial gives accurate results for 2^x:

Range: [0,.25]   Relative accuracy: 6.53 decimal digits

```
    p0= 0.9999997065661
    p1= 0.6931858515857
    p2= 0.239443309321
    p3= 0.060504944251
```

Range: [0,.5]   Relative accuracy: 7.08 decimal digits

p0= 1.00000008129674
p1= 0.69313862988812
p2= 0.24036734524543
p3= 0.0547058964282
p4= 0.01142364474288

Cosine, Sine, and Tangent

Computing equations of motion to drive a robotic arm, drawing diagonal lines on a plotter, computing a phasor in an ac circuit—the fundamental trig functions underlie these and almost all geometrical calculations.

Most programmers (particularly those without mathematical backgrounds) think in terms of degrees, with 360 forming a circle. The radian is used almost exclusively in mathematical texts and is a more natural unit of measurement for angles. Radians are based on π, the number that relates diameter to circumference and ties all of trigonometry together.

A circle consists of 2π rad. Thus, π rad corresponds to 180°, $\pi/2$ to 90°, and so forth. The formal relationship between degrees and radians is

$$2\pi \text{ rad } = 360°$$

so,

$$\text{radians} = (\pi/180) \cdot \text{degrees}$$

To put this in easier-to-understand terms, one radian is about 57°.

The trig libraries used by different languages seem to almost arbitrarily support radians or degrees. The following discussion is in radians.

The standard trig functions are interrelated as follows:

$$\sin(x + 90) = \cos(x) \qquad \text{(in degrees)}$$
$$\sin(x + \pi/2) = \cos(x) \qquad \text{(in radians)}$$
$$\tan(x) = \sin(x)/\cos(x)$$

There's little reason to develop approximations for both the sine and cosine, since it is so easy to convert between them. Use these relations, write one approximation function, and save coding time and memory.

For those whose trig is a little rusty, Fig. 7.4 illustrates the relation-

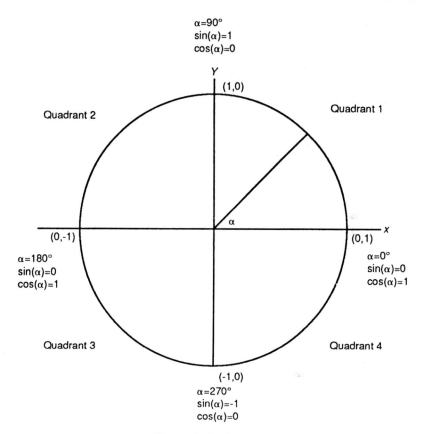

$\alpha=90°$
$\sin(\alpha)=1$
$\cos(\alpha)=0$

Y

(1,0)

Quadrant 2

Quadrant 1

α

(0,-1) x

(0,1)

$\alpha=180°$
$\sin(\alpha)=0$
$\cos(\alpha)=1$

$\alpha=0°$
$\sin(\alpha)=0$
$\cos(\alpha)=1$

Quadrant 3

Quadrant 4

(-1,0)
$\alpha=270°$
$\sin(\alpha)=-1$
$\cos(\alpha)=0$

Figure 7.4 The circle.

ship between the sine and cosine. Position ($y = 0$, $x = 1$) is arbitrarily assigned to 0°. Rotating around counterclockwise, at ($y = 1$, $x = 0$) the angle is 90° or $\pi/2$ rad. Continuing around, ($y = 0$, $x = -1$) corresponds to 180° or π rad. The 6 o'clock position is 270° (1.5π rad). As you plot the sine or cosine function at each position on the circle, the famous sine wave, so beloved of late-night science-fiction programs, appears (Fig. 7.5).

Figure 7.6 shows a C function that computes the cosine of an angle x in radians. The accuracy is measured in absolute terms and slightly exceeds 9.6 decimal digits.

It's interesting to compare this to the polynomial approximations for the log and square root. These functions abruptly stop at zero where

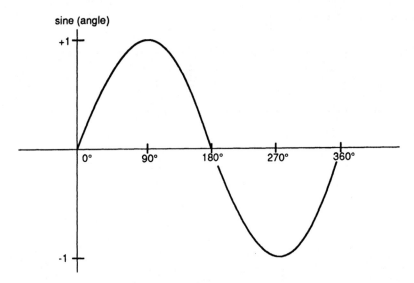

sine (angle)

Figure 7.5 Sine wave.

they are discontinuous. The accurate range of the approximating polynomial stops well before zero, as discontinuities disrupt all efforts to fit
a function. The sine and cosine, though, are continuous and symmetrical through zero, leading us to the reasonable and correct assumption
that the approximating range could go to 0. The polynomial in Fig. 7.6
does indeed approximate the cosine over the range 0 to $\pi/2$, or for the
circle's first quadrant.

Variable **quad** assumes the values 0, 1, 2, or 3, corresponding to the
quadrant that x lies in (see Fig. 7.4). The routine decomposes the input
angle x into **quad** and **frac**, where **frac** lies between 0 and $\pi/2$, the
range of the polynomial.

The form of the polynomial is a bit different than those explored so
far. The coefficients p_0 to p_5 build an equation of the form $\cos(x) =$
$p(x^2)$. In other words, the equation is

$$p_0 + p_1 x^2 + p_2 x^4 + p_3 x^6 + p_4 x^8 + p_5 x^{10}$$

Different systems require a wide range of accuracy, from low-pre-
cision fast approximations for real-time imaging to slow but ultra precise numbers for orbit corrections. Following are a number of coefficient sets with different speed/accuracy trade-offs. All coefficients
cover the same range as the function shown; they plug directly into the
code in the Fig. 7.6. Of course, where a coefficient is zero, remove that
entire term from the polynomial to save two floating-point operations.

```
double cosine(double x)
{
double p0,p1,p2,p3,p4,p5,y,t,absx,frac,quad,pi2;

p0= 0.999999999781;
p1=-0.499999993585;
p2= 0.041666636258;
p3=-0.0013888361399;
p4= 0.00002476016134;
p5=-0.00000026051495;
pi2=1.570796326794896;          /* pi/2 */

absx=x;

if (x<0) absx=-absx;            /* absolute value of input */
quad=(int) (absx/pi2);          /* quadrant (0 to 3) */
frac= (absx/pi2)-quad;          /* fractional part of input */

if(quad==0) t=frac * pi2;
if(quad==1) t=(1-frac) * pi2;
if(quad==2) t=frac * pi2;
if(quad==3) t=(frac-1) * pi2;

t=t * t;
y=p0 + (p1*t) + (p2*t*t) + (p3*t*t*t) + (p4*t*t*t*t) +
p5*t*t*t*t*t);

if(quad==2 | quad==1) y=-y; /* correct sign */

return(y);

};
```

Figure 7.6 Function to compute cos(x).

Range: [0,pi/2]   Absolute accuracy: 3.22 decimal digits

```
        p0=  0.99940307
        p1= -0.49558072
        p2=  0.03679168
        p3=  0.0
        p4=  0.0
        p5=  0.0
```

Range: [0,pi/2]   Absolute accuracy: 7.33 decimal digits

```
p0=   0.999999953464
p1= -0.499999053455
p2=   0.041663584677
p3= -0.001385370426
p4=   0.0000231539317
p5=   0.0
```

Range: [0,pi/2]   Absolute accuracy: 12.12 decimal digits

```
p0=   0.99999999999925182
p1= -0.49999999997024012
p2=   0.04166666647338454
p3= -0.00138888841800042
p4=   0.00024801040648456
p5= -0.000000275246963843
p6=   0.000000001990785685
```

Inverse Trig Functions

The inverse trig functions (arcsin, arccos, arctan) are the complements
of sine, cosine and tangent. That is

$$x = \arcsin[\sin(x)]$$
$$x = \arccos[\cos(x)]$$
$$x = \arctan[\tan(x)]$$

They are related by the identities

$$\arcsin(x) = \arctan\left(\frac{x}{\sqrt{1-x^2}}\right)$$

$$\arccos(x) = \frac{\pi}{2} - \arcsin(x)$$

$$\arctan(x) = \arcsin\left(\frac{x}{\sqrt{1+x^2}}\right)$$

It is certainly possible to compute polynomial approximations for each
of the inverse trig functions, but in practice most arcsine and arccosine
routines use these equations and a single arctangent function.

Figure 7.7 is a function that computes the arctan for any value of x
with a relative accuracy of about 9.5 decimal digits. The polynomial is

```
double atana(double x)
{
double tan_pi_12,pi6,pi2,sqrt_3,y,x1;

tan_pi_12=      0.2679491924311227;  /* tan(pi/12) */
pi2=            1.570796326794896;   /* pi/2 */
pi6=            pi2/3;               /* pi/6 */
sqrt_3=         1.73205080757;       /* sqrt(3) */

if (x<0)
    {
    x=-x;        /* abs(x) since atan(x)=-atan(-x) */
        if (x>1)
    {
            x=1.0/x;
        if (x> tan_pi_12)
            {
            x1=((x * sqrt_3)-1)/(sqrt_3+x);
            y=atana_step4(x1) + pi6;
            }
            else
            {
            y=atana_step4(x);
            };
            y=-y + pi2;
        }
        else
        {
        if (x> tan_pi_12)
            {
            x1=((x * sqrt_3)-1)/(sqrt_3+x);
            y=atana_step4(x1) + pi6;
            }
            else
            {
            y=atana_step4(x);
            };
        };
    y=-y;
    return(y);
    };
```

Figure 7.7 Function to compute arctan(x). (*Figure continues.*)

```
if (x>1)
    {
        x=1.0/x;
    if (x> tan_pi_12)
            {
            x1=((x * sqrt_3)-1)/(sqrt_3+x);
            y=atana_step4(x1) + pi6;
            }
            else
            {
            y=atana_step4(x);
            };
        y=-y + pi2;
    return(y);
    };

if (x> tan_pi_12)
    {
    x1=((x * sqrt_3)-1)/(sqrt_3+x);
    y=atana_step4(x1) + pi6;
    }
    else
    {
    y=atana_step4(x);
    };
return(y);
}

double atana_step4(double x)
{

double p0,p1,p2,p3,p4,t,y;

p0=   0.99999999971301;
p1= -0.33332423445;
p2=   0.199977320113;
p3= -0.14195746243;
p4=   0.0963034789;

y=x*x;
t=p0 + (p1*y) + (p2*y*y) + (p3*y*y*y) + (p4*y*y*y*y);
t=t*x;

return(t);
}
```

Figure 7.7 (Continued)

good only over the range [0,tan(pi/12)], so a rather complicated range reduction is called for.

The algorithm implemented in Fig. 7.7 works as follows:

Step 1:
If $x < 0$, then
Do steps 2, 3, and 4 with the argument $= -x$.
Negate the result, since $\arctan(x) = -\arctan(-x)$.
Return.

Step 2:
If $x > 1$, then
Do steps 3 and 4 with the argument $= 1/x$.
Negate the result, and add $\pi/2$ since

$$\arctan(x) = \frac{\pi}{2} - \arctan\left(\frac{1}{x}\right).$$

Return.

Step 3:
If $x > \arctan(\pi/12)$, then

Do step 4 with the argument $= (x\sqrt{3} - 1)/(\sqrt{3} + x)$
since:

$$\frac{x\sqrt{3} - 1}{\sqrt{3} + x} \le \arctan\left(\frac{\pi}{R}\right)$$

when $x > \arctan(\pi/12)$.
Add $\pi/6$ to the result.
Return.

Step 4:
The argument is in the range 0 to tan(pi/12). Solve the polynomial approximation.

Need more accuracy? Over the same range of [0,tan(pi/12)] the following coefficients yield 13.2 digit precision:

```
Range:  [0, tan(pi/12)]     Relative accuracy: 13.2 digits
    p0=  0.999999999999936736
    p1= -0.33333333324648299
    p2=  0.1999999805073221
    p3= -0.142855498296859
    p4=  0.1110447484328
    p5= -0.089522032997
    p6=  0.06222172411
```

CHAPTER 8

Interrupt Management

It is not only an interruption, but also a disruption of thought.—Arthur Schopenhauer

Wise amateurs fear interrupts. Normal sequential code is hard enough to understand, code, and debug. Toss in a handful of asynchronous events that randomly change the processor's execution path, perhaps thousands of times per second, and you have a recipe for disaster.

Yet interrupts are an important fact of life for all real-time systems. No experienced programmer would dream of replacing a clean interrupt service routine with polled I/O, particularly where fast response is needed.

Interrupts are both the best and worst feature of any microprocessor. Well thought out interrupt-driven code will be reasonably easy to write, debug, and maintain. A poorly conceived interrupt routine is probably the most hideous software to work on. Interrupts are crucial to embedded systems—become proficient with their use.

Interrupts

It's hard to generalize about interrupts and interrupting devices. This field is so broad! Thankfully, there are some common denominators between the most popular processors and their peripherals.

We software people forget that an interrupt is far more than just an asyncronous input that invokes a service routine. Every interrupt is an exquisite ballet of hardware and software, each interacting in a complex way to produce a very simple result.

A device signals its need for attention by asserting the processor's interrupt signal. Sometimes an interrupt controller IC stands between the peripherals and the CPU. The controller generally prioritizes multiple interrupt priorities, sorting through perhaps several conflicting demands for service, and presents the one that is most important. If the hardware is properly designed, the interrupt signal stays asserted until the CPU acknowledges its acceptance. At this point the peripheral removes the signal, freeing the common interrupt line for other assertions.

Meanwhile, the processor stops execution of code, saves the program counter and perhaps status information on a stack, and branches (usually indirectly through a vector table) to a service routine. Only the stack and execution path change; the rest of the machine's context remains the same.

The interrupt service routine (or ISR, an important acronym in this business) first pushes all of the registers it will modify. Then it handshakes with the hardware. After taking care of whatever the interrupt is supposed to do, the ISR exits by popping the registers and executing a return. If all goes well, the original program resumes exactly where it left off with no changes to its registers or variables.

The processor responds to level-sensitive interrupts only if asserted during the window while the microcode samples the signal. The processor could miss a very short pulse coming outside of the window. With edge-sensitive interrupts, the CPU latches the rising or falling edge of the pulse, saving the transition until the machine is ready for it. All edge-sensitive interrupts will be serviced, no matter how short.

Processors handle interrupts in wildly different ways. A few examples follow.

68000

Motorola's 68000 processor accepts a 3-bit signal that encodes the priority of the interrupt (or, in 68000 parlance, the exception). If all three bits are zero, no action is taken. Any other input will initiate an interrupt whose priority is given by the code. Seven is the highest level and corresponds to a nonmaskable interrupt since it can never be disabled.

The CPU's internal status register maintains a similar 3-bit code that indicates the system's current priority. An interrupt request that is of a lower priority than the current state is deferred until the software lowers the state to that level.

If the processor accepts the request it immediately pushes the status register and program counter on the system stack and toggles to supervisor mode (where no instruction is privileged). The processor's microcode sets the priority in the status register to that of the interrupt, masking lower priority exceptions but leaving a window open to those more important. The processor then fetches a vector number from the peripheral. It reforms this 8-bit value into a 32-bit address by left-shifting it twice and zero-filling the high-order bits. This is an index into the software's interrupt vector table. By reading the address stored at the index the CPU finds the start of the interrupt service routine.

Unlike most other processors destined for embedded work, the 68000 never really disables interrupts. The priority may change, but higher order requests can always be honored. Interrupt-intensive applications should take advantage of the multiple priorities that the CPU offers.

Z80/64180/Z180

In an attempt to be all things to all people the Z80 family supports three distinct modes of interrupt operation. None are as powerful as those of the 68000, but the simpler modes do make ultra cheap simple systems possible.

Mode 2 most resembles the architecture of the 68000. An interrupting device pulls the request line low, initiating an interrupt-acknowledge cycle at the end of the current instruction. The device supplies an 8-bit vector during this cycle (always even: address line 0 must be 0), which the CPU combines with an internal register to form a 16-bit index into the interrupt vector table. As on the 68000, the processor extracts the address of the ISR from the table. It stacks the program counter, globally disables all interrupts, and then starts the ISR.

Some Z80 peripherals contain built-in support for a crude priority scheme. By daisy chaining the peripherals' interrupt enable in/out (IEI and IEO) lines together, smart I/O devices can hold off their interrupt if a higher priority device is issuing a request. Device priority is determined by the peripherals' electrical position on the daisy chain; the device closest to the processor is more important than those farther away.

Mode 0 interrupts have the least CPU support. The requesting device supplies an instruction to the processor in response to the interrupt-acknowledge cycle; the CPU then executes this instruction. It does not automatically stack the program counter, fetch a vector, or transfer to an ISR. The interrupting device generally provides one of the single-byte CALL instructions, which acts much like a vector transfer. Once, way back in the 8008 and 8080 days, this was the only way to handle interrupts.

The 8008 carried this to extremes. Hardware resets just halted the processor. To start running after reset very smart electronics asserted an interrupt and painfully jammed a three byte jump onto the data bus. We've come a long way in 15 years.

Mode 1 interrupts CALL location 38 without generating an acknowledge cycle. Single-interrupt systems can sometimes save a lot of hardware by using mode 1 since no vector is needed.

80x88

The 80x88 family's response to interrupts is somewhere between that of the 68000 and the Z80. All devices share a single interrupt pin on the processor. When asserted, the computer completes the current instruction and pushes the program counter (consisting of a 16-bit offset and 16-bit segment) and flag register. The interrupting device supplies an 8-bit vector, which forms a pointer to the interrupt table when multiplied by four. The processor disables all maskable interrupts and branches to the ISR whose address is found in the table.

Some of the higher integration versions of the family include several request pins and a built-in interrupt controller. They function much like the discrete combination of the CPU and an external controller (like the 8259 as used in all PCs).

8051

No discussion of embedded systems is complete without reference to the venerable and still immensely popular 8051 family. The original 8051 core handles five different interrupts, three of which come from on-board peripherals and two from external inputs. All of the dozens of derivitive chips respond in the same way to interrupts.

Any request pushes the program counter and starts the ISR corresponding to that interrupt. All ISRs are at predefined, unchangeable locations. What could be easier? A mask register lets you selectively enable or disable each interrupt. You can assign one or two priority levels to each interrupt source.

Interrupt Service

Interrupt service routines all take on more or less the same form:

1. Push all registers that the ISR will change onto the stack. Save other critical variables like the floating-point accumulator. This keeps the ISR from altering the context of the interrupted program.

2. If the interrupt is part of a wired-OR structure (that is, more than one device could have presented one signal, all giving the same vector), determine which peripheral requires service. In some complex devices (like SCSI controllers), the code might read a register within the peripheral to determine the cause of the interrupt. Perhaps a data byte is ready; maybe a transmission error occurred.

3. Some hardware devices need explicit software service. The code might have to clear an error condition, read data, or just toggle the peripheral's chip select to make it deassert the interrupt signal.

4. Now the ISR can take care of all of its nonreentrant duties like altering global variables.

5. The ISR reenables interrupts or (in the case of the 68000) changes priority masks. Only at this point is it safe to receive another interrupt.

6. All other reentrant servicing finally takes place. Schedule off a task or queue up a handler if the ISR will be very long.

7. With all of the real work done, the ISR can pop the registers and machine state and return to the mainline code.

ISRs are the home of tight, fast code. Nowhere else is speed quite so important. Before reenabling interrupts, the machine is effectively shut down, dedicated to servicing just that one request; all others are blocked out. In a system with only a single slow interrupt this is not a concern. Others deal with dozens of interrupt sources, each of which will asyncronously demand processor time.

Compilers are now so good that it's often practical to code the ISR in C. Truly speed-critical applications do continue to demand the use of assembly, a situation that will probably never change as applications keep pace with skyrocketing processor speeds.

Sometimes an embedded application must respond to extremely high-speed interrupts coming perhaps hundreds of thousands of times per second. This rate will overwhelm the capability of most microprocessors since there is so much overhead and latency associated with processing each interrupt. After all, before the processor can even initiate an interrupt cycle it must complete execution of the current instruction. In the middle of a big divide, possibly tens of microseconds might elapse before the instruction is done and the CPU is even interruptable. Then a vectored interrupt issues an acknowledge cycle to get the interrupt source, several PUSHes to stack a return address and other context information, and an indirect read through the vector table. All of this takes time—sometimes quite a few microseconds.

Consider using the processor's oddball interrupt modes (if they exist) where extremely fast requests are a problem. While the Z80 is usually used in its most useful mode 2 vectored configuration, mode 0 (where the external hardware jams an instruction onto the data bus in response to the acknowledge cycle) bypasses all conventional interrupt processing. It can be very fast indeed.

The following code takes advantage of a jammed NOP instruction.

```
loop:
      halt          ; wait for interrupt
      <process interrupt>
      jmp  loop
```

The interrupt does nothing but exit the halt condition and execute a NOP. The response delay is just the processor's raw interrupt latency, which is usually only one or two machine cycles. With no interrupt servicing overhead the code runs about as fast as possible.

This technique can be improved a bit where speed is a real problem. Suppose the code counts the number of interrupts received until some number is exceeded. Keep the count in the HL register pair. Jam an INC HL instruction instead of an NOP. This single-byte opcode will perform some useful work, slightly increasing the system's performance.

The 64180 has an even better way to process fast interrupts. Its very low-power mode is initiated by executing the SLP (sleep) instruction. SLP is rather like HALT, except for the lower current drain.

SLP has an unusual mode that is poorly documented deep in the chip's hardware description. Like HALT, only an interrupt will exit a sleep condition. Like HALT, SLP will initiate conventional interrupt servicing if the processor is using vectored interrupts. However, if the global interrupts are disabled (via a DI instruction), but an individual peripheral interrupt enable bit is on, then an interrupt will exit sleep mode without starting an interrupt acknowledge cycle. The code will just flow past the SLP instruction into the next opcode, effecting just the sort of fast response we need without having extra hardware to jam a special instruction.

Nonmaskable Interrupts

If interrupts are tough to work with, then the nonmaskable interrupt (NMI) is the true monster of the business.

When timing gets tight the code can easily disable a conventional interrupt. Indeed, the very assertion of the interrupt signal automatically turns all interrupts off until the software explicitly reenables them, giving the code a clean window to process a high-priority task. Not so with NMI. An NMI at any time will interrupt the CPU—no ifs, ands, or buts. As long as hardware supplies NMIs to the processor, the processor stops whatever it's doing and vectors through the NMI handler.

The very fact that NMI can never be disabled makes it ideal for handling a small but vital class of extremely high-priority events. Chief among these is the power-fail interrupt. If a system must die gracefully, then hardware that detects the imminent loss of power can assert NMI to let the software park disk heads, put moving sensors into a safe state, copy important variables from RAM to nonvolatile storage, and so forth.

Modern power supplies have little reserve capacity. Old linear designs employed massive filtering capacitors that acted like batteries with several seconds of stored charge. Today's off-line switchers use comparatively tiny capacitors—smart electronics does the filtering. When AC power goes down, the switcher's output quickly follows suit.

A standard maskable interrupt could be disabled for the entire time power trails off. Only the NMI is guaranteed to be available all of the time. Power fail is such an important event (in some systems) that NMI is really the only option for notifying the software of its impending demise.

Perhaps more should be said about power-fail circuits at this point, since so many suffer from serious design flaws. Most embedded systems ignore power fail. Running ROM-based code with no dangerous or critical external hardware, embedded systems can restart when power resumes from the top of the program without harm. Two types of systems do require power-fail management hardware and software. In the first category are those systems controlling moving objects; a disk controller should park the head, a robot should stop all motors, and an x-ray system should shut down the beam.

The other class are systems that must preserve transient data through a power-up cycle. A data acquisition system might need to keep logged data even when power goes down, an instrument sometimes has to preserve painfully collected calibration constants, and a video game should remember high-scoring individuals' initials and totals.

Far too many designs rely on nothing more than battery-backed-up static RAMs or some nonvolatile device like an EEPROM to store data through multiple on/off cycles. Let's consider what happens when the ac line power fails.

At first the computer circuitry itself will be unaware of the impending disaster. It takes some time for the system's 5-V supply to decay. Without ac, the power supply stops work. The computer continues to run from the energy stored in the supply's output capacitor. The amount of time left before the computer goes haywire is proportional to the size of the capacitor in microfarads and inversely proportional to the amount of current consumed by the electronics.

The computer continues to run properly until the supply decays to about 4.75 V. At this point most of the system's chips are no longer operating in their design region. No one can predict what will happen with any certainty.

At about 4.8 to 4.9 V the well-designed power-fail circuit will inject an NMI into the computer (some detect missing ac cycles, a better but more expensive approach). Probably the system has only milliseconds before decaying to the 4.75-V region of instability. The NMI routine should quickly shut down external events and save critical variables.

The voltage level continues to decline past 4.75 V, eventually reaching zero. Unfortunately, the supply's capacitor decays exponentially. It will provide something between 0 and 4.75 V for a comparatively long time—perhaps seconds.

What does the CPU chip, memories, and glue logic do with, say, 2 V applied? No one knows. No vendor will guarantee any behavior under the 4.75-V level. Frequently the program just runs wild, executing practically random instructions. Your carefully saved data or meticulously protected I/O could be destroyed by rogue code!

No power-monitoring circuit is fail-safe unless it clamps the reset line whenever power is less than the magic 4.75-V level. A suitable design keeps the CPU in a reset state, preventing wild execution from corrupting the efforts of the NMI power-save routine. Motorola sells a three-terminal reset controller, for less than a dollar, that will assert reset in all low V_{cc} conditions.

Consider another case: Suppose the power grid's sadly overloaded summertime generating capacity gives a short brownout. If the line drops from 110 V ac to, say, 80 V, what happens to the +5-V output from your system's power supply? Most likely it will go out of regulation, giving perhaps 3 or 4 V until the 110-input level is reestablished. Hopefully the power-fail logic will assert an NMI to the processor chip. The conventional resistor/capacitor unclamped reset circuit will droop reset only to the 3- to 4-V level, not nearly low enough to reset the CPU when power comes back. A correct clamping circuit would not only keep the CPU in a safe state; in this brownout case it will also insure that the system eventually restarts properly.

Regardless, NMI is the only reasonable interrupt choice for power-fail detection. Unfortunately, it is widely abused as a general-purpose interrupt. Use NMI only for events that occur infrequently. Never substitute it for poor design.

It's not unusual to see a peripheral driving NMI, generating hundreds or thousands of interrupts per second. Usually these designs start life using a reasonable maskable interrupt. As the programmer debugs the system, he or she finds that the CPU occasionally misses an interrupt and switches to NMI. This is a mistake. If the code misses interrupts there is a fundamental flaw in its design that using NMI will not cure.

Your code will ignore interrupts only if some bottleneck keeps them disabled for too long. Always design the code to keep interrupts disabled only while servicing the hardware. Reenable them as soon as possible. With good reentrant design, interrupts should never be off for more than a few tens of microseconds.

Quite a few processors implement NMI as an edge-sensitive interrupt. This guarantees that even a breathtakingly short pulse will set the CPU's internal NMI flip-flop, causing several kinds of problems.

Suppose the input comes from the real world, perhaps after having been transmitted a few feet. Without proper pulse-shaping circuitry, the signal might have ragged edges or even multiple, closely spaced transitions. Maskable interrupts live quite happily with short bouncing on their lines, since the first transition will make the processor disable the input and start the ISR. Even the fastest code will take a few microseconds to service and reenable the interrupt, by which time the transients will be long gone. NMI cannot be disabled; every bit of bounce will reinitiate the NMI service routine. The result: one real interrupt might masquerade as several independent NMIs, each one pushing on the stack and recalling the ISR.

Edge-sensitive inputs respond when the input voltage crosses some threshold. Imperfect digital circuits give a rather broad window to the threshold. If the NMI input signal is perfectly clean but moves slowly from the idle to the asserted state, it will stay within the threshold region for far too long, sometimes causing multiple NMI triggers.

The edge-sensitive nature of NMI renders it susceptible to every stray bit of electrical noise. A clean NMI driven by a gate on the other side of a circuit board might pick up unexpected transients on the PCB track as it transits the board. Edge-sensitive NMI inputs must be clean, noise free, and should switch quickly and without glitches.

Remember that debugging NMI service routines is sometimes tough. As mentioned in Chapter 4, some tools will create false NMI edges. Others use NMI to force a breakpoint, effectively preempting its use. Some processors respond oddly to NMI. On the Z80, for example, until the NMI service routine executes the RETN instruction, your peripherals may be in an indeterminate state. Be aware of this when setting a breakpoint within the NMI ISR.

Queue Handling

How will ISRs communicate with each other and with the mainline code? Conventional parameter passing is just not an option, since no part of the code calls the interrupt handler. The same problem exists for intertask communication whenever a real-time operating system is in control.

The obvious solution is to allocate sections of global memory for parameter passing. Unless managed properly this is difficult to maintain. Each task or ISR will have different and conflicting data needs. Some will change dynamically, depending on who passes data to whom.

Certain data structures and techniques used in other areas of software engineering will make synchronizing intertask events and passing data much easier. Chief among these is the queue. A circular queue is a sort of stack with a head and a tail. One task inserts data at the queue's head; another extracts it from the tail.

While queues are well known, embedded systems put a new wrinkle on their implementation. It's important that one task cannot corrupt the queue while another is using it. For example, an 8-bit computer may take several cycles to get data from the queue and update the pointers. If this task is interrupted in the middle of the update another may use incorrect values. Consider the following queue handler:

```
add_q_data:
        ld      hl, (q_head_pointer)
        ld      (hl),c
        inc     hl
        ld      (q_head_pointer),hl
```

An interrupt and context switch anytime after the first instruction will be a disaster if the **add_q_ptr** routine is reentrantly invoked by another task. It will use the old, incorrect value of **q_head_pointer.**

It's easy to simply disable interrupts for one or two instructions, as follows:

```
add_q_data:
      di
      ld    hl, (q_head_pointer)
      ld    (hl),c
      inc   hl
      ld    (q_head_pointer),hl
      ei
```

Interrupts might spend a lot of time disabled if significant amounts of data are transferred. A better solution is to assign semaphores to signal that a particular queue handler is busy. This is easier said than done, for at any time in the code another interrupt could come along and issue a request for the same queue. Murphy's law of the perversity of nature insures the interrupt will come at the worst possible time.

Add a section of code to the queue handler that loops if another task or ISR is using the queue. Every queue will need its own semaphore, a sort of "in-use" flag that indicates whether or not it is busy. But we need a bit more information than this; consider the following addition to a queue handler:

```
loop:
Step A:    Test queue-in-use flag.
Step B:    If the queue is busy, go to loop.
Step C:    Set queue busy.
Step D:    Do queue activities.
```

A pathological interrupt occurring just after step A might invoke another request for the queue. At this point the in-use flag is not set; both ISRs read the flag, see the queue is available, and then assume that they have sole control of it. In other words, the time between testing the flag in step A and setting it to the "it's mine!" state in step C is a window of vulnerability where another task or ISR can mistakenly try to gain control.

It's better to assign an identifier to every possible requester, whether task or ISR. Insert that ID in the busy flag and retest it after making the preliminary decision that the queue is available. Another interrupt will at worst insert its own ID. The retest of the busy flag will indicate that someone else assumed control.

```
loop:
        Test queue-in-use flag.
        If the queue is in use, go to loop.
        Set our ID in the queue-in-use flag.
        Test queue-in-use again.
        Go to loop if the ID is not ours.
```

Recoding the earlier example (now the caller passes an ID in register b):

```
add_q_data:
        ld    a, (semaphore_mask)
        or    a
        jr    nz, add_q_data        ; loop till queue not in use
        ld    a, b                  ; OR in request ID
        ld    (semaphore_mask), a   ; set our request in the mask
        ld    a, (semaphore_mask)   ; see if anyone else requested
        cp    a, b                  ; if mask=our ID, we own queue
        jr    nz, add_q_data        ; loop till ready
        ld    hl, (q_head_pointer)
        ld    (hl), c
        inc   hl
        ld    (q_head_pointer), hl
        ld    a, 0
        ld    (semaphore_mask), a   ; free queue up
```

This illustrates the difficulty of transferring data when interrupts are enabled. Much of the problem goes away if only one routine or ISR can queue data at any time. In multitasking systems this is hard to enforce.

Some processors include instructions designed to ease some of the pain. The 68000's test and set does an uninteruptable read-modify-write cycle. It is ideal for semaphore handling since another ISR can't sneak in and change the flag.

An important variation on the standard queue is one with a "test-if-data-is-available" feature, somewhat like the data ready bit on an I/O device. In multitasking, one can never assume that a queue has data in it; any of a number of problems might slow down the task expected to add data. In addition to conventional **add_q_data** and **remove_q_data** routines, include a **test_q_data_available** function. An easy way to do this without adding an (expensive) extra data field is to compare the queue head and tail pointers. If equal, the queue is empty.

Knuth (see the Bibliography) is one of the most complete sources of information about data structures. Sedgewick and others include related useful algorithms. Queue management is a standard part of the software repertoire that is covered in most books on computer science.

Problem Areas

This chapter started with an admonition to be wary of interrupt-driven code, especially if you are new to the field. Most ISRs differ little from other code; their complexity lies in how they behave, being as they are invoked asyncronously to the rest of the system.

Most problems with interrupts lie in one of four areas: completion, latency, stack corruption, and reentrancy. Debugging these problems is one of embedded programming life's little (very little) pleasures.

COMPLETION PROBLEMS

Whenever two or more activities run concurrently and share resources all sorts of conflicts might occur. No one would dream of partially filling a data structure and then calling another routine that works on the same uncompleted bytes. Yet that is exactly what happens whenever an ISR shares data with the mainline code or other ISRs.

Use queues and semaphores to transfer data between ISRs and tasks. These techniques automatically, though tediously, protect your major data structures. Minor structures are just as much of a problem.

How do you safely change a 16-bit variable that is global to the mainline code and one or more ISRs? Suppose, working on an 8-bit machine, you update the variable with two single-byte store instructions. An interrupt coming between the two stores will invoke another ISR with the variable only partially modified; if the ISR refers to those locations, totally corrupt data will result.

One solution is to use 16-bit load/store instructions on all global word-sized variables. This doesn't help much with a 32-bit item. Or you could protect the data structure with a reentrant driver routine, shared by all of the code, that disables interrupts around accesses. Consider using a smarter routine that minimizes latency with a semaphore.

This is a particularly thorny problem when working in C, as you might have little control over the instructions that the compiler generates. Check the code your compiler writes to be absolutely sure partial loads/stores cannot occur. This is a point in favor of object-oriented programming, where you can more easily define an object that behaves well in an interrupt environment. Minimize global variables, both to reduce interaction between routines and to reduce the number of places where interrupts will cause problems.

I/O suffers from a similar problem. Suppose your system has an 8-bit parallel output port with 1 bit assigned to each of eight different control functions. An ISR might have to set or clear one of these bits. Unfortunately, the mainline code might modify them as well. Two concurrent routines that set the bits asyncronously could create a problem like the one that we explored with queues.

For example, suppose the bits assignments are

Bit 0: Enable light 0
Bit 1: Enable light 1
Bit 2: Enable light 2
Bit 3: Enable light 3
Bit 4: Enable light 4
Bit 5: Enable light 5
Bit 6: Enable light 6
Bit 7: Enable light 7

An I/O instruction sets the entire port—all 8 bits at once. To turn light four on, the code must read the port, OR in a 1 to enable the lamp, and then do the output:

```
INPUT register
OR register with 10h (i.e., set bit 4)
OUTPUT register
```

An interrupt occurring between the input and output will corrupt the port data if the ISR services the same port.

Sometimes it's impossible to read data back from an output port. In this case maintain a memory image that is updated with each output. Either way, the problem remains the same.

A crude solution is to disable interrupts around the I/O routine. The software artist will use semaphores, which, while admittedly slower, keep interrupts enabled to minimize latency.

Any shared resource is subject to completion problems. Always reduce the number of things shared across interrupt boundaries. Write drivers for every one of these devices or memory locations. Finally, use semaphores or (gasp! simple systems only) disable interrupts as needed.

LATENCY

Few systems can tolerate missed interrupts, yet too many programmers carelessly leave them disabled for extended periods of time. Latency is defined as the time it takes to respond to an interrupt. Sometimes this can be an infinite number of seconds.

Before considering the software components of latency it makes sense to look at proper hardware design. How should we present an interrupt to the processor? Only one solution is correct: Assert the interrupt-request line until the CPU responds with an acknowledgement of that particular interrupt. If the event is short, say, a fast pulse from an encoder, then by all means latch the signal in an external flip-flop, which is not cleared until the interrupt is serviced. Quite a few systems just strobe the interrupt line, hoping the CPU will be ready when the event is asserted. Just decoding the CPU's interrupt-acknowledge machine cycle is not enough—some other interrupt may have won the priority struggle.

With this said, sometimes recurring costs make embedded designers fight a battle for every gate and resistor. That extra latch might require an additional chip. One can avoid the extra logic altogether in a simple system with little latency. It's not an easy thing to do. You have to know the worst-case latency and insure that the pulse width is at least that long. Then, if the interrupt input is level sensitive (most are), the ISR must keep interrupts off for at least the length of the pulse so that one assertion doesn't cause multiple interrupts.

The key to minimizing latency in any system is to minimize times when interrupts are disabled. Never, never invoke a 2000-line subroutine from within the ISR. Never execute a loop of any length unless interrupts are on.

The 68000 and other processors include a hardware priority scheme that lets the system disable only low-priority interrupts. This is great as long as external hardware remembers the pending interrupt. If not, keep the priority mask to a low level as much as possible.

Where should your code reenable interrupts? Turn them on as soon as nonreentrant and hardware-sensitive processing is done. However, the enable interrupt instruction, no matter what it is called on any processor, takes effect *after* the next instruction executes. If the routine is very simple it might make sense to delay it an instruction or two. For example

```
ISR_routine:
        Do a single output instruction
        Enable interrupts
        Return
```

might be better than

```
ISR_routine:
        Enable interrupts
        Do a single output instruction
        Return
```

In the second instance a very fast source of interrupts can reinvoke the ISR before the return executes, possibly eventually blowing the stack. The first code fragment prevents this by delaying the next interrupt cycle until after the stack is cleaned up.

If the ISR really must start some very complex activity, design a real-time operating system into your code (see Chapter 9). The ISR should schedule off a complicated task and quickly exit, letting the task complete at its leisure.

Another option is a forked interrupt system, which can be used when an interrupt starts some very complex activity—something more than you'd care to include in the ISR. The forked structure closely resembles a real-time operating system. It is simpler, and is highly tailored to servicing interrupts as they arrive.

In a forked system every ISR is split into two parts. The first handles only what must be taken care of as soon as the interrupt arrives: acknowledgment, device handling, and the like. The second part takes care of lower tier activities like processing input from the device.

The first section places a request for second-level service into a fork queue. A very simple sequencer invokes routines from the queue. If the second-level routine is reentrant many incarnations of it can be active at any time. Suppose that occasionally a device will send a few interrupts faster than a conventional ISR could accept them. The forked approach will queue off requests for service for each of the interrupts very quickly. Of course, the code can't keep this up forever; if the interrupts don't slow down the system will be quickly overloaded.

The *C User's Journal* (April 1990) includes a complete set of fork drivers.

STACK CORRUPTION

Without stacks the whole concept of reentrant interrupt service crumbles. The processor's hardware saves the return address whenever any interrupt occurs.

The first rule in servicing interrupts is to be sure there is plenty of stack depth available to handle all possible levels of interrupt nesting. Bear in mind that each incarnation of a routine will most likely push additional temporary data.

Some processors support separate user and system address spaces, usually giving each area its own hardware stack pointer. Interrupts generally affect only the system stack and automatically drive the processor into system mode. User applications (in embedded systems these are generally just tasks) don't have to supply interrupt stack space.

Be sure to pop the same amount of data you push in every routine so the code doesn't return to a data item. This is equally true in ISRs or mainline code, but it bears repeating as unmatched pushes and pops are a constant source of debugging headaches.

In word machines, word or double-word align the stack pointer. Depending on the memory's speed and number of wait states, odd aligning the stack pointer can cost 30 to 40% of the processor's execution time. On some CPUs odd alignment is simply illegal.

A more insidious form of stack corruption plays havoc with fast and miscoded interrupts. If interrupts come so quickly that no ISR has a chance to run to completion, then the stack will eventually overflow as service requests back up. Adding a stack checker that signals stack overflow errors makes a lot of sense.

It seems every novice embedded programmer stumbles on a variant of the stack overflow problem. Some devices, notably UARTs, assert the "transmit-buffer-empty" interrupt during the time when they are ready to accept a character to transmit. A conventional ISR that services this interrupt and passes the UART another character will work fine until there is no data to transmit. Then the constant presence of this signal will reinvoke the ISR as fast as the computer can acknowledge interrupts. The solution is to mask off the interrupt when the code has nothing to transmit, reenabling it when a character becomes available.

Never expect data to stay in the same place on the stack between invocations of the same ISR.

We almost lost a big emulator sale when a customer complained that the unit didn't handle interrupts properly. Digging through his program we discovered that the code saved data on the stack and then expected it to be in the same place on the next interrupt. Perhaps all would have been well in a single-interrupt environment. In this case, the timer interrupt came along once in a while and pushed a return address over his not-so-carefully saved information.

REENTRANCY

If your system uses interrupts, be sure to plan what sort of reentrancy every scrap of code will need to support. It's awfully hard to find reentrancy bugs.

Usually the mainline code can be nonreentrant. It executes constantly and is never restarted by an external event. Even the ISRs may not have to be reentrant if they will always run to completion.

Three rules define reentrancy requirements:

1. No routine can call itself or be called by multiple threads (including an ISR) unless it is reentrant.

2. Do not call a nonreentrant subroutine from more than one place if it is possible that an interrupt or recursive call could make two or more calls active at one time.

3. Never use self-modifying code, unless you can guarantee that only one incarnation of the code will be active at any time.

C solves many reentrancy problems. Automatic variables have no fixed address, being assigned offsets from the current stack frame pointer. Programs that use only automatics are thus by their nature reentrant. Some compilers, particularly those for microcontrollers, generate static code even when automatics are called for. While this greatly increases the software's speed, it destroys all hope of reentrancy.

Software floating-point packages are a prime source of reentrancy problems. They usually maintain a data area, the floating-point accumulator (FPA), on which all operations take place. It's rather like a calculator's display register. If more than one activity uses floating point, save the FPA and all other floating-point temporaries. Treat the FPA just like a register: ISRs should push every register they use. Push (or save) the FPA as well. Otherwise an ISR that uses floating point will corrupt other calculations.

Watch out for temporaries of any sort. A routine that might be invoked more than once before running to completion can not use static variables. Allocate them off the stack. Subroutines are particularly insidious, since an ISR might share a simple routine with other ISRs or the mainline code. Be absolutely sure that these shared routines do not use statics!

On some processors, working off the stack is very cumbersome. Without explicit stack-relative instructions the code will run slowly and eat up lots of memory. An alternative is to write routines that dynamically allocate and manage statics.

Years ago I wrote a multitasking BASIC compiler for Z80 and 80x88 systems. It included a complete real-time operating system that let a user write and run dozens of independent tasks in BASIC. For the sake of speed I wanted to store partial results of complex BASIC assignment statements in static areas of memory (Z80 stack-relative operations are painstakingly slow). The compiler allocated a block of temporaries to each of the BASIC tasks. Every time it generated code that needed a temporary it used the next few bytes within that task's temporary area. This insured that no two tasks could share the same data (see Fig. 8.1).

Strings, though, posed a bigger problem. Some string operations result in a need for one or two temporary buffers, each of which could be huge. To keep memory requirements reasonable the compiler generated code that dynamically requested a 128-byte string temporary. If one of the run-time package's string-temporary areas was free, then the allocation routine returned its address to the caller. The entire task was blocked if all areas were in use.

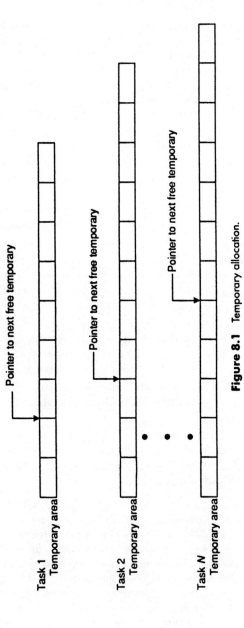

Figure 8.1 Temporary allocation.

DEBUGGING ISRs

Interrupt-driven code is hard to debug and maintain. While you're finding problems in one section of the software, other ISRs continue to run asyncronously, perhaps (if there is a bug) destroying important variables in an almost random and hard-to-catch fashion.

Consider the debug problems from the outset of your design. If the system uses a lot of interrupts, look for ways to run it, perhaps degraded, with some or all of them turned off. Otherwise you'll have a hard time pinning problems down to specific routines.

When your debugger or emulator is stopped at a breakpoint it probably won't service interrupts. If an ISR controls a critical piece of hardware, a breakpoint could bring the whole system crashing down. Talk to the vendors to see if their products will support some kind of interrupt service even when not emulating the program.

Watch out for interaction between the tools and your code. Single stepping is one source of frustration in interrupt-driven systems. A lot of debuggers and emulators single step by setting a breakpoint on the next instruction and restarting the code. Between steps, a lot of time goes by—seconds or more, more than enough time for another interrupt to occur. The debugger will attempt to service the interrupt when the step starts, executing perhaps thousands of instructions in the ISR before returning and executing the one instruction that was at the program counter address.

One customer called with just this problem. While single stepping through an ISR, the registers would sometimes suddenly change for no apparent reason. It turns out that the ISR he was debugging immediately reenabled interrupts, long before all nonreentrant section of code had executed. As he stepped through the code another interrupt reinvoked the ISR. The nonreentrant software destroyed registers!

CHAPTER 9

Real-Time Operating Systems

The wasting of time is an abomination to the spirit.—Ptahhotpe

Many embedded systems manage what amounts to a number of individual and distinct sets of software. In a controller, some code handles the data acquisition, other updates the display, and still more computes results based on various inputs. Though all of the code shares data, often each section is largely independent of the rest.

A big monolithic program tries to handle all of these functions using carefully constructed logic to sequence all activities and (perhaps) interrupts to drive some of the I/O operations. The logic that starts off as a beautiful, highly organized structure usually crumbles into a convoluted mess with each new feature and bug fix.

One solution that is singularly appropriate to the embedded world is the real-time operating system (RTOS). Like the state machines discussed in Chapter 3, an RTOS makes it easy to structure your code as a collection of many small pieces, each running tiny parts of the big problem.

Everyone is familiar with conventional operating systems like DOS for PCs, VMS for the VAX, and hundreds of other variations. Big operating systems manage many of the same problems as an embedded RTOS. However, most RTOSs provide no disk or mass storage support and little if any protection from malicious or accidental coding mistakes.

Tasking and Scheduling

As we saw in Chapter 8, interrupts are the natural means by which to avoid the biggest time waster of all—polling for completion of external I/O events. Interrupts shift the burden of indicating a device is ready to the hardware where it rightfully belongs.

Interrupt-driven I/O addresses only the tip of the CPU utilization problem. Sometimes complete processes must essentially go to sleep until some number of seconds goes by or until a combination of external and internal events come to pass. Some real-time systems run what amount to several programs that must run more or less simultaneously. A protocol converter might have several serial channels. When a particular input stream occurs on any channel, some event is initiated.

In effect, these systems run many more or less independent programs that all share the same resources. Each program (or task) may be heavily dependent on the others, but each is a separate element competing for CPU time. Without an RTOS, one massively complex program executes all tasks as an intertwined whole, generally yielding code that looks like the twisted mess it is. Structuring the code around an RTOS lets you write each task as an independent module. The RTOS takes care of sequencing between activities.

In lieu of multiple processor architectures and superscaler CPUs, only one task can actually execute at a time. The RTOS uses a fast regular clock interrupt to suspend the execution of the current task and start or resume another. The computer is so fast that it appears that each task has sole control of the processor. In a four-task system, the RTOS allocates so many milliseconds per second to each of the four.

A regular timer interrupt forms the heartbeat of the RTOS. Years ago the universal "tic" interrupt was the 60-Hz wall power. Today's cheap hardware lets us use any convenient frequency.

The nucleus of the RTOS is the context switcher, which is responsible for stopping the execution of one task and invoking another. The context switcher is an interrupt-driven section of code that is invoked by the tic or when specifically called by some task.

Every RTOS uses one of a number of scheduling algorithms to decide what to do when the tic comes along. All tic-based scheduling algorithms are preemptive, since the interrupt abruptly stops one task and starts another.

Sometimes a task might reach a point where it is blocked, waiting for some resource to become available. This could be an I/O device, or the completion of another task's activity. Rather than execute a null loop (burning CPU time wastefully while waiting for the resource), the task signals the RTOS its need to suspend execution for a time. To the RTOS, this bonus CPU time is a bonanza that can be allocated to other tasks.

The following requirements define the central nucleus of the RTOS. To provide proper task execution, the RTOS must

1. Switch execution time between tasks, so every task gets its fair share of time. This is called time slicing.

2. Provide a mechanism whereby tasks can go into an idle state for specified periods without wasting CPU time. WAITing and scheduling are the most common methods used.

3. Allow any task to alter its execution order when some important event occurs. That is, the tasks must be able to raise and lower their priority.

TASKS

A task is a logically complete program that runs independently of all other code. It may use services provided by other tasks; it will certainly make calls to the operating system for device-specific help. However, no task ever calls code in another (although any task can invoke, or spawn, another complete task). Each task runs asynchronously with respect to the others; no task knows or cares what runs when.

In effect, each task thinks it is always in control of the CPU. The context switcher will in fact partition execution time between the tasks, but this process is mostly invisible. The tasks run concurrently—they compete for computer time.

Any task can be in one of 5 states:

Dormant: The task has no need for CPU time.

Ready: The task will require the CPU when its reschedule interval (defined later) has elapsed. It is not immediately a contender for execution time.

Active: The task is executing. Obviously, only one task can be ACTIVE at any time.

Waiting: The task requested a delay. After the delay time is up it again becomes available for execution.

Suspended: All conditions are satisfied for the task to run, and the task was indeed at one time running. It was suspended by an interrupt from the timer tic. The task is anxiously awaiting its next slice of CPU time from the context switcher.

Figure 9.1 is the state diagram of a typical RTOS. The circles represent each possible task state. The arrows show the events causing transitions between states. Since many tasks are competing for time, Fig. 9.1 is somewhat of a simplification of reality; in effect, this should be a three-dimensional drawing, with one layer of depth added for each task. Since only one can be active at any time, there will be only one ACTIVE circle for the entire picture; ACTIVE serves as the hub around which all task sequencing flows.

Tasks start life in the DORMANT state. The context switcher is aware of DORMANT tasks but ignores them until an ACTIVE task commands a DORMANT one to go to the READY state. The process of raising a DORMANT task to the READY level is called spawning.

When a task enters the READY state it is not immediately eligible for execution (i.e., cannot go directly to ACTIVE). Every task has a reschedule interval associated with it that signals to the operating system how long to delay before making the READY task eligible for the ACTIVE state.

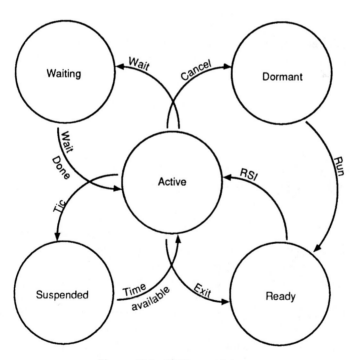

Figure 9.1 RTOS state diagram.

Consider the case of using software to refresh an LED display. Every 100 msec or so the RTOS must invoke the same refresh task. Rather than have a fairly complex time-tracking task waiting for 100-msec intervals, why not let the operating system do the work?

Whoever spawns a task must specify the task's reschedule interval (RSI). During execution of the spawned task the RSI is ignored. Once the task runs to completion and exits, the RTOS counts time until the RSI elapses and then restarts it. The best analogy is to reincarnation, except the task is always reborn as software and not as a higher animal.

When a READY task's RSI is up it is eligible for execution. Subject to demands made by other competing tasks, the operating system will raise the task to ACTIVE and start executing it as time permits.

Very short tasks may complete before another tic comes. If this happens, the task is placed back into the READY state where it remains until its reschedule interval once again elapses. This process repeats forever unless the applications program commands a change via the CANCEL or WAITING operating system calls.

Many tasks will take more than one tic's worth of time to complete. Indeed, some may run forever (if they include an infinite loop—perfectly legal and valid in a multitasking system). What is the RTOS to do? Remember that the *raison d'etre* for a real-time operating system is to wisely allocate limited processor resources to many competing tasks. Although a task may want 100% of the processor's time, it simply won't get it.

The RTOS has only one option: put the ACTIVE task in a SUSPENDED state and give another a chance to run. SUSPENDED means exactly what it implies. The task needs more computer time but has been put on hold. The context switcher very carefully preserves the complete state of the task, including all of its registers, stack, and flags, so the task can be resumed without ever being aware it had been interrupted.

A READY task makes no demands for CPU time (it is waiting for the RSI to elapse), a DORMANT task practically doesn't exist, and as we'll see a WAITING task is also in limbo. Only those SUSPENDED are engaged in competition for processor time.

Sometimes a task should go idle until an external event occurs. One approach is to exit, going back to the READY state until the RSI goes by. The task will be completely restarted when it goes ACTIVE. It will run from the top—perhaps not what we really want. It's better to place the task in suspended animation for a time. Obviously a null loop will do just this but at the expense of burning computer time.

The WAITING state permits any task to delay for a fixed time and then to restart from the point where the delay was issued. The applications program initiates a WAIT by issuing an RTOS call, requesting the ACTIVE task be placed in a WAITING state for a specified number of tics. The context switcher will not give the task access to the CPU until the wait count elapses.

Any task can return to the DORMANT state, taking it completely out of contention for computer time. Since a task doesn't truly die by running to completion (it will be reincarnated after the RSI elapses), another mechanism (a call to the RTOS to cancel the task) removes it from the execution stream.

Cancelling doesn't abort the task; rather, it signals the operating system that the task should be allowed to complete and then never be reincarnated.

ROUND-ROBIN SCHEDULING

Exactly how does the context switcher decide which of the competing tasks to elevate to ACTIVE? After all, when a tic invokes the context switcher possibly dozens of tasks could be suspended, WAITING (with the wait count elapsed), and READY (also with RSI up).

If more than one task is eligible for execution the context switcher must pick one to run in such a manner as to satisfy two conditions:

(1) Every task must get a fair chance to run.
(2) Certain crucial tasks are more eligible than others and must be given more opportunity to execute.

The RTOS maintains a pointer to the last task it executed, ensuring that every task gets the same chance to run. When a tic invokes the context switcher it attempts to run the next sequential task. If that task is not eligible for execution, then the operating system continues searching for one that is ready. In other words, it tries to execute the task that has not been ACTIVE for the longest amount of time. This is called round-robin scheduling and is the basis for most operating systems.

The round-robin scheduling algorithm always guarantees that every task gets an equal chance to run, but suppose the applications program defines a task so important that when it is ready to go ACTIVE it absolutely must gain control of the processor? For example, a task used to track time MUST execute every so many tics or else the clock will get behind.

Most operating systems assign task execution priorities. Generally the task gets an initial priority when defined. It can alter the priority at any time by issuing a call to the RTOS.

Why would you want a task to have low priority? In embedded systems data acquisition is usually the most important activity since the data is available only for a limited amount of time. Many tasks may be needed to gather data, analyze it, actuate a controller (perhaps for a closed-loop system) and update the CRT or LEDs. The display task might run at an extremely low priority so that the real meat of the application will never lose control at a critical moment. The display activity may get suspended for long periods, but these delays will not be noticeable to the operator. Suppose a 200-msec update rate occasionally becomes 210 msec?

A high-priority task is a dangerous beast, since it can easily monopolize all of the processor's time. It's much better to elevate a task to a high priority only for the time a critical event is being serviced then to keep it high at all times.

The priority scheme, then, alters the round-robin algorithm. Instead of just starting the next eligible task, the context switcher first examines the current priority level of all tasks that are READY (with their RSI up), WAITING (with the wait count elapsed), and SUSPENDED. It starts the highest priority task it finds that satisfies these conditions.

If several tasks are eligible and have equally high priority, the context switcher uses the round-robin concept to alternate execution between the high-priority tasks until all become ineligible. Then the next priority level is checked. This algorithm defaults to simple round robin if all tasks are of equal priority.

High-priority tasks will own the CPU! Be sure that they exit, wait, or get cancelled fairly often so others get a shot at running.

Round-robin scheduling is not the only context switching algorithm. One of the more interesting alternatives is rate monotonic scheduling (RMS), which allocates time to tasks based on their expected execution time.

Assuming you know how long each task that executes (yet another reason for using performance analysis!), RMS theory lets you calculate the maximum safe processor loading, which will be somewhat higher than that achievable using traditional round-robin methods. Given the time each task takes to execute and how frequently each must be invoked, a formula given in Silverthorn (see Bibliography) lets you compute whether each will meet its execution deadline.

Implementing the method is trivial. Set the task priorities in decreasing order of task execution period. The most frequently executed task is assigned the highest priority, and the least frequently invoked gets the lowest.

Using an RTOS

In many ways the RTOS twists our programming thinking inside out. Instead of partitioning a problem into subroutines, break it up into complete executable units. Think in terms of concurrent activities, not routines that execute only when called.

Referring back to the microwave oven example used in Chapter 3, consider using an RTOS to replace the state machine described. While this example is so simple there is no compelling reason to use the RTOS, it does show how one's thinking changes when working with concurrently executing tasks.

Make one task a keypad handler. Let it run all of the time, passing keypad results to other tasks through a data structure. This eliminates the numerous cumbersome calls to check for keystrokes used by big monolithic programs. The keypad handler spawns the COOKING task when the proper buttons are pressed. COOKING either exits when done or spawns an error task and then exits if the oven's door opens unexpectedly.

Some embedded systems use an RTOS just to simplify keypad handling. With the key scanning task always READY or ACTIVE, dispatching new actions is almost trivial. An added benefit is the modeless operation of the resulting product.

A popular Loran navigation unit obviously uses some sort of RTOS in its 8051-based software. Despite its rather complicated nested menu design, pressing the four function keys always aborts the current task and starts another, without worrying about stack corruption and the like. It makes for a very simple user interface that works the same way no matter what menu or mode the unit is operating in.

Interrupt latency is a problem in most fast systems. Missing any interrupt is usually a disaster! Non-RTOS-driven software usually services interrupts with one huge homogeneous routine, possibly having thousands of lines of code. Complex interrupt handlers running under an RTOS should simply service the hardware, reenable interrupts, and spawn off a task to take care of the more time-consuming details.

Sometimes interrupts come in groups—say, two quickly with a pause between them. A slightly more intelligent interrupt service routine could spawn off multiple copies of the handler, servicing burst interrupts much faster than normal.

Remember that tasks operate under a tighter set of constraints than conventional code. Be wary of sharing subroutines between tasks—some RTOSs will not permit this, particularly if some form of memory management is supported. In some operating systems the tasks must all be reentrant, since one copy of the task code might be running under several incarnations at once.

Especially when home brewing an RTOS, consider how you'll debug the operating system itself and the tasks. Some big-machine kernals include smart debuggers designed specifically for isolating tasking problems. If debugging several tasks, snapshot dumps and the other logging routines discussed in Chapter 4 will be useless unless you include the task's ID or name in the logged information.

Always keep the system's task control data structures well documented and readily available (i.e., in a public area), so you can quickly access them with your debugging tools. In cases where the structures are very complex it makes sense to maintain a simpler status word. You'll spend a lot of time looking at the state of the tasks—make your life as easy as possible.

Sometimes it's important to monitor overall task scheduling. Try writing a simple task that runs, say, once per second and that shows the contents of the task control data structures. You'll be kept apprised of the state of all tasks, measuring the RTOS's behavior.

Commercial Operating Systems

Although the next section includes a simple RTOS that is adequate for many applications, it does make sense to consider purchasing a commercial operating system. Reinventing the wheel is almost always a bad idea.

Be sure you get one targeted specifically for the chip you are using. Generic public-domain operating systems written in C don't take advantage of special processor features that can drastically reduce task overhead. For example, some processors include instructions to save and restore all of the registers. Others have multiple stack pointers.

Find out what the RTOS's interrupt latency is. In the middle of a context switch interrupts will probably be off for a while. If too long, your other high-priority interrupts will be lost or delayed excessively. Similarly, find out how long it takes to perform a complete context switch. If the CPU spends 50% of its time deciding what task to run, your code won't get much chance to run.

In embedded systems the RTOS's size will be of prime concern. No matter how big your CPU's address space is the RTOS will likely run from limited ROM space. Be sure it will fit. Sometimes you can pick and chose features to reduce the system's size. Few vendors tell you just how big each part of the RTOS is, information you need to make informed decisions before committing to their code.

Especially when using a microcontroller, be wary of RAM as well as of ROM requirements. Each task will have a data structure associated with it. Some commercial products use linked lists to handle an unlimited number of tasks. Your RAM size may impose an early and arbitrary limit on the number of usable tasks.

Look at features: how are messages passed between tasks? Can you allocate a resource (say, an I/O port) exclusively to one task so there is no contention problem with two or more activities trying to update the same value at one time? How much speed does this cost? How will you link to the RTOS? Whether written in C or assembly, you'll probably compile and link it right into your code. Is the source code compatible with your compiler and debugger tool chain?

A Poor Man's RTOS

Before writing an operating system, consider either purchasing one from a reputable vendor or using one of the hundreds of public-domain versions published in various magazines over the years. Refer to the Bibliography for other sources. It is instructive to see how an RTOS is structured.

The 64180 source code in Fig. 9.2 completely implements an RTOS. Though small, it has been used in a number of commercial applications. The RTOS consists of two major segments: the context switcher, which is responsible for starting, stopping, and sequencing tasks, and the task control code, which initiates various task operations. It does not include semaphores or other locking mechanisms.

This RTOS is designed to reside in low memory as a separate section of code distinct from the application program. The context switcher should not be accessed by the user's code; it is invoked only on an interrupt from the processor's internal timer. A number of routines can be called by applications programs to request task servicing.

The RTOS uses the 64180's timer 0 to sequence all task activities. It is programmed by an initialization routine to generate a tic interrupt every 10 msec. The currently executing task is suspended and the

```
        public  os_define, os_run, os_exit, os_cancel, os_wait, os_priority
        public  context_switch, os_init
        public  tcb, tcbptr
;
;  This is a real-time operating system for the 64180-series
;  CPUs. The code is copyrighted by Jack G. Ganssle but may be
;  used in noncommercial applications without prior permission.
;
;  The operating system is segmented into the following sections:
;        Initialization
;        Context Switcher
;        Task control - which is further broken into:
;                Task DEFINE
;                Task RUN
;                Task EXIT
;                Task CANCEL
;                Task set PRIORITY
;                Task WAIT
;
; Define IN0 and OUT0 macros to get to internal 64180 devices
;
in0     macro   arg
        defb    0edh, 38h, arg
        endm
out0    macro   arg
        defb    0edh, 39h, arg
        endm
;
; I/O ports
;
il      equ     33h             ; interrupt vector register
bbr     equ     39h             ; MMU bbr register
cbr     equ     38h             ; MMU cbr register
cbar    equ     3ah             ; MMU cbar register
tcr     equ     10h             ; timer control register
tmdr01  equ     0ch             ; timer data low register
tmdr0h  equ     0dh             ; timer data high register
rldr01  equ     0eh             ; timer reload register low
rldr0h  equ     fh              ; timer reload register high
;
; misc things
;
numtsk  equ     16              ; max number of tasks allowed
tic     equ     4608            ; timer divisor to get 100 tics/sec
cbar_data equ   84h             ; RTOS CBAR value
```

Figure 9.2   RTOS listing. (*Figure continues.*)

```
;
; Task state Definitions
;
waiting equ    1              ; task is in a WAIT mode
suspend equ    2              ; task has be interrupted so another can
                                be serviced
active  equ    4              ; task currently has control of the CPU
ready   equ    8              ; task was started by a RUN & is ready to
                                execute
none    equ    10h            ; task not defined
dormant equ    20h            ; task is defined but has nothing to do
;
; offsets into each TCB entry to get specific values
;
t_state equ    0              ; task state
t_cancel equ   1              ; cancel flag
t_bank  equ    2              ; task's MMU bank
t_priority equ 3              ; task's priority
t_rsi   equ    4              ; task's reschedule interval
t_rsc   equ    6              ; task's reschedule count
t_wait  equ    8              ; task's wait count
t_start equ    10             ; task's start address
t_sp    equ    12             ; task's stack pointer
;
; ********************************************************************
;
; Interrupt Linkages
;
        aseg
        org    0e4h           ; locate vectors here
        defw   context_switch ; tic vector

        cseg
;
;
; ********************************************************************
;
; Initialization
;
; This code sets up the TCB and other variables. It MUST be
; called on initial reset BEFORE enabling interrupts.
;
; Note that each task is defined at state NONE. The TCB must be
; one entry larger than needed so the last, unused task will always
; be NONE.
;
```

Figure 9.2 (Continued)

```
os_init:
          ld      hl,tcb
          ld      (tcbptr),hl       ; set pointer to tcb=start of tcb
          ld      b,numtsk          ; max number of tasks allowed
          ld      de,15             ; # bytes to add to get to next entry
init1:                              ; in this loop we init the tcb
          ld      (hl),none                 ; set state of each task=NONE
          inc     hl
          ld      (hl),0            ; zero cancel bit
          add     hl,de             ; pt to next task
          djnz    init1             ; do all tcb entries

          ld      a,cbar_data       ; set cbar for co=0-3fff, b=4000-7fff,
                                      c1=8000-ffff
          out0    cbar
          ld      a,0               ; set RAM at physical 8000
          out0    cbr
          out0    bbr               ; set tasks at physical 0000+load offset

          ld      ix,tcb            ; since task 0 not defined, do it here
          ld      (it+t_state),active; task 0 always active
          ld      (ix+t_priority),32; set middle level priority
          ld      (ix+t_rsc),0      ; set task 0 rsc=0
          ld      (in+t_rsc+1),0
          ld      (ix+t_bank),0     ; set task 0 bank=0

          ld      a,11h
          out0    tcr               ; enable timer 0 for interrupts
          ld      a,low tic         ; set low tic divisor
          out0    tmdr01
          out0    rldr01
          ld      a,high tic        ; set high tic divisor
          out0    tmdr0h
          out0    rldr0h
          ld      a,0e0h            ; set start of interrupt table
          outo    il                ; set IL register
          im      2                 ; run mode 2 interrupts
          ei
          ret
```

Figure 9.2 (Continued)

```
;  **********************************************************************
;
;  Context Switcher
;
;  This code sequences all task activities.
;
;  Up to NUMTSK tasks can be defined. Each of these tasks requires an
;  entry in the Task Control Block (TCB) of 16 bytes. Each entry
;  takes the form:
;
;  Byte 0 STATE - Indicates which state this task is in
;       1 CANCEL - set non-zero if this task has been canceled
;       2 BANK - What memory bank the task is in
;       3 PRIORITY - task relative priority (63=highest, 1=lowest)
;       4 RESCHEDULE INTERVAL - time in tics between automatic
;                 rescheduling of this task
;       6 RESCHEDULE COUNT - # tics to go before restarting the task
;       8 WAIT COUNT - # tics to go till we can resume a waiting task
;      10 START ADDRESS - start address of this task
;      12 STACK POINTER - this task's SP at the time it is interrupted
;
;  The TCB is defined with 16 bytes per entry, leaving 2 spares for
;  future expansion.
;
;
;  This is where the execution goes on an interrupt from the
;  timer.
;
;  The interrupt will first be serviced. Two reads are required to service
;  the 64180 timers.
;
context_switch:
        push    hl              ; push all registers
        push    de
        push    bc
        push    af
        push    ix
        push    iy
        exx
        push    hl
        push    de
        push    bc
        exx
        ex      af,af'
        push    af
        ex      af,af'
        in0     tcr             ; read tcr to clear interrupt
        in0     tmdr01          ; also must read tmdr to clear intr

        ld      ix,(tcbptr)     ; pt to current task's tcb entry
        ld      (ix+t_state),suspend; suspend the task
```

Figure 9.2 (Continued)

```
cs:      ld       hl,0
         add      hl,sp            ; hl=stack pointer for this task
         ld       (ix+t sp),l      ; save sp low in tcb
         ld       (ix+t_sp+1),h    ; save sp high in tcb
         call     dec_cnts         ; decrement tcb counts
         call     inc_rr_ptr       ; increment the round robin pointer
         call     find_tsk         ; find a task to execute
         ld       (tcbptr),ix      ; reset tcbptr
         ld       l,(ix+t_sp)      ; get low sp
         ld       h,(ix+t_sp+1)    ; get high sp
         ld       sp,hl            ; set the task's sp
         ld       a,(ix+t_state)   ; ix pts to task to run; get state
         ld       (ix+t_state),active; set task will now be active
         cp       ready            ; possible states: ready, suspended, waiting
         jr       nz,css1          ; j if not ready
         ld       l,(ix+t_start)   ; get low start address
         ld       h,(ix+t_start+1) ; get high start address
         call     remap            ; set proper bank
         push     hl               ; push start address
         ei
         reti                      ; start task
css1:    cp       suspend          ; suspended?
         jr       nz,csw1          ; j if not; must be waiting
         call     remap            ; set bank for this task
         ex       af,af'           ; restore registers
         pop      af
         ex       af,af'
         exx
         pop      bc
         pop      de
         pop      hl
         exx
         pop      iy
         pop      ix
         pop      af
         pop      bc
         pop      de
         pop      hl
         ei
         reti                      ; resume suspended task
csw1:    call     remap            ; remap to resume task that was waiting
         ei
         reti                      ; restart task

;
; remap - Subroutine to remap the MMU. This is entered with ix pointing
; to the tcb entry for this task.
;
```

Figure 9.2 (Continued)

```
remap:    ld      a,(ix+t_bank)    ; get this task's bank
          out0    bbr              ; set bbr for this task
          ret
;
; dec_cnts - This subroutine decrements all reschedule and wait
; counts in the entire tcb. IX must be preserved.
;
dec_cnts:
          ld      iy,tcb           ; pt to tcb start
dc0:      ld      a,(iy+t_state)   ; get task state
          cp      none             ; if none, end of used entries
          ret     z                ; ret if no more tasks to do
          ld      l,(iy+t_rsc)     ; set hl=reschedule count
          ld      h,(iy+t_rsc+1)
          ld      a,l
          or      h                ; if rsc=0, don't dec it
          jr      z,dc1            ; j if rsc=0
          dec     hl               ; rsc-1
          ld      (iy+t_rsc),l     ; restore rsc
          ld      (iy+t_rsc+1),h
dc1:      ld      l,(iy+t_wait)    ; now dec the wait count
          ld      h,(iy+t_wait+1)
          ld      a,l
          or      h                ; if wait=0, don't dec it
          jr      z,dc2            ; j if wait=0
          dec     hl               ; dec wait count
          ld      (iy+t_wait),l    ; save count
          ld      (iy+t_wait+1),h
dc2:      ld      de,16            ; adder to next tcb entry
          push    iy
          pop     hl
          add     hl,de            ; pt to next entry in tcb
          push    hl
          pop     iy
          pop     iy
          jr      dc0
;
; inc_rr_ptr - Increment round robin pointer. IX points to
; just-suspended task. Add 16, modulo the table size. Make
; sure the pointer is aimed at a task that is available for
; execution.
;
```

Figure 9.2 (Continued)

```
inc_rr_ptr:
          ld        de,16                ; table size
inc1:     push      ix
          pop       hl
          add       hl,de                ; pt to next entry
          push      hl
          pop       ix
          ld        ; a,(ix+t_state) ; get task's state)
          cp        none                 ; if none, recycle to start of table
          jr        nz,inc2              ; j if not table end
          ld        ix,tcb               ; recycle table
          ld        a,(ix+t_state)       ; a=task's state
inc2:     and       ready+suspend+waiting; only these are avail for exec
          jr        z,inc1               ; if not one of those, go to next task
          ld        a,(ix+t_rsc)         ; if available, rsc=0
          or        a,(ix+t_rsc+1)
          jr        nz,inc1              ; j if rsc<>0
          ld        a,(ix+t_state)       ; a=task's state
          cp        waiting              ; is the task in a wait?
          ret       nz                   ; ret if suspended or ready
          ret       nz                   ; ret if suspended or ready
          ld        a,(ix+t_wait)        ; to be available, wait=0
          or        a,(ix+t_wait+1)
          jr        nz,inc1              ; j if wait count not up
          ret                            ; ok- waiting task now ready
;
; find_tsk - find the next task to run.
;
; In this subroutine, the following registers will be maintained:
;         IX- Pointer to highest priority task so far
;         IY- TCB pointer
;         E - Highest priority found so far
;         D - Task counter
;
find_tsk:
          push      ix
          pop       iy                   ; start search at current task
          ld        d,2                  ; loop thru the tcb till NONE found twice
          ld        e,0                  ; highest P so far=0
ft1:      ld        a,(iy+t_state)       ; get state of task
          and       ready+suspend+waiting
          jr        z,ft3                ; j if not in any of those states
          ld        a,(iy+t_rsc)         ; see if rsc=0
          or        a,(iy+t_rsc+1)       ; if 0, rsc=0
          jr        nz,ft3               ; j if rsc <>0
          ld        a,(iy+t state)       ; get task state
          cp        waiting              ; is this task in a wait mode?
          jr        nz,ft3               ; j if the task is ready or suspended
          ld        a,(iy+t_wait)        ; see if wait count=0
          or        a,(iy+t_wait+1)
          jr        nz,ft3               ; j if wait not -
```

Figure 9.2 (Continued)

```
ft2:    ld      a,(iy+t_priority); a=task's priority
        cp      e               ; if this one > last biggest found?
        jp      m,ft3           ; j if this one is < last biggest
        jr      z,ft3           ; also skip if equal priorities
        ld      e,a             ; set new highest priority
        push    iy
        pop     ix              ; set new text-tsk-to-do
ft3:    ld      bc,16
        push    iy
        pop     hl
        add     hl,bc           ; make iy pt to next entry
        push    hl
        pop     iy
        ld      a,(iy,+T_state) ; get state of next task
        cp      none            ; if none, we need to recycle table
        jr      nz,ft1
        ld      iy,tcb          ; recycle table
        dec     d               ; dec # times to go thru table
        jr      nz,ft1          ; if more, go test
        ret
;
;   ****************************************************************************
;
;   This group of routines are those called by executing programs
;   to request service by the operating system.
;
;   The following requests are supported:
;   DEFINE, RUN, EXIT, CANCEL, PRIORITY, WAIT
;
;   os_define - define a task. This routine doesn't start a task
;   executing; rather, it simply makes the task known to the
;   operating system so the context switcher can start it at
;   the proper time.
;
;   Entered with
;       HL=task's start address
;       DE=task's top of stack
;       C =task's runtime bank (bbr value)
;       B =task's initial priority
;       A =task number (0 to numtsk-1)
;
os_define
        call    pt_to_task      ; set ix to task entry
        ld      (ix+t_state),dormant; dormant till a RUN commanded
        ld      (ix+t_bank),c   ; set bank
        ld      (ix+t_priority),b; set initial priority
        ld      (ix+t_start),1  ; set start address
        ld      (ix+t_start+1),h
        ld      (ix+t_sp),e     ; set top of stack
        ld      (ix+t_sp+1),d
        ret
```

Figure 9.2 (Continued)

```
;
; os_run - put a task into the READY state.
;
; This task is entered with A=task number, and DE=reschedule interval
;
os_run: call    pt_to_task      ; set ix=tcb entry
        ld      (ix_state), ready; elevate task to READY
        ld      (ix+t_rsi),e    ; set rsi=de
        ld      (ix+t_rsi+1),d
        ld      (ix+t_rsc),e    ; set rsc=de
        ld      (ix+t_rsc+1),d
        ld      (ix+t_cancel),0 ; make sure cancel not set
        ret
;
; os_exit - put a task back in the dormant state (if CANCEL
; was set) or back to READY.
;
os_exit:ld      ix, (tcbptr)    ; point to the tcb entry
        ld      a, (ix+t_rsi)   ; get low reschedule interval
        ld      (ix+t_rsc),a    ; set rs count=rs interval
        ld      a, (ix+t_rsi+1) ; do the entire 16 bits
        ld      (ix+t_rsc+1),a  ; I'd give 5 bucks for a 16 bit load
        ld      (ix+t_state),dormant; set dormant
        ld      a, (ix+t_cancel) ; a=1 if cancelled
        or      a
        jp      nz,cs           ; j if cancelled
        ld      (ix+t_state),ready; put task in ready state
        jp      cs              ; exit to context switcher
;
; os_priority - set a task's priority. Entered with
; B= new priority to assign (0 to 63).
;
os_priority:
        ld      ix, (tcbptr)
        ld      (ix+t_priority), b; set new priority
        ret
;
; os_cancel - Cancel the task whose task number is in
; A (0 to NUMTSK-1).
;
os_cancel:
        call    pt_to_task      ; set ix=tcb entry
        ld      (ix+t_cancel),1 ; cancel task
        ret
;
; os_wait - put the task  into a WAIT state.
; The Wait count is passed in DE (1 to 32767).
;
```

Figure 9.2 (Continued)

```
os_wait:ld        ix,(tcbptr)      ; set ix=tcb entry
        ld        (ix+t_state),waiting; put task to sleep
        ld        (ix+t_wait),e    ; set wait count
        ld        (ix+t_wait+1),d
        jp        cs               ; goto context switcher after pushes
;
; pt to task - With an entry parameter of the task number (0 to
; numtsk-1) in A, return IX pointing to the TCB entry of the task.
; Preserve all registers except A.
;
pt_to_task:
        push      hl
        push      de
        ld        hl,tcb           ; pt to tcb entry
        ld        de,16            ; # bytes/entry
pttsk1: dec       a
        jp        m,pttsk2         ; j if done
        add       hl,de            ; pt to next tcb entry
        jr        pttsk1
pttsk2: push      hl
        pop       ix               ; set ix=entry pter
        pop       de
        pop       hl
        ret
;
; Data area for the operating system
;
        dseg
tcbptr: defs      2                ; pter to current tcb entry
tcb:    defs      numtsk*16        ; task control block
        end
```

Figure 9.2 (*Continued*)

context switcher invoked every time this interrupt occurs. The RTOS supports all five task states discussed earlier: DORMANT, READY, ACTIVE, WAITING, and SUSPENDED.

Tasks are initially defined using subroutine **OS—DEFINE**, which makes an entry in the task control block (TCB) for the task. Tasks are initially DORMANT. The context switcher is aware of DORMANT tasks but ignores them until an ACTIVE task commands a DORMANT one to go to the READY state. This can only happen as a result of the ACTIVE task issuing a call to the operating system's **OS—RUN** subroutine. When a task enters the READY state it is not immediately eligible for execution (i.e., it is not allowed to go directly to ACTIVE).

Call **OS—RUN** with the task's reschedule interval. It can't start until the number of tics specified in the reschedule parameter elapses.

RTOS operations revolve around one data structure, the TCB. All scheduling information is kept in the TCB; all requests for service are made through it. The TCB has one 16-byte entry for each task. Its format is

Byte 0: Task state

Byte 1: One if a cancel was requested for this task. If this byte is set the task becomes ineligible for further rescheduling when it exits.

Byte 2: Task bank. This is the BBR value for the task. Required to support memory management (described later).

Byte 3: Task priority. Legal values are 1 to 63.

Byte 4: Task reschedule interval (RSI). Given when the task is first requested for execution.

Byte 6: Task reschedule count. This is set to the RSI every time the task exits, so the context switcher can begin counting down again.

Byte 8: Wait count. If the task is WAITING, this count is decremented to 0, at which time it again becomes eligible for execution.

Byte 10: Task start address. This is the task's entry point. When a READY task is elevated to ACTIVE, it starts at this address.

Byte 12: Task stack pointer. The current value of the SP
is saved for all tasks so the context switcher can
completely restore the task's state.

TCBPTR always points to the currently ACTIVE task. It implements the round-robin algorithm.

The first TCB entry is for task 0, the main routine that must exist just to spawn other tasks. Task 0 is never explicitly created; the RTOS forces it to exist when a call to the operating system's initialize routine is executed. The last TCB value (TCB + 2) is the task's current stack pointer. Every task MUST use its own, distinct stack. If one stack were shared between many tasks, after several tics the stack would become a horrible jumble with no way to determine which values belong to which task.

When a tic interrupts a task, the context switcher pushes the entire state of the machine (all registers and flags) on the current stack (i.e., that which belongs to the task just interrupted). The stack pointer is then saved in the TCB. When another task starts, that task's SP is recovered from its saved position in the TCB and used. POPs in the reverse order balance the stack and recover the task's register set. In this way the registers, flags, and stack are preserved, guaranteeing the integrity of the task's operation. In effect, it never knows it was interrupted. This has an important implication: each task *must* define an initial stack pointer via **OS_DEFINE.** Further, the stacks must be in logically distinct areas.

Call the initialization routine **OS_INIT** before the application issues any other RTOS calls. **OS_INIT** sets up the TCB so subsequent calls to other routines will find the TCB in a known, safe state. This involves setting all tasks to a default NONE, or nonexistent, state except for task 0. **OS_INIT** also programs the processor's timer to interrupt every 10 msec.

CONTEXT_SWITCH has two functions: decrement the RSI and wait counts of each task requiring such service and finding a task to execute.

Subroutine **DEC_CNTS** decrements the RSI and WAIT interval of every task in the TCB. The counts bottom out at zero; **DEC_CNTS** will not decrement past zero.

INC_RR_PTER increments the round-robin pointer. It makes sure the pointer will be aimed at a task that is available for servicing, not one that has no need for CPU time.

FIND_TSK searches the entire TCB, starting at **TCBPTR,** for the highest priority task to execute. It selects only tasks that qualify for execution time. If all tasks are the same priority, the task selected is the one at **TCBPTR,** thus implementing the round-robin scheduling algorithm.

READY tasks begin at the start address given in the TCB. WAITING tasks resume from the call to **OS_WAIT.** SUSPENDED tasks resume from the point of suspension, with all registers restored.

Figure 9.3 shows a series of macros that simplify access to the operating system. (Why laboriously code multiple identical register loads when the assembler can do the work for you?)

This RTOS includes one extra feature to demonstrate how even an 8-bit microprocessor can easily support a huge address space. As mentioned in Chapter 6, memory management units are an important component of some modern microprocessors. Unfortunately, they are without exception difficult and confusing to use. If you locate all memory management within the operating system itself, then individual tasks need never concern themselves with the complexities of memory allocation. Even better, you'll only have to troubleshoot the difficult-to-debug mapping code once.

Tasks are logically complete sections of code; since only one task can be ACTIVE at a time, only the active task needs to be mapped into

```
;
; Include file for 64180 RTOS.
; This file should be INCLUDED in all RTOS applications.
; It contains the macros that ease access to the RTOS itself.
;
        external        os_define, os_run, os_exit, os_cancel
        external        os_wait, os_init, os_priority
;
; This routine must be called before any other RTOS
; call is made.
;
; rt_init  (no arguments)
;
rt_init macro
        call    os_init
        endm
;
; rt_define - Make a task known to the operating system
;
; rt_define must be called before any other commands are issued
; for the task.
;
; rt_define start, stack, bbr, priority, number
;       start   = start address
;       stack   = top of stack for this task
;       bbr     = task's bank
;       priority= task's initial priority
;       number  = task number (1 to NUMTSK-1)
;
rt_define macro start, stack, bbr, priority, number
        ld      hl, start               ; set start address
        ld      de, stack               ; set top of stack
        ld      bc, priority*256+bbr; set priority and bank
        ld      a, number               ; task number
        call    os_define
        endm
;
; rt_run - Put a task in the READY state.
;
; tr_run number, rsi
;       number  = task number
;       rsi     = reschedule interval
;
rt_run  macro   number, rsi
        ld      de, rsi                 ; set reschedule interval
        ld      a, number               ; set task number
        call    os_run
        end
```

Figure 9.3   RTOS macros listing. (*Figure continues.*)

```
;
; rt_exit   - Exit the current task
;
; rt_exit   (no arguments)
;
rt_exit macro
        call    os_exit
        endm

;
; rt_priority - Set the current task's priority
;
; rt_priority priority
;        priority= task's new priority (1 to 63)
;
rt_priority macro         priority
        ld      b,priority
        call    os_priority
        endm

;
; rt_cancel  - Cancel a task
;
; rt_cancel number
;        number  = task number (0 to NUMTSK-1)
;
rt_cancel macro number
        ld      a,number        ; set task number
        call    os_cancel
        endm

;
; rt_wait   - Put the current task into a WAITING state
;
; rt_wait count
;        count   = number of tics to wait (1 to 32767)
;
rt_wait macro       count
        ld      de,count        ; set count
        call    os_wait
        endm
```

Figure 9.3 (Continued)

the current space at any time. The RTOS takes advantage of this by assigning each task to a separate map. The operating system automatically resets the MMU after every context switch, bringing the proper code into view. The RTOS's memory map is configured as three separate banks. In keeping with standard 64180 programming practice, common 0 starts at location 0 and runs to logical address 3FFF. The bank area starts at 4000 and goes to 7FFF. Common 1 runs from 8000 to the end of memory. This configuration gives the operating system and other utilities 16k of memory starting at 0. All tasks typically start at logical 4000 and can be as long as 16k each. Common 1 is the RAM data area.

Common 0 (the operating system) and the RAM area are always visible in the logical map; they are never mapped out. The bank area, where all tasks are stored, is the only section affected by remapping. It is usually remapped for each task to bring new ones into view.

16k is reserved for the RTOS and other important global routines. 32k is available for variables. The rest of memory, almost 1 Mbyte, can be tasks. 16k per task is almost always enough. Tasks by their nature should each be simple; it's better to have a lot of simple tasks than a few big complex ones.

Some applications may require other memory configurations. More RAM might be needed or larger or smaller task sizes accommodated. The only things sacred about the map outlined are that the RTOS starts in low memory and is never mapped out, and that RAM is available somewhere and it too is never remapped. The value **CBAR_DATA** in the code can be changed at will, within these constraints, to suit other requirements.

The 64180 MMU's 12 bits of resolution implies that each task will use at least 4k of memory space. This does not mean that a program with four short tasks will need 16k. The TCB contains two values that affect mapping. A BBR (bank base register) is stored for each task, so the MMU can be remapped to this address. However, every task's start address is also saved. If all tasks began at 4000 logical a start address would not be needed.

By saving a start address, many tasks can coexist in one map. In the extreme case, when the entire program will use only 64k, set all BBR values the same, store each task at a different address, and set the proper start addresses within the TCB (using the **OS_DEFINE** routine). Thus, the RTOS gives the user all possibilities; mapping can be defined in virtually any fashion or it can be completely ignored simply by setting all BBR values to 0.

Be aware that since tasks can be assigned to maps, no task should ever call or access an address in another task. That address may not exist when the task is running!

Figure 9.4 is a simple multitasking program that illustrates the use of the RTOS and the various system calls that request task servicing. It is a five-task program (remember, task 0, at ROOT, exists by default). Task 0 does nothing; it runs an infinite loop. Task 1 increments a

```
        .z80
        cseg
;
        public  root,start,task1,task2,task3,task4,hex4,cout,inituart
;
;
        include osmaroc.mac      ; include rtos macros
;
; 64180 IN0 and OUT0 macros
;
in0     macro   arg
        defb    0edh,38h,arg
        endm
out0    macro   arg
        defb    0edh,39h,arg
        endm
;
; uart
;
baudrate equ    21h              ; 9600 baud
baudport equ    3                ; baud rate port
uartinit equ    1                ; uart init port
uartstat equ    5                ; uart status port
uartout equ     7                ; uart output port
;
;   This program is a test driver for the 64180 Real Time
; Operating System.
;
start:  ld      sp,t0sp
        call    inituart         ; initialize the uart

        ld      hl,0
        ld      (counter),hl     ; zero counter

        rt_init                  ; initialize the os

        rt_define task1,t1sp,0,40,1; define task 1
        rt_define task2,t2sp,1,32,2; define task 2
        rt_define task3,t3sp,2,32,3; define task 3
        rt_define task4,t4sp,3,32,4; define task 4

        rt_run  1,5              ; start task 1
        rt_run  2,300            ; start task 2
        rt_run  3,1000           ; start task 3
        rt_run  4,50             ; start task 4
root:   jr      root
```

Figure 9.4 RTOS application program listing. (*Figure continues.*)

```
;
; inituart - init the uart to 9600 baud
;
inituart:
        ld      a,64h
        out0    uartinit        ; set up 8 data, 1 stop, no parity
        ld      a,baudrate
        out0    baudport        ; set baud rate
        ret
;
; task 1- increment a counter
;
        aseg
        org     4000h
task1:  ld      sp,t1sp
        ld      hl,(counter)
        inc     hl
        ld      (counter),hl
        rt_exit                 ; end task
;
; task 2 - reset the counter to 0
;
        org     5000h
        .phase  40000h
task2:  ld      sp,t2sp
        ld      hl,0
        ld      (counter),hl    ; zero counter
        rt_exit                 ; end task
        .dephase
;
; task 3 - cancel task 2 after a while
;
        org     6000h
        .phase  4000h
task3:  ld      sp,t3sp
        rt_cancel       2       ; cancel task 2
        rt_cancel       3       ; cancel ourselves
        rt_exit
        .dephase
;
;
; task 4 - display the counter
;
        org     7000h
        .phase  4000h
task4:  ld      sp,t4sp
        ld      hl,(counter)    ; number to display
call    hex4                    ; hex4 displays the number in HL
                                ; and then prints a CRLF
        rt_exit
```

Figure 9.4 (Continued)

```
;
; data
;
          dseg
counter: defs    2          ; tic counter for task 1
          defs   100        ; task 0's stack
t0sp:     defs   1          ; end of stack for task 0
          defs   100        ; task 1's stack
t1sp:     defs   1          ; end of stack for task 1
          defs   100        ; task 2's stack
t2sp:     defs   1          ; end of stack for task 2
          defs   100        ; task 3's stack
t3sp:     defs   1          ; end of stack for task 3
          defs   100        ; task 4's stack
t4sp:     defs   1          ; end of stack for tack 4

          end
```

Figure 9.4 (Continued)

memory-based counter once every five tics. It runs at a high priority, established when the task was defined by the macro **RT_DEFINE.** Task 2 runs infrequently (once every 300 tics). It resets the counter to zero. Task 3 cancels task 2 after 1000 tics, effectively killing off the resetting of the counter to zero. It also cancels itself, since once task 2 is killed, task 3 is done forever. Task 4 prints **COUNTER** twice a second. (**HEX4** prints the number in HL in hex.) This lets you see the effect of task interaction. The counter value will be generally increasing, since task 1 runs often. Once every 3 sec task 2 resets it to zero. After 10 sec, task 3 cancels task 2, so the count is never again reset to zero.

Each of the tasks runs in its own memory map. They're small, so they do waste most of the address space allocated to them. However, this illustrates the use of the RTOS with memory management and of loading tasks in different maps.

Every task is assigned to logical address 4000 and occupies exactly 1000 bytes (the mapping resolution of the MMU). The BBR values increment from 0, so the physical addresses of the tasks are 4000 (task 1), 5000 (task 2), 6000 (task 3), and 7000 (task 4).

The tasks can not be assembled at their physical addresses, since internal jumps won't go to the logical address, which is where the program really runs. Tasks cannot be defined at their logical addresses because then all of the tasks would be at the same address, causing assembly errors.

The solution is to use an ORG to set the physical address of the task, and .PHASE and .DEPHASE to force the assembler to assume the code is really somewhere else—in this case at the execution address (4000). The code is loaded at the correct physical address, but it is assembled at the proper logical spot.

CHAPTER 10

Signal Sampling and Smoothing

Badness you can get easily, in quantity.—Hesiod

Though we digital folks long for a realm where everything is digital, our code often reads and analyzes signals from a noisy, drifty analog world. Whenever a system includes an analog-to-digital converter (ADC), we have to make sense of readings that include parasitic effects on top of the real data we're looking for.

The noise problem is getting worse. While the analog world continues with the same innate disagreeable amount of randomness, systems once content to use a 10-bit ADC now sport 16 or more bits of resolution. Each bit might represent a mere 100 μV. Customers are pushing us into the noise floor whether we like it or not! Linear circuits have improved a lot in the last decade but not enough to render signal smoothing obsolete. Even if the electronics were perfectly quiet, quantization errors and resolution limitations will always induce undesired signal characteristics that must be filtered out.

The demand for higher precision seems to outstrip the ever-improving electronics. Clever software algorithms that extract meaning from what often appears to be little more than noise can save lots of expensive circuitry. A related problem is that of calibrating digital equipment that models complex physical phenomena. Many of the same techniques used to smooth data apply directly to establishing calibration constants.

Radio and TV receivers are astonishing devices. We go nearly insane trying to remove a few millivolts of noise from our latest widget while the radio plays a crystal-clear violin concerto. Often the station's signal is only a few microvolts at the antenna, buried in many millivolts of noise and rock 'n' roll. Why do we fight so hard when digitizing nearly dc data, yet a receiver works so well with a thousand times less signal?

The music we hear is modulated on the station's carrier frequency. Marvelously designed RF filters easily notch out virtually everything that is not at almost exactly the carrier's center frequency. The noise is distributed over a huge bandwidth; the filters remove all but a tiny portion of that bandwidth, taking the noise out as well.

By contrast, most analog presented to a digital system is at a very low frequency. Indeed, most is a nonperiodic, nearly dc voltage. No carrier exists; all of the bandwidth carries important information.

Analog data processed in embedded systems falls into one of two categories: single-point readings, where only the instantaneous value of the signal is important, and periodic signals, where the varying but more or less repetitive shape of the input conveys information.

An example of a single-point input is the slowly changing output of a potentiometer (perhaps mounted at a robot's elbow joint). The signal moves slowly with time—for all intents it is dc. Usually the computer goes to the ADC for a reading when something happens. If a limit switch commands "take a reading NOW," then the computer probably gets one quick measurement and carries on with its computations. Other examples include the output of a digital voltmeter, the photocell voltage in a security system, and thermistor resistance in a temperature sensor.

Periodic signals are like those displayed on an oscilloscope. The waveform is a swept signal; one axis is time and the other voltage. Each sweep is usually almost identical to the previous one, or at least has a similar shape.

Many real-world instruments generate scope-like data. A spectrophotometer optically scans amplitude versus wavelength. A spectrum analyzer shows amplitude versus frequency. An EKG monitor measures voltage versus time. The signal repeats only very slowly (by computer standards).

In all of these cases the input envelope changes sluggishly with respect to the sweep time—each cycle of an EKG output closely resembles the previous one. The output is a two-dimensional plot generally represented in the computer as an array of amplitudes. During every sweep the computer reads data and digitizes it into an array.

Most of us filter this sort of data by averaging lots of successive sweeps. Perhaps not so obviously, we can smooth the data within any one sweep along the implicit axis (the axis implied by array position—*time* for an oscilloscope or EKG, *frequency* for a spectrum analyzer or spectrophotometer).

This discussion is limited to data that are continuous along the implicit axis. This means there are no sharp discontinuities from one point to the next. In other words, for any point i, point $i + 1$ will be approximately the same value or will be generally changing in the same way the previous one was. This characteristic is true of most physical phenomena.

Averaging

A digital instrument reading single-point dc-like voltages (as in the case of the robot arm pot) will most likely average multiple ADC readings to minimize noise. Little else is possible.

Pick an intelligent averaging technique. Most programmers opt for a running average, also known as a boxcar. Only the latest n readings are included in the average, so very old data can't skew the results. After all, presumably the robot's arm moves regularly; the output is meant to noiselessly reflect its current position. The value n is chosen large enough to generate quiet data but must be small compared to the arm's speed. If the arm can move 30°/sec, then averaging for 5 sec will give hopelessly inaccurate data.

Each new sample replaces the oldest in a circular buffer. Once the buffer is initially filled the system can provide a smoothed output by taking only one reading and computing the average of the buffer's contents. In other words, any reading $D(i)$ is a function of some number n of past and future values:

$$D(i) = \frac{1}{n} \sum_{k=i-n/2}^{i+n/2} RAW(k)$$

How can we have a future reading? In effect the output value is delayed in time. Point $D(i)$ isn't available until n additional samples are read. Where this is just not possible, then $D(i)$ might be computed as

$$D(i) = \frac{1}{n} \sum_{k=i-n}^{i} RAW(k)$$

Be sure n is small enough to ensure that it doesn't skew reading $D(i)$ in favor of old values. A better approach is outlined later.

Any simple averaging technique reduces noise at a rate proportional to the square root of the number of samples in the average. Using 100 samples yields an order of magnitude improvement in noise figure. Since any system will eventually be bound by the computer and ADC speed, averaging results in a sort of diminishing return. Increasing the number to 1000 gives only a factor-of-three improvement in noise over using 100. Noise reduction always involves a trade-off between system response time and quietness.

Now consider sweeping systems. Suppose your EKG processes noisy analog data, but you want to display a glitch-free output. If the code reads each sweep into the two-dimension array RAW(i,n) (where i is the index into the sweep and n is the sample number—see Fig. 10.1), then the smoothed value at any point is

$$D(i) = \frac{1}{n} \sum_{k=i-n/2}^{i+n/2} D(i,k)$$

In other words, each point is averaged with the all of the points at the same index in the array. Smart software fills array RAW(i,n) with the latest n samples, dropping the oldest every time a new sweep is read. This is no different than the way we averaged single-point data, except that the output is a number of array elements.

If the instrument takes a long time to acquire a sweep, averaging multiple sweeps to smooth the data is simply out of the question. In this case the only option is to average in the i dimension.

For a spectrum analyzer this dimension is frequency—a sample is taken every so many hertz. The data behaves as a continuous function. There are no sharp discontinuities between data points. Any point $D(i)$ is much like its neighbors, so averaging over the implicit axis doesn't create too much distortion. In an EKG the implicit axis is time. Averaging for 1 sec will completely obliterate heartbeat information, but little is lost by averaging a hundred readings over the course of a few milliseconds.

This is profoundly different from averaging multiple sweeps, where the fear is blurring sweep-to-sweep changes. Smoothing over the baseline axis smears adjacent points a bit but yields much faster answers. You don't have to wait to gather the next n sweeps.

Imagine the digitized data is in array RAW(i), where i runs from 0 (the first point of the current scan) to k (the last point). Smooth the data by computing a new array $D(i \ldots k)$. Every element $D(i)$ is the average (for a five-point smoothing function) of RAW($i - 2$), RAW($i - 1$), RAW(i), RAW($i + 1$), RAW($i + 2$). This is exactly the same as the box-

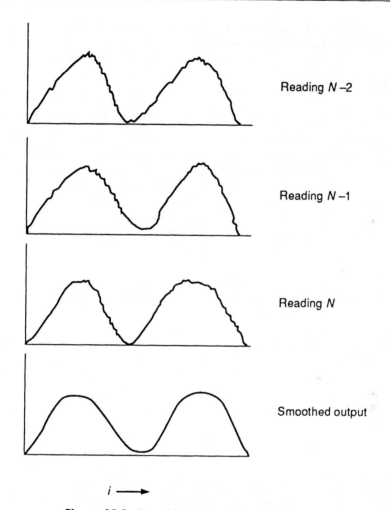

Reading N – 2

Reading N – 1

Reading N

Smoothed output

i ———▶

Figure 10.1 Smoothing by averaging multiple sweeps.

car average, except that it is applied over the sampling axis. Mathematically,

$$D(i) = \frac{1}{n} \sum_{k=i-n/2}^{i+n/2} \text{RAW}(k)$$

The output data will be a little smeared; sharp peaks will be somewhat flattened. If the n is small and the signal changes slowly with increasing *i*, then the flattening will not be significant. Can we define an averaging strategy that will avoid this side-effect?

Convolutions

The previous equation generates an output for each point *i* that is the average of all the points in the vicinity of *i*. In effect, for each *i* we make an output by multiplying the input waveform by a unit step function and summing the results at each point. We then slide the step one point to the right and repeat the algorithm. Adjusting the number of points included in each average simply changes the width of the step. Wider steps (i.e., a bigger *n*) give more noise-free data, but at the price of greater smearing. Narrow steps give noisier signals that are more faithful to the input data. A step exactly one-point wide doesn't smooth or change the input in any way.

The technique of iteratively replacing any point *i* with a function of the points around *i* is called *convolution*. The unit step in Fig. 10.2 is the very simplest of convolutions. Most of the convolving points are 0; the rest form the narrow unit step and are 1.

Instead of using the crude step shown in Fig. 10.2, why not convolve the input data with a function that resembles the expected signal? In other words, pick a set of weights that accentuate the midpoint and include reduced levels of the more distant values. If the convolving function looks rather like the expected input signal, then less smearing will result.

Figure 3 illustrates a triangular convolution. Computationally this involves multiplying each point in the vicinity of *i* with a weighting factor and then averaging the results. The triangle is always centered on the point being smoothed, which, since it has the greatest weight, affects the output far more than the adjacent data. Points far away from the center play a much less significant role in the result but do contribute to smoothing. The result is a smoothed output waveform more faithful to the real input.

A triangular five-point smoothing function (i.e., the output value depends on the point we're on and two points to the right and left) is

```
D(i)=(RAW(i-2)*.33 + RAW(i-1)*.66 + RAW(i) +
RAW(i+1)*.66 + RAW(i+2)*.33) / 3.0
```

Where do these coefficients come from? The values .33 and .66 [and the implicit 1 that multiplies RAW(*i*)] define the shape of the triangular convolver; plotting .33, .66, 1, .66, and .33 gives a triangle. As you'd

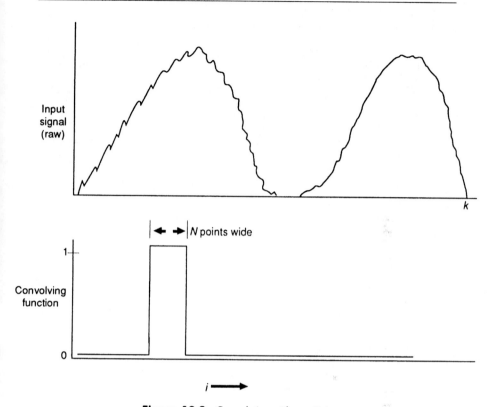

Input
signal
(raw)

k

|← →| *N* points wide

1

Convolving
function

0

i ⟶

Figure 10.2 Convolution with a unit step.

expect the points furthest away from the center value contribute less to
the answer than those nearby (i.e., RAW(i − 2) and RAW(i + 2) are
multiplied by a measly .33). The entire equation is divided by 3.0,
which is the weighted average of the points. With the unit step, we
divided by the number of points in the smooth to get a true average.
Now, with the oddball triangle shape, we divide by a number factored
to compensate for the shape of the waveform.

The whole point of convolutions is to define a set of weighting values that gives a truer picture of the system's input while minimizing
noise. These numbers can be chosen to anticipate the system's output
and thus bias the results in a favorable direction.

Since the sweep's data is continuous we can represent it over a very
small interval with a polynomial of sufficient degree. Even noncontin-
uous signals are often piecewise continuous; given a small enough in-

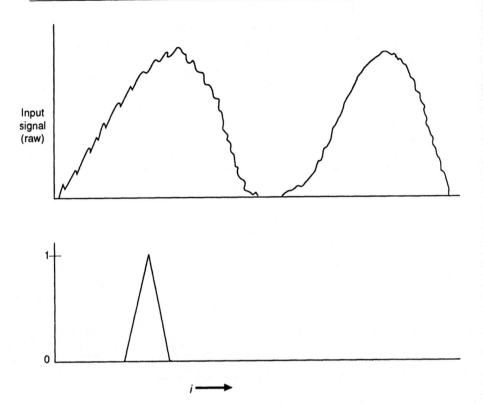

Figure 10.3 Convolving a signal with a triangular function.

terval their shape will resemble a polynomial. This is exactly analogous to the approximating functions in Chapter 7.

Remember that the sweep is noisy. Even if the sampled signal were a perfectly smooth waveform, by the time the computer reads the data the less-than-perfect analog circuits and ADC quantization problems may have corrupted its integrity. We must fit a curve through the data to generate a more realistic model of the signal. No one point is assumed to be correct; the curve defined by a collection of points will yield data that is, on the average, closer to the truth.

Many curve-fitting techniques exist. In most instances the goal is to reduce the "amount of error" in the data. We can use the technique of least squares to find coefficients for a polynomial describing a curve that fits the data in such a fashion that the sum-square error is minimized. That is, the square root of the sum of the squares of the error at each point is a minimum. From the standpoint of smoothing, this means we try to fit points onto an ideal curve; the raw data describes about what the curve will be in the region of the approximation.

Computing a least-squares polynomial at each point of a sweep is computationally very expensive. At realistic data rates no micro could ever keep up with the workload. Fortunately, the concept of convolutions can be extended to perform the least squares automatically.

The derivation of the method is rather involved—refer to the paper by Savitzky and Golay (see Bibliography) for more details. Suffice to say that we'll use a set of integers that, when convolved with an input signal, gives an output waveform that is a least-squares fit to an ideal signal over a narrow range.

This is really the best sort of noise reduction. The sampled data is idealized, and each output point is then picked off the smooth curve. There is no magic with the method; noisy data will not be transformed into a perfect representation of the input signal. However, a much better result can be obtained than that with a unit step convolution (i.e., a boxcar average). We don't have to average multiple sweeps so data can be smoothed immediately.

The following sets of integers define convolving functions that yield least-squares fits to input data. The table fits a cubic (third-order) polynomial over a region of the data. Use the broad convolutions (e.g., 21 or 25 points) where the data is smooth and changes slowly over a wide region. Use the narrower ones for faster changing data.

Points	25	21	17	13	9	5
$i - 12$	-253					
$i - 11$	-138					
$i - 10$	-33	-171				
$i - 9$	62	-76				
$i - 8$	147	9	-21			
$i - 7$	222	84	-6			
$i - 6$	287	149	7	-11		
$i - 5$	322	204	18	0		
$i - 4$	387	249	27	9	-21	
$i - 3$	422	284	34	16	14	
$i - 2$	447	309	39	21	39	-3
$i - 1$	462	324	42	24	54	12
$i + 0$	467	329	43	25	59	17
$i + 1$	462	324	42	24	54	12
$i + 2$	447	309	39	21	39	-3
$i + 3$	422	284	34	16	14	
$i + 4$	387	249	27	9	-21	

(*Table continues*)

Points	25	21	17	13	9	5
$i+$ 5	322	204	18	0		
$i+$ 6	287	149	7	-11		
$i+$ 7	222	84	-6			
$i+$ 8	147	9	-21			
$i+$ 9	62	-76				
$i+10$	-33	-171				
$i+11$	-138					
$i+12$	-253					
Norm	5175	3059	323	143	231	35

It's easy to use the convolution coefficients. The set of 5 integers creates a polynomial that smooths signal D(i) by computing:

```
D(i)= (RAW(i-2)*(-3) + RAW(i-1)*12 + RAW(i)*17
+ RAW(i+1)*12 + RAW(i+2)*(-3))/ 35
```

A seven-point smooth takes the form

```
D(i)=(RAW(i-4)*(-21) + RAW(I-3)*14 + RAW(i-2)*39
+ RAW(i-1)*54 + RAW(i)*59 + RAW(i+1)*54 + RAW(i+2)*39
+ RAW(i+3)*14 + RAW(I+4)*(-21))/ 231
```

Notice that the equation is divided by the norm—the sum of the coefficients. Also notice that the shape is symmetrical; on either side of the center point the coefficients are identical, just as common sense suggests. Further, the center point is always the biggest number, making that piece of data contribute the most to the result.

If the data is very busy (i.e., over only a few sample points it undergoes a lot of maxima and minima), then use a small set of integers (e.g., 9 rather than 21). The method does attempt to fit a curve to a short segment of the input data; busy data is all but impossible to fit under any circumstances. Data that changes slowly can use the larger sets of integers and reap the rewards of more smoothing.

The following code fragment creates an array D that is a five-point least-squares smooth to data in RAW using coefficients from the table:

```
for(i=2; i<array_size-2; ++i)
        D(i)= (RAW(i-2)*(-3) + RAW(i-1)*12 + RAW(i)*17 +
        RAW(i+1)*12 + RAW(i+2)*(-3))/ 35;
```

Note that the smoothing operation ignores the end points, since for $i = 0,1$, and at the last two points we can't solve the equation. If $i = 0$ then RAW($i - 2$) is negative, creating havoc with the compiler's array computations. Probably the easiest solution is to use unsmoothed data at these points.

Differentiation

Some systems compute the derivative of the input data. Most embedded programmers are aghast at the thought of using calculus in a ROM-based system, but in fact it is rather common. Remember that the first derivative of a function is its rate of change (e.g., velocity is the derivative of position), and the second derivative is the rate of change of the change (acceleration).

One example of an application where calculus is important is image processing, where the edge-detection algorithms all rely on a convolution to compute the derivative of brightness levels. Another is the spectrophotometer, which uses derivatives to measure amounts of compounds in a sample. On a spectrum analyzer the derivative shows the quality of the transmitted signal's carrier; this is essentially the Q factor used in so many RF calculations.

The convolution can help compute derivatives. Convolutions have an important property, namely

$$f'(t) = g(t) * h'(t)$$

and

$$f'(t) = g'(t) * h(t)$$

where * represents the convolution process and the prime marks indicate the derivative. This means to both smooth and differentiate a signal you can convolve the signal with the derivative of the convolving function. You never need to explicitly differentiate the input signal, a task that might use far too much computer power to be practical.

This means we can compute the derivative of a continuous signal by convolving it with the derivative of the unit impulse (a step one-point wide). Unfortunately, this derivative can't be expressed in a set of integers usable by a computer.

Remember that the convolving process primarily smooths input data. We can convolve the derivative of a smoothing function with the input signal to both smooth and take the input's derivative in one step. A single convolution does both.

The following table is a set of integers that both smooths and differentiates the data by least squares. Use these values as previously described.

Points	25	21	17	13	9	5
$i-12$	30866					
$i-11$	8602					
$i-10$	-8525	84075				
$i-9$	-20982	10032				
$i-8$	-29236	-43284	748			
$i-7$	-33754	-78176	-98			
$i-6$	-35003	-96947	-643	1133		
$i-5$	-33450	-101900	-930	-660		
$i-4$	-29562	-95338	-1002	-1578	86	
$i-3$	-23806	-79564	-902	-1796	-142	
$i-2$	-16649	-56881	-673	-1489	-193	1
$i-1$	-8558	-29592	-358	-832	-126	-8
$i+0$	0	0	0	0	0	0
$i+1$	8558	29592	358	832	126	8
$i+2$	16649	56881	673	1489	193	-1
$i+3$	23806	79504	902	1796	142	
$i+4$	29562	95338	1002	1578	-86	
$i+5$	33450	101900	930	660		
$i+6$	35003	96947	643	-1133		
$i+7$	33754	78176	98			
$i+8$	29236	43284	-748			
$i+9$	20982	-10032				
$i+10$	8525	-84075				
$i+11$	-8602					
$i+12$	-30866					
Norm	1776060	3634092	23256	24024	1188	12

The convolution principle can be generalized to any derivative and to any number of sample points.

Linear Calibrations

One of the weakest points of any system is the analog electronics. In the digital world a one is a one is a one—we rarely worry about voltage levels and the like. Not so in an analog front end. Drift, aging, and even humidity and cleanliness can dramatically affect the response of an analog circuit. Since the entire system will be only as good as any of its parts, removing front-end inaccuracies is just as important as having the proper software algorithms.

Traditional analog circuits use potentiometers (variable resistors, colloquially known as "pots") to remove most errors. A technician calibrates the unit by carefully setting each pot. With one or two pots this is usually not a big deal, but some systems have dozens. Worse, one pot can affect the setting of all of the others. For example, setting the gain pot usually requires readjustment of the offset. This is an iterative process, driving the technician into a pot-twiddling frenzy.

It's nice to think that a product consists of a bare minimum of analog electronics all of which are a front end to the processor. More often than not the raw signals must be amplified, smoothed, and sometimes translated before being fed to the ADC. One or more operational amplifiers are usually wired together before the ADC (unadjusted, all contribute some amount of analog error to the digitized data, as will the ADC itself).

High-accuracy systems (those with a 10-or-more-bit ADC) will almost certainly require calibration. In a purely analog world there may not be a good alternative to a multitude of pots, but embedded systems can take advantage of the power of the computer to mathematically eliminate most error sources. After all, a pot is really an analog memory device. We can replace all of these expensive components with clever code and perhaps some trivial electronics. The benefit? Each removed pot reduces system size, increases reliability, and eliminates the labor associated with its adjustment. This also increases overall system accuracy since the computer can recalibrate itself continuously, far more frequently than is feasible with manually adjusted pots.

Offset is an undesired dc bias. (For example, when you expect 0 V out, the circuit gives 0.25.) Gain is the amplification factor. A system that relies on a gain of 5.0 may not work properly if the gain is really 5.1. Mathematically speaking, gain is the algebraic quantity "slope" and offset is the intercept. Remember that the equation of a line is defined by $y = mx + b$, where m is the slope and b is the intercept.

Many analog circuits are well described by this equation. Even an ADC can be pretty well characterized this way. Although we wish an ADC would have the ideal characteristic $y = x$ (output digital representation is exactly the same as the input), most will exhibit small gain and offset errors. High-precision converters have a provision for trimming these parameters via external pots.

The op amps have errors, the ADC is suspect, and even the sensors themselves rarely measure precisely what we want. Thermistors and thermocouples change sensitivity with age. Photocells drift with age and temperature.

We designed a system years ago with lead sulfide photodetectors. Unfortunately the sensors were an order of magnitude more sensitive to temperature than to the infrared light we were trying to measure! It seems that a sensor for measuring almost any physical parameter to a reasonable degree of accuracy will, uncorrected, lead to significant errors.

    Eliminate pots! Try to design your system to be self-calibrating. Sensors and analog circuits will probably always need some sort of alignment but try to come up with a purely digital approach. If the self-calibrating routine is invoked every second, day, or week, the end product will ultimately give much more accurate results than a painstakingly hand-tuned front end whose last calibration was half a decade ago.

    Given that most systems use linear sensors (or at least sensors that are mostly linear in the operating range) and linear circuits, it follows that we can use a linear correction to remove essentially the errors. Even some nonlinear circuits can use a linear correction if the operating range is sufficiently restricted.

    A self-calibrating system needs two ingredients: some known value, which is injected into the front end during the calibration, and an algorithm to correct the overall transfer function to meet these known values.

    Before considering the problem of introducing known values into the system, let's look at how we might do the math involved in the calibration.

    Suppose we're measuring the light from a star in a telescope. The input to the computer will be a number of bits representing voltage x. This quantity will certainly include both gain and an offset errors. We compute light intensity by replacing x with the formula

$$x' = mx + b$$

where x' is the corrected (linearized) value of x, m is the correction to the system's gain, and b is the correction to the system's offset. The values for m and b are computed every time we recalibrate.

    Elementary algebra tells us that to solve for the two unknowns m and b we need at least two equations. A technician would adjust the pots by inserting 0 V for the offset correction and a full-scale reading for the gain correction. We should do the same.

    If we take a measurement with very different values, say, one at each extreme of the sensor's range, then we'll get two formulas:

$$y_1 = mx_1 + b \quad \text{(first reading)}$$

$$y_2 = mx_2 + b \quad \text{(second reading)}$$

Solving for m:

$$m = \frac{y_1 - y_2}{x_1 - x_2}$$

And for b:

$$b = y_1 - mx_1$$

Again, x_1 and x_2 are the values read from the ADC; and y_1 and y_2 are their known correct values.

Every time we take a reading from the ADC we should correct the reading by applying

$$\text{output} = \frac{y_1 - y_2}{x_1 - x_2} \cdot x + y_1 - x_1 \cdot \frac{y_1 - y_2}{x_1 - x_2}$$

While this might seem a bit cumbersome, all of the coefficients can be computed at calibration time, so the computational burden is small.

Nonlinear Calibrations

A linear calibration, one that uses just an offset and gain, is adequate for many simple systems where a line models the transfer function of the input signal. Some of what we measure with embedded systems is far more complex than this. Often several independent inputs make up the output value—for example, a colorimeter uses at least three frequencies of light (red, green, and blue) to determine color.

I once worked at a company that used different wavelengths of light to measure protein in wheat. No magic formula exists to compute protein in this manner, but it turned out that over a small range (say, 11 to 19% protein), a linear relation does exist between the measured light and protein. In other words, if f_1, f_2, and f_3 are responses at each of three frequencies:

$$\text{Protein} = k_0 + k_1 f_1 + k_2 f_2 + k_3 f_3$$

Unfortunately, the coefficients k_0 to k_3 vary from instrument to instrument. By running dozens of wheat samples with known protein concentrations and measuring the f_1, f_2, and f_3 values, we could compute the k coefficients by doing a least-square fit of the f data to the known protein levels.

In this case and many others the empirical data obtained during the instrument's calibration is used as a predictor for future measurements. The calibration determines the k coefficients, and then the instrument uses these coefficients to measure unknown samples.

A similar application is precision temperature monitors. The response of some thermistors is not linear—temperature may not be directly related to the thermistor's resistance. Some electronic thermometers operate by forcing the user to present known temperatures (typically through a specific chemical state change) to the instrument and letting the unit calibrate itself using least squares.

In effect, this self-calibration procedure is heuristic—the instrument learns from its mistakes. On initial power-up the device is a blank slate, with the potential of measuring some parameter but without the detailed knowledge of the world (represented by coefficients of an equation) needed to do the job. Calibration to known samples provides these coefficients.

LEAST SQUARES

All curve-fitting techniques attempt to find a formula that relates one or more inputs to a single output. In other words, a function f is found such that

$$g = f(v_1, v_2, v_3 \ldots)$$

where g is the output and v_1 to v_n are input signals.

Some form of the function must be assumed; generally, a polynomial is selected since practically any function can be approximated (at least over some interval) by a polynomial. That is, the function f looks like the following:

$$f(v_1, v_2, v_3 \ldots) = k_0 + k_1 v_1 + k_2 v_2 + k_3 v_3 \ldots$$

Frequently there is really only one input value (say x), and we're looking for a function f that fits x despite a perhaps very bizarre behavior of x over some range—it might be a sharp parabola. Then, f will be of the form

$$f(x) = k_0 + k_1 x + k_2 x^2 + k_3 x^3 \ldots$$

This traditional polynomial form can be used to fit any continuous function over some range.

By definition, least squares constructs a function that minimizes the sum-square error between the measured samples and the "real" value of the sample. To be more exact, it minimizes the function

$$\sum_{i=1}^{m} [x(i) - x'(i)]^2$$

where m is the number of samples in the calibration, $x(i)$ are the predicted values, and $x'(i)$ are the computed x values.

Least squares operates by recognizing the impossibility of an exact fit; it tries to keep the average error as small as possible.

Least squares is by far the most common way to fit curves but is by no means the only method. Another is the Chebyshev approximation. Chebyshev minimizes maximum error; no point is allowed to exceed some maximum value. This doesn't mean Chebyshev is more accurate than least squares since typically the average error will be higher.

We compute the k coefficients by setting the sum-square formula to 0 and figuring the partial derivatives of it with respect to each of the terms. This gives a matrix of equations called normal equations and represents a linear system of multiple simultaneous equations.

Deriving the least-squares process is a fascinating exercise that is beyond the scope of this book. Use the cookbook approach shown in Fig. 10.4 to fit a least-squares curve to experimental data. This program is in BASIC to encourage playing with it in an interactive development environment. The program solves for a formula of the form

$$y = k_0 + k_1 x_1 + k_2 x_2 + k_3 x_3$$

In other words, the program finds the **k** values that match the experimental data x_1, x_2, and x_3 to the known **y** data.

In the program, variable **p** is the number of terms in the equation. If the maximum coefficient is 3 (as above), then **p** will be 3. The variable **n** is the number of experimental samples being used to create the formula.

This program assumes that the array **f** will be loaded with the experimental data before it is invoked. Array elements are arranged in the following order (if **p** = 3):

	x1	x2	x3	y
Sample 1:	f (1, 2)	f (1, 3)	f (1, 4)	f (1, 5)
Sample 2:	f (2, 2)	f (2, 3)	f (2, 4)	f (2, 5)
Sample 3:	f (3, 2)	f (3, 3)	f (3, 4)	f (3, 5)
		.		
		.		
		.		
Sample n:	f (n, 2)	f (n, 3)	f (n, 4)	f (n, 5)

Note that the first column of the array is empty; the program fills it with ones during the computation.

When the program terminates, the coefficients **k0** to **kn** are stored in the right-most row of the **a** matrix. In other words, **a(1,p + 2)** is **k0**, **a(2,p + 2)** is **k1**, etc.

```
n=number of experimental samples
p=number of terms in equation
f=experimental data (dimensioned f(n,p+2))

10  dim a(p+2,p+2)
15  ' Clear out Normal Matrix
20  for i=1 to p+2
30    for k=1 to p+2
40      a(i,k)=0
50    next k
60  next i
100 ' Build Normal Matrix
110 for t=1 to n
120   f(t,1)=1
130   for j=1 to p+2
140     for k=1 to p+2
150       a(j,k)=a(j,k)+f(t,j)*f(t,k)
160     next k
170   next j
180 next t
1000 ' Do a Gauss Jordan elimination
1001 k=1
1010 j=k
1020 s=a(k,k)
1030 a(k,j)=a(k,j)/s
1040 j=j+1
1050 if j <= p+2 then 1030
1060 if k >= p+1 then 2000
1070 i=k+1
1080 j=k
1090 s=a(i,k)
1100 a(i,j)=a(i,j)-s*a(k,j)
1110 j=j+1
1120 if j <= p+2 then 1100
1130 i=i+1
1140 if i <= p+1 then 1080
1150 k=k+1
1160 goto 1010
2000 if k <= 1 then 3000
2010 i=k-1
```

Figure 10.4 Program to compute a least-square fit. (*Figure continues.*)

```
2020 j=k
2030 s=a(i,k)
2040 a(i,j)=a(i,j)-s*a(k,j)
2050 j=j+1
2060 if j <= p+2 then 2040
2070 i=i-1
2080 if i >= 1 then 2020
2090 k=k-1
2100 goto 2000
3000 stop
```

Figure 10.4 *(Continued)*

To give an example application, suppose we're measuring the quality **world__peace,** which is (for argument's sake) a function of **number__of__wars, number__of__civil__liberties,** and **number__ of__aggressive__posturings.** If we have some *a priori* knowledge that these are related linearly by the function (the "**number__of__**" prefix has been dropped for clarity)

```
world_peace= k0 + k1*wars + k2*liberties
+ k3*posturings
```

then we can measure **world__peace** at any time if we know the coefficients **k0** to **k3.** This does assume that **world__peace** can be quantified.

To determine the coefficients we start with a known data set. Suppose a think tank gave us the following table:

Country	Peace	Wars	Liberties	Posturings
1	2	2	2	20
2	10	0	10	0
3	0	5	0	100
		.		
		.		
		.		
30	5	1	3	30

Thus, we have 30 samples, one for each of 30 countries, that relate **world__peace** to the three parameters we've defined. The variable **p** in Fig. 10.4 is 3 (we have three factors making up the equation), and **n,** the number of samples, is 30. Array **f** is organized as

	f (i, 2)	f (i, 3)	f (i, 4)	f (i, 5)
i=1	2	2	20	2
i=2	0	10	0	10
i=3	5	0	100	0
			.	
			.	
			.	
i=30	1	3	30	5

Column **f(i,5)** is the known value of **world_peace** for the calibration set. All 30 samples go into the makeup of array **f**.

After invoking the program, set the **k** coefficients to

```
k0=  a(1,5)
k1=  a(2,5)
k2=  a(3,5)
k3=  a(4,5)
```

Now (assuming there is some meaning to this relationship!) our utopia gauge can predict **world_peace** for any other country by computing

```
world_peace= k0 + k1*wars + k2*liberties
+ k3*posturings
```

Note that the program in Fig. 10.4 solves for a linear combination of terms (**k0 + k1*x1 + k2*x2**, etc.) and not a polynomial combination of them. The variables **x1** to **xn** are assumed to be independent: for example, absorptions at different wavelengths. If a polynomial fit were used, only one independent term (corresponding to a single physical parameter), raised to incremental powers (**k0 + k1*x + k2 * x**2 + k3*x**3**), would be included. Modify the program to fit polynomial data by replacing the input with the terms raised to the appropriate powers.

Least squares can fit data with remarkable, but never perfect, accuracy. It is always important to evaluate just how well the computation worked. The great peril of computing is that the algorithm becomes a black box whose inner operations are hidden; it may not be easy to get a quick sanity check on its operation.

Fortunately, the science of statistics provides us with a great range of "goodness of fit" measures. Different applications require different yardsticks, but certainly one of the easiest to comprehend is standard deviation, which is defined by

$$S.D. = \sqrt{\frac{\sum_{i=1}^{n} [x(i) - x'(i)]^2}{n - 1}}$$

If the real (x) and predicted (x') values are identical at all points, then the standard deviation will be 0. This is a perfect fit.

If the distribution of errors follows the standard Gaussian distribution (pretty much true for most systems), then 68% of the samples fall within one standard deviation; 95% within two, and 99.7% within three standard deviations.

No mathematical technique, especially one as complex as least squares, can be indiscriminately applied to any situation. Take care to ensure that the input data and results are truly meaningful.

The algorithmic nature of least squares (in a computer) tends to mask the details of its operation. Least squares works well only if the number of samples used in finding the coefficients is much larger than the number of coefficients. I've seen people try to solve for five unknowns (coefficients) with only four or five samples. With smooth, easy to fit data, 20 would be more reasonable. Noisy data requires far more samples.

After finding the coefficients be sure that samples presented to the instrument have values that lie within the calibration range. For example, if you calibrated the instrument with a set of samples that ranged from 10 to 20 pF (when measuring capacitance), then don't try to use the equation to solve for 30 pF. The fit is often quite poor outside of the calibration range.

Finally, be wary of the number of terms used in the equation. More terms yield a set of normal equations that is harder to solve. Small errors due to noise or even to the resolution of the computer's floating-point package can give wildly incorrect values. The Hilbert determinant gives a relative idea of the difficulty of getting a good solution as a function of the number of coefficients:

Number of terms	Hilbert determinant
1	1
2	8.3×10^{-2}
3	4.6×10^{-4}
4	1.7×10^{-7}
5	3.7×10^{-12}
6	5.4×10^{-18}
7	4.8×10^{-25}
8	2.7×10^{-33}
9	9.7×10^{-47}

With nine terms the equation is about 10^{47} times more difficult to solve than with one term. It's generally a bad idea to use too many terms. If the data is so hard to fit that a huge polynomial is needed, segment the problem into several smaller ranges and create a polynomial for each range.

If the data is not too noisy the spline fit will save calibration and computation time where multiple polynomials are needed. At the point where we switch from one polynomial to the next the two polynomials must, by definition, give identical answers. This property simplifies the matrices and yields an easier result. Refer to the Bibliography for more information about spline curve fitting.

Standards

None of these techniques work unless you have some way to inject samples with known values into the instrument's measuring path. Both the linear and nonlinear calibrations use a number of predetermined values (or standards) to compute the coefficients. Just how does one go about injecting known values for the sake of calibration?

If your system measures an electronic quantity like voltage or current (with no sensor), a purely electronic solution is practical. Put a computer-actuated analog switch in the front end. Position 1 might be the normal input, position 2 a good zero level (ground), and position 3 a precision full-scale value. The computer can then use these two calibration points to establish gain and offset corrections using the formulas described earlier.

If the instrument already uses an analog multiplexer to sample readings from several sources, just dedicate two of the multiplexer's channels to calibration parameters.

Some systems use a digital-to-analog converter (DAC) feeding the multiplexer so the computer can generate any calibration voltage. This is a nice approach, but you must be sure that the DAC is accurate enough to avoid skewing the calibration results. I'm not a big fan of this unless the system needs a high-accuracy DAC for some other reason.

Drifty sensors will make the calibration procedure more complicated. It's hard to create a standard physical parameter (like temperature or a light level) with precision. This makes sensor calibration difficult at best, but remember that such calibration is needed regardless of the instrument's technology—smart code still saves pots. For example, how do you calibrate a thermistor? The user inserts it in a controlled temperature bath and then enters the bath temperature into the computer. To get another calibration point (two equations in two unknowns) the process is repeated in a bath of another temperature.

Tedious? Yes. Avoidable? Not really, given that the thermistor requires some sort of calibration.

Every sensor does have its unique calibration requirements. In cases where the computer can automatically insert known readings, by all means do so. The frequent recalibration will yield a better product. If some manual intervention is needed, say, by making the user subject the sensor to known values, then self-calibration is still worthwhile. A little code saves several pots and completely eliminates tedious pot twiddling.

Sometimes, due to the expense or complexity of inserting accurate standards, a two-point calibration is not feasible. We just can't get around the fact that two equations are needed to solve for two unknowns, but you can at least correct either the gain or slope by using one standard.

Before the microprocessor age I worked on a colorimeter that was packed with analog circuits. The electronics simply could not maintain the accuracies the designers strove for, so they included a rotating white standard shaped like a bow tie. Many times a second the standard was in view, blocking light from the user's samples but returning a precision white value to the photodetectors. The electronics used this information to recompute the amplifiers' gains. The presumption was that offset contributed only a small part of the error. The white bow tie constantly corrected for gain errors.

Drifty sensors and electronics demand these awkward mechanical calibration methods. Other options are always available. If the input data changes slowly with time you can use a simple analog switch (or even relay) to occasionally inject a known voltage into a sum node of the first stage of amplification. For example, if the system has an input range of 0 to 10 mV, the code can wait for a midrange reading to occur (5 mV or so). Then have it momentarily actuate the switch to add another few millivolts to the signal. Since this additional value is known (precision voltage references are cheap), it's easy for the code to compute a gain-correction factor.

An option for single-point gain corrections is to provide a single manually inserted standard. In an updated version of the colorimeter I referred to earlier we supplied each unit with a white tile with known reflectances. The user put this on the instrument for a daily gain-only recalibration. Another possibility is to add an analog switch in the feedback loop of an op amp. If the switch reduces the amplifier's gain by half, then it is easy to compute an offset correction.

It's a lot harder to supply standards where a least-squares curve fit defines the instrument's transfer function. With a bit of noise and perhaps four polynomial coefficients (**k0** to **k3**), you'll need typically 20 to 50 standards. The accuracy of the system is no better than the accuracy of the calibration, so don't scrimp on these standards!

The protein measurement instrument I described earlier was quite noisy, so a 50-standard calibration was the norm. Being organic, the ground-up wheat samples changed almost daily. We had a lab carefully prepare standards and chemically analyze their protein content. During calibration we inserted each one and let the instrument read raw reflectance readings prior to figuring the constants.

Another instrument irradiated a sample of metal with a small pellet of americium. A detector measured how much radiation passed through the sample to determine its thickness. This is far from a linear relationship, so we used a dozen thickness-controlled pieces of steel to calibrate it. Each standard was mounted on a solenoid. The computer could insert standards as needed to gather data for a calibration. Since it really needed 30 or 40 different thicknesses for a good curve fit, we had the computer inject two or three standards at a time to create additive thicknesses.

In one steel thickness gauge we combined multiple-point and single-point calibrations. This system included a number of self-calibration features, including a multiple-point regression as just described. In addition, every minute or so the system automatically blocked all x-rays from its sensor by inserting a heavy hunk of lead in the beam. During this brief dark time the computer made a number of A/D readings, averaged them, and recomputed the system's offset.

Conclusion

Sometimes using least squares is more of an art than a science. Picking the right number of terms requires knowledge of the physics of the measurement and some experimentation. The form of the equation (linear, polynomial, or even a combination of complex functions) must also be selected, generally using some *a priori* knowledge of the system.

Least squares can be a bit complicated to apply, especially for the non-mathematically inclined. It is worth the trouble, especially since the results are easy to test. If the calibration sample set is run through the instrument after calibration and crazy results are obtained, then there is a flaw in the code or in the selection of terms.

CHAPTER 11

A Final Perspective

No man is an island, entire to itself. Every man is a piece of the continent, a part of the main.—John Donne

Schedule Panics

The consumer, our customers, are so acclimated to the benefits of the technology that they lose sight of the miraculously complex nature of the products. They have no idea of just how difficult it is to bring a product to market. Embedded systems are getting much more expensive to design, test, and market. Now the development process is often the single most important and expensive concern in planning new products.

We engineers sometimes lose sight of the fact that our profession is really a business discipline. It is one (very important) ingredient of making a company successful. Engineering is not an activity that operates in isolation; it dovetails into other aspects of the business's strategies and plans. Just as strategic planners cannot operate without input from accounting, marketing and sales rely heavily on engineering's decisions and trade-offs.

Perhaps one of the most important business issues faced by engineers is the development schedule. In our rapidly changing industry, products must be brought to market in breathtakingly short times. What might seem an arbitrary deadline from marketing may indeed be crucial to gaining market share; ultimately, making the schedule can be vital to each engineer's job security!

This does not mean that the specifications handed down from marketing's ivory tower are necessarily sacrosanct. Marketing managers often work in a vacuum, coming up with a product's features without the benefit of the expert advice available from engineering. How many times have we seen product concepts that were totally unmanageable? Or those that cost astronomical amounts of money to develop? We engineers blame marketing for these debacles; perhaps we are also partially to blame.

Interdepartmental rivalries seem to be a part of big company corporate culture, but ultimately they serve to make everyone's jobs harder and the products less successful. Marketing needs our expert feedback to tune their desires. Is the design too expensive to manufacture? Tell them! Can some clever trade-off be made to decrease cost or increase performance? Tell them! John Donne's famous "No man is an island, entire to itself" applies equally to individual people and entire high-technology departments. Feedback should be an iterative process that accommodates the needs of all groups within the company. For example, if a particular trade-off impacts testability get the test group involved.

In no other area does the engineering department have more control than in defining and meeting the development schedule. When software is involved, as it is in all microprocessor-based projects, it seems that schedules are treated with a certain irreverence or a form of mild contempt that is perhaps justified since so few software projects are completed on or near schedule. While this sad fact is sometimes due to an impossible schedule imposed by outside forces, it is just as common in cases where each member of the development team agrees to the milestones in advance.

"The unexpected" is frequently cited for delays. Tools fail, prototype hardware is flaky, and unknown coding issues arise. True—unexpected problems will impact any schedule. But why do we continue to schedule projects with no room or plan for dealing with these problems? Why do we continue to make the same mistakes over and over again? Have you ever started a project, using a new toolset (compiler, linker, etc.) and found some sort of fatal incompatibility between tools? Why does this happen with every project?

While writing code for an embedded environment is perhaps not much more difficult than for a conventional desktop or mainframe computer, debugging it is much harder. The environment is much less interactive, much less stable (e.g., flaky hardware), and much more subject to real-time concerns. Yet how many times have you seen a schedule with a single line called "debugging?" Much of the uncertainty in scheduling a project can be removed by carefully planning the development, and especially the debugging, process.

Much has been written about structured analysis and design. This is crucial to the development of every product, from a simple controller to the space shuttle. Surprisingly little research has been applied to the back end of the project, debugging, where little room is left for schedule slippages (since debugging nearly always takes place late in the game).

Most embedded code takes life incrementally, with little or no thought given to debugging it until late in the project when things are going terribly wrong. Debugging embedded code is much more complicated than debugging conventional systems. Two sins are endemic to this arena. First, the debugging part of the project is almost never given the careful planning it deserves. Second, debugging is always scheduled optimistically—everyone assumes the code will be nearly perfect and that no unexpected problems will arise. In this industry little is immune from change, but these two rules certainly are: (1) things will be worse than you figure at debug time, and (2) you will spend far more time debugging than you ever guessed.

Scheduling enough time to a proper debugging job is an important factor to timely product introduction. Unfortunately, no one seems to really understand what elements go into coming up with a sound schedule. In some ways high-level design and coding are easier to plan since these activities don't require making something work; there is no good measure of the quality of the job. Structured code walk-throughs are one approach to insuring accuracy, but in fact most embedded systems are done by small groups or individuals working alone. They have neither the resources nor the discipline to engage in the careful design reviews characteristic of large Department of Defense projects. Of course, these big jobs seem to get in just as much trouble . . .

Careful initial design and coding will reduce errors tremendously. Interestingly, surveys conducted by Tom DeMarcos and Timothy Lister reveal that the fastest programmers are often also the most accurate. Further, the best performers are not necessarily superprogrammers. Rather, they share one trait: they have few interruptions. It seems one of the best ways of improving performance is to keep phone calls, noise, and other interruptions to a minimum. This easy-to-implement approach typically yields about a 2.5 to 1 improvement in both speed and accuracy! Surprisingly few companies adopt it, preferring to corral groups of programmers into noisy cubicles. *Peopleware*, by DeMarcos and Lister, is an eminently readable account of their analysis. It contains recommendations that every manager should consider.

A company is like a growing organism, adapting and changing to suit its competitive environment. Like the organism, we should make an effort to learn from our past history, to improve ourselves as a result of experience. Does your company use past project performance to close the feedback loop of scheduling? It's fine to make mistakes, but only if we learn from them. Conduct a postmortem examination on a late project, not to condemn the guilty, but to find out what went wrong. Where were the slippages? What were they a result of? Sometimes it is just overoptimistic scheduling—use this as feedback into the next project. Were there tool problems? Was the magnitude of the project just not understood?

Crucial to all of this analysis is a careful record of where time is spent. While timecards are shunned as nuisances demanded by accounting, they do form a fantastic database of information. Of course, if all time is just charged to the project, with no subcategories (like design, debug, integration), you won't get useful information. Part of the planning process for any project is data collection for the next: come up with rules and methods for gathering the information you'll need next month or next year.

It's pretty rare to see a project that comes in significantly ahead of schedule. Even on small projects build in a little time for unexpected problems. People get sick. Tools fail. Algorithms sometimes just don't work or get much more complicated than initially envisioned. Sometimes it is best to not advertise that a margin of error is built into the schedule. After all, the Peter Principle states (accurately) that a job will expand to fill the amount of time allocated to it.

The old adage that 90% of the work is in the last 10% of the job is so frequently true that it simply must not be neglected when initially planning a project. The 90% figure indicates that something went wrong with the rest of the job—the problem is almost always planning-related. Either the job was poorly specified, poorly designed, or unrealistic assumptions were made about the schedule.

Many projects are rescued by dedicated engineers and programmers working long, hard hours. Ours is a creative discipline, but as Edison said, creativity is 1% inspiration and 99% perspiration. While everyone gripes about the hard work, I think it is what separates us in our profession from the obscurity of unionized blue-collar employees.

Make Yourself More Valuable

Think: what makes you valuable as a programmer? What can you do to be more useful, ultimately getting more job security and pay? Everyone wants big raises; few consider that a raise implies something in exchange. Presumably, your usefulness to the company should increase in step with salary growth. The economic climate of the 1990s will preclude free rides.

Honing one's skills is a lifelong process. Don't stop learning just because your formal schooling is over! Every so often stop and take a break; mentally marshall your resources. What is your competitive position in the employment market? Programming savvy is but one ingredient—the well-rounded embedded-programmer's repertoire should include all of the following:

Hardware Knowledge: In no other area of computer science are we so closely coupled to the hardware. It's impossible to do any sort of embedded development without at least some hardware experience. Programmers adept at manipulating chips and boards will always be in great demand.

Keen Design Capabilities: An incisive mind that can decompose conflicting requirements into a neatly structured program is an asset to every programming organization. Coding is secondary to overall design.

Methodologies: Professional programmers bring structured programming disciplines to the embedded world. Methodologies are essential to the health of the industry. Someday CASE (computer-aided software engineering) will be as useful as the schematic capture and PC layout programs hardware engineers use. Stay abreast of developments in this field.

Diverse Language Background: C is the most important language in the embedded world, but assembly still plays an important role. Some applications will always use every last bit of CPU horsepower, keeping assembly alive for the foreseeable future. Become proficient at it as well as new high-level languages like C++.

Libraries: Develop a library of algorithms and completed code that you can draw from to make your job easier. Try to avoid reinventing the wheel. Save your own algorithms as well as those collected from every possible source so you can benefit from others' experience.

Tools: We all work with a variety of tools, ranging from editors to compilers, linkers to debuggers. Don't be content to understand only the five most commonly used commands! Spend a few minutes a week becoming expert with your most important tools. Look for other ways to automate tedium and speed development.

Attitudes are just as important as skills. No one likes a prima donna, but this industry seems to breed them. Be a can-do individual. Look for ways to get a job done, not for reasons for why it is impossible.

Stay informed about the company's products so your work fits into the framework of the business's competitive position. Learn to communicate effectively with management and customers. Realistically look at your capabilities in each of these areas and find ways to improve. Software gurus are made, not born.

The Future of Embedded Systems

In the course of 20 years this industry has gone from birth to maturity. In 1970 no one would have dreamed of including a computer into virtually every electronic product. Now we can't imagine how we could get along without an embedded processor in even the simplest appliance. Who can say what the future will bring?

Languages come and go, but the embedded world is still dominated by assembly and C. ADA seems doomed to DOD-only programs, and Forth's popularity is sustained only by a dedicated die-hard fringe element. I find assembler and C to be totally inadequate. Both are ideal for writing complex real-time controllers and both perfectly suit getting a specific project done. Neither language inherently solves a business's long term problem, that of efficiently getting a lot of different projects out over the course of years.

C++ might be a step in promoting software packaging. The mantra of the 1990s will be "inheritance, encapsulation, polymorphism." Why rewrite the same routines time after time? C++, and a strong-armed programming discipline, just might make the concept of reusable packages a reality.

Reusable software is our only hope of dealing with increasing software complexity. Let's face it: at some point our own code will be simply too convoluted for anyone, including ourselves, to understand. It's simply naive to expect that by itself a new language will create some magic ability to handle bigger systems. The solution is to adopt new levels of abstraction.

Why is it so much easier to design an embedded system's hardware than its code? Conventional wisdom holds that the hardware is simpler, that designers just glue a lot of chips together, but software engineers must solve much tougher problems. Balderdash! Sure, programming is hard. But look at relative levels of complexity. Your 30,000 lines of code might be running in a system with over 100 million transistors. Which is more complicated? Which would you expect to be harder to design?

The hardware community is much better than their software counterparts at defining and living with levels of abstraction. No one designs a computer from scratch for an embedded system. We use an off-the-shelf processor. Need some memory? Pick one of thousands of standard chips. I/O is just as simple—hundreds of different kinds of peripherals lie at our fingertips, with yet more hundreds of variations of each type. Any one chip might be supremely complex, but each is easy to use.

Programmers decompose a problem into its functional blocks and then laboriously code each block. The hardware engineer also partitions the problem into functional blocks. Then he uses a few standard parts to implement each section. Suppose there is no chip that does just exactly what is needed. In very simple cases the engineer will design a custom solution using a bit of glue logic. Otherwise, he'll modify the design until it fits some combination of standard parts.

The problem of hardware complexity has been mastered by standard parts and (perhaps more importantly) a will to use them even if the design must be altered to fit that which is available.

No matter what the level of complexity, a chip comes with a well-defined interface bounded by some number of pins. Voluminous data books describe the action of the device in gory detail. While the unit's internal operation might be glossed over, its interface is documented with timing diagrams, input and output levels, and the like. Doesn't this sound a bit like object-oriented programming?

We need software counterparts to the huge data books supplied by the chip vendors. Need a fast regression? Pull down a data book and look at the choices. Perhaps graphs will show performance versus the size of the data matrix. Where chip manuals describe the package type, our software data books will list object module formats supplied: OMF, COFF, or the like.

Just think of how much easier programming will be. You'll never again reinvent the wheel. We'll tie standard components together. Perhaps someday a sort of universal software bus will become common, letting us just hang modules together, rather how peripherals now drop onto more or less standard address, data, and control busses.

It seems like a dream, yet something of this sort simply must come to pass. The motivating factor will be money. Software should be priced like integrated circuits. You won't spend $595 for an unlimited runtime license to a window manager; you'll buy it a copy at a time, for $1.34 each. Like the hardware, faster versions will have a premium price. A 27-μsec context switcher will cost half that of one rated at 18 μsec.

Software companies will take a cue from the history of marketing and develop distribution channels. A gaggle of software peddlers will be knocking on your door, pushing their latest interrupt-driven UART routine ("it's 200 bytes smaller than the competition's!"). Second sources will give your company the assurance that even if one company folds, the code your product so desperately needs will still be available.

A high-integration processor is a computer core surrounded by peripherals. Everyone using that chip deals with the same peripherals, yet most IC vendors don't supply driver code. Doesn't it seem ludicrous that thousands of different companies pay programmers to develop the same code? Intel now gives away an expert system for their 80196 CPU that automatically writes the driver code for you. This is certainly the direction of the future.

The only thing we can be sure of is that the future will bring totally unexpected new ideas and products. Be prepared to meet the accompanying challenges.

Magazines

The embedded microprocessor world changes quickly. Sometimes profound changes occur in a matter of weeks or months. Subscribe to industry publications (see following list) to stay abreast of the latest developments.

The C User's Journal, R&D Publications Inc., 2601 Iowa, Lawrence, KS 66046, (913) 841-1631.

Arguably the best source of information about the C language in the industry.

Computer Design, Pennwell Publishing Company, One Technology Park Drive, P.O. Box 990, Westford, MA 01886, (508) 692-0700.

Focuses on both hardware and software issues in micro, mini, and mainframe computer systems. Free to those in the industry.

Computer Language, Miller Freeman Publications, 500 Howard Street, San Francisco, CA 94105, (415) 397-1881.

Not quite so specialized as its title would seem to indicate. Contains a wealth of algorithms, and addresses object-oriented programming, C++, and the like.

EDN Magazine, Cahner's Publishing Company, 275 Washington Street, Newton, MA 02158.

Covers the entire electronics industry from analog-to-digital to embedded programming. Free to those working in the business.

Electronics, Penton Publishing, 611 Route #46 West, Hasbrouck Heights, NJ 07604, (201) 393-6060.

Free publication that addresses all aspects of electronic circuits.

Electronic Engineering Times, CMP Publications, 600 Community Drive, Manhasset, NY 11030.

Weekly newspaper-format magazine that is free to qualified subscribers and is an ideal way to stay on top of fast-changing developments. Has a decided bent toward the business aspects of the profession. Almost every week there is a story about the latest, most advanced technologies, giving a glimpse into the not-too-distant future.

Embedded Systems Programming, Milier Freeman Publications, 500 Howard Street, San Francisco, CA 94105, (415) 397-1881.

Free to those working in the industry and well worth studying monthly. The only magazine targeted directly at the embedded market.

Personal Engineering & Instrumentation News, Personal Engineering Communications, Box 430, Rye, NH 03870, (617) 232-3625.

Complements *Embedded Systems Programming's* software bias with its extended coverage of hardware issues. Free to qualified subscribers.

File Format

Intel hex and Motorola S-Record are the two most common de facto standards for storing object files. Many other formats are important as well, but little standardization exists.

The biggest shortcomings of these formats is their lack of debugging information. IEEE-695, COFF, and others include complete structural information about C and assembly programs, but they are very complex and are implemented differently by various vendors.

Intel Hex Format

Intel hex files are composed of a series of one-line records that include a record start character (a colon), the record length, address of where to start storing data, a record type field, the data items themselves, and a checksum.

The form of a record is

: LLAAAATTDDDDDDDDDDDDDDCC

where

$$\begin{aligned}
: &= \text{Record start character} \\
LL &= \text{Number of data bytes in record} \\
AAAA &= \text{16-bit load address of line} \\
TT &= \text{The record type} \\
DD &= \text{HEX data bytes} \\
CC &= \text{Checksum}
\end{aligned}$$

The checksum is formed by adding each of the record's bytes, including the byte count, address, record type, and data fields, and then computing the two's complement.

Example record:

: 02053E00B30503

This record consists of two data bytes (B3 and 05), which are to be stored at address 053E. The record type is 00. The checksum is 03.

Type 00 records contain data. Type 1 is the so-called "end record," or the last record in the file. The end record has 0 length, an unused address field, and no data. It always appears as

: 00000001FF

Note that the checksum is correct.

With only four digits for the address field, program sizes are limited to 64k. The extended address record, type 02, lets us expand the address range.

Type 02 records have an unused address field. The data field gives the high 16 bits of the segment for all subsequent addresses. This follows the segmented architecture used by the 80x88-series processors, where the effective address is formed by

```
Address=segment*16 + offset
```

Whenever a type 02 record is encountered, all succeeding data records (until the next type 02) start at an address computed by using the segment in the type 02 and adding the address in the individual data records. Suppose a type 02 record gives a segment of 1234. Then, add 12340 to the address in all of the following data records. An example type 02 record is

: 020000021234B6

The record is comprised of 02 data bytes, four unused address bytes (all set to zero), the type 02 identifier, and a data field of 1234, which is the segment for all following addresses. The checksum is B6.

Some tools produce symbols embedded into the hex file. Intel's standard method puts three fields on each symbol line. The first is always a zero. Field two contains the symbol name, followed by its address in the third field. The address is a hex number with a leading 0 and a trailing "H" suffix. An example follows:

```
0  SYMBOL1  0123H
0  SYMBOL2  0EFFFH
0  SYMBOL3  03H
$
```

The final dollar sign indicates the end of the symbols.

Motorola S-Records

Motorola's S-Records contain much the same information as Intel hex but in a much different format. 68000, 68HC11, and 6800 processors commonly make use of this file type.

Motorola prefixes every record with a record type that is indicated by a capital S followed by a one-digit record type. Legal types are

    S0   Start record
    S1   Data record (with 4 digit address)
    S2   Data record (with 6 digit address)
    S3   Data record (with 8 digit address)
    S7   End record (when using 8 digit addresses)
    S8   End record (when using 6 digit addresses)
    S9   End record (when using 4 digit addresses)

Every record is formatted as follows:

    STLLAAAA.... CC

ST is an S followed by the one-byte type.

LL is the record length, which is the number of bytes used by the address, data, and checksum fields. This is the number of bytes in binary form; it is half of the actual character count in the file, since each byte is represented with two ASCII digits. The checksum is formed by adding up all of the bytes in the length, address, and data fields, and then taking the one's complement.

Start records normally just signal that data records follow but can optionally contain identifying information about the program. With none of this information, it takes the form

    S0030000FC

That is, type is 0, length is 03, address is 0000 (not used), and checksum is FC. If identifying information is included it is stored in the data field that normally comes after the address.

Three different types of data records are supported. All three are identical with the exception of the length of the address field. Given a 4-byte data stream of DF 1B 34 4D, then typical records look like the following:

    S1071234DF1B344D37

where type is 1, length is 07, address is 1234, data is as above, and the checksum is 37.

    S208123456DF1B344DE0

where type is 2, length is 08, address is 123456, and checksum is E0.

    S30912345678DF1B344D67

where type is 3, length is 08, address is 12345678, and checksum is 67.

The end of a series of data records is indicated by an end record. Normally the address field is 0. Any other value means the field contains the program's start address.

Just as there are three types of data records, so there are three end records. The reason is the same—different types are needed to express differently sized address fields. A typical end record looks like the following

    S9030000FC

where type is 0, length is 03, address is 0000, and checksum is FC.

Serial Communications

Serial communications interfaces are ubiquitous in the embedded world. It seems all of our hardware tools cable together via some sort of serial link, generally RS-232. A lot of embedded systems themselves include some form of the protocol.

RS-232, as has been extended for microcomputer communications, defines signal levels, transfer parameters, and cabling to insure that all forms of equipment work together. Different vendors implement various aspects of the standard in different ways, so devices hardly ever work together.

ASCII

Most nonbinary serial communications take place using ASCII codes (American Standard Code for Information Interchange). This is a 7-bit pattern. Many vendors have extended it to 8 bits, usually using the extra 128 characters for special symbols and graphics (the PC's "smiley face" may be the best known of these).

The 7-bit set is divided into four symmetrical groups of characters as shown in Fig. C.1. Codes under 20h are all nonprinting characters that cause special actions like carriage return, form feed, etc. Those lying between 20h and 3fh include numbers and most punctuation marks. The letters eat up most of the rest of the codes: 41h to 5Ah are the upper case letters, and 61h to 7Ah are lower case.

You can make an uppercase letter by ORing 40h with the lowercase equivalent. To go from uppercase to the control characters (e.g., Ctrl-C), just remove bit 40h. If C is 43h, then control-C is 03h.

char	hex	char	hex	char	hex	char	hex
NUL Ctrl-@	00		20	@	40	'	60
SOH Ctrl-A	01	!	21	A	41	a	61
STX Ctrl-B	02	"	22	B	42	b	62
ETX Ctrl-C	03	#	23	C	43	c	63
EOT Ctrl-D	04	$	24	D	44	d	64
ENQ Ctrl-E	05	%	25	E	45	e	65
ACK Ctrl-F	06	&	26	F	46	f	66
BEL Ctrl-G	07	'	27	G	47	g	67
BS Ctrl-H	08	(	28	H	48	h	68
HT Ctrl-I	09	)	29	I	49	i	69
LF Ctrl-J	0a	*	2a	J	4a	j	6a
VT Ctrl-K	0b	+	2b	K	4b	k	6b
FF Ctrl-L	0c	,	2c	L	4c	l	6c
CR Ctrl-M	0d	-	2d	M	4d	m	6d
SO Ctrl-N	0e	.	2e	N	4e	n	6e
SI Ctrl-O	0f	/	2f	O	4f	o	6f
DLE Ctrl-P	10	0	30	P	50	p	70
DC1 Ctrl-Q	11	1	31	Q	51	q	71
DC2 Ctrl-R	12	2	32	R	52	r	72
DC3 Ctrl-S	13	3	33	S	53	s	73
DC4 Ctrl-T	14	4	34	T	54	t	74
NAK Ctrl-U	15	5	35	U	55	u	75
SYN Ctrl-V	16	6	36	V	56	v	76
ETB Ctrl-W	17	7	37	W	57	w	77
CAN Ctrl-X	18	8	38	X	58	x	78
EM Ctrl-Y	19	9	39	Y	59	y	79
SUB Ctrl-Z	1a	:	3a	Z	5a	z	7a
ESC Ctrl-[	1b	;	3b	[	5b	{	7b
FS Ctrl-\	1c	<	3c	\	5c	|	7c
GS Ctrl-]	1d	=	3d	]	5d	}	7d
RS Ctrl-^	1e	>	3e	^	5e	~	7e
US Ctrl-_	1f	?	3f	_	5f	DL	7f

Figure C.1 ASCII character set.

RS-232 Data Transmission

Data transferred over an RS-232 link goes one bit at a time. Figure C.2 outlines the transmission format.

All communications take place at some baud rate agreed on by both the

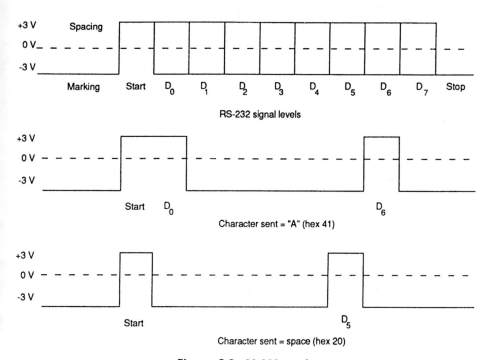

Figure C.2 RS-232 signals.

driver and receiver. 9600 baud means that each bit of the character stream takes 1/9600 sec to transmit.

When the link is idle (no data being sent) it is in the marking state (the line is more negative than −3 V). The start bit, which puts the line into the spacing state for 1-bit period, is sent first and serves to announce that a character is on the way.

Data bits follow start. The least significant (data bit 0) goes first. After the entire character has been transferred the line goes to the marking state for the length of the stop bit—one or two bit times, depending on the protocol agreed to by the communicating devices. A logic zero data bit is transmitted as a spacing line condition (positive voltage); ones go as marking bits (negative).

The RS-232 standard defines pinouts for data communications equipment (DCE) and data terminal equipment (DTE). Terminals are DTE. Computers seem to be DTE or DCE, depending on the whim of the designer. The IBM PC is DTE. Fig. C.3 shows the RS-232 pins most often used on microcomputer gear for both 9- and 25-pin connectors.

Pin Number		Direction	Pin Name
DB-9	DB-25		
5	7		Ground
	1		Frame ground (not used on 9 pin connectors)
3	2	DTE to DCE	Transmitted data from DTE
2	3	DCE to DTE	Received data from DCE
8	5	DCE to DTE	Clear to send (DCE ready)
7	4	DTE to DCE	Request to send (DTE ready)
6	6	DCE to DTE	Data set ready
4	20	DTE to DCE	Data terminal ready

Figure C.3 RS-232 pins. (Note: the PC is a DTE.)

Bit Banging

Ultralow-cost embedded systems might be too pressed for recurring costs to include a UART. Or, maybe you really want to have a UART just for debugging and maintenance purposes but can't con the hardware group into adding one. A really cheap solution is the "bit banger"—a UART implemented entirely in software.

UARTs convert parallel bytes of data from the program into a serial stream of bits and vice versa. They handle a lot of other RS-232 interface chores like double buffering the data, automatic handshaking, etc. If you can get by with a minimal noninterrupting serial interface that eats up all of the processor's time when sending and receiving characters, then the bit banger is a natural choice.

A tiny amount of hardware complements the code. One output bit and one input bit are all that is needed. Connect them through RS-232 level shifters (say, one MAX232 chip) to a 9- or 25-pin connector and you have a complete serial interface.

Figure C.4 shows the three subroutines needed to transmit, receive, and initialize the baud rate. This code is written in Z80 mnemonics, but will run equally well on the Z80, 64180, 8085 and NSC800 processors. The principle of operation is simple. At powerup issue a call to **BRID** and type a space character on the keyboard. After **BRID** detects a start bit it waits for start to go away (i.e., for the line to return to a logic 0) and then counts how many loop iterations during the six zero periods before the logic one (space is hex 20) occurs. This count is then transformed into a bit time, the basis of all timing in the transmit and receive routines.

COUT sends a character by toggling the serial line high (a start bit), delaying for one bit time, and then sending data bits one at a time. It also transmits two stop bits at the end of the character.

```
;
;   BRID - Determine the baud rate of the terminal. This routine
; actually finds the proper divisors BITTIM and HALFBT to run CIN
; and COUT properly
;
;   The routine expects a space. It looks at the 6 zeroes in the
; 20h stream from the serial port and counts time from the start
; bit to the first 1.
;
;   serial_port is the port address of the input data. data_bit
; is the bit mask.
;
brid:
        in      a, (serial_port)
        and     data_bit
        jp      z, brid         ; loop till serial not busy
bri1:   in      a, (serial_port)
        and     data_bit
        jp      nz, bri1        ; loop till start bit comes
        ld      hl,-7           ; bit count
bri3:   ld      e, 3
bri4:   dec     e               ; 42 machine cycle loop
        jp      nz, bri4
        nop                     ; balance cycle counts
        inc     hl              ; inc counter every 98 cycles
                                ; while serial line is low
        in      a, (serial_port)
        and     data_bit
        jp      z, bri3         ; loop while serial line low
        push    hl              ; save count for halfbt computation
        inc     h
        inc     l               ; add 101h w/o doing internal carry
        ld      (bittim), hl    ; save bit time
        pop     hl              ; restore count
        or      a               ; clear carry
        ld      a, h            ; compute hl/2
        rra
        ld      h, a
        ld      a, l
        rra
        ld      l, a            ; hl=count/2
        ld      (halfbt), hl
        ret
```

Figure C.4 Bit banger UART. (*Figure continues.*)

```
;
;
;  Output the character in C
;
;   Bittime has the delay time per bit, and is computed as:
;
;   <HL>' = ((freq in Hz/baudrate) - 98 )/14
;   BITTIM = <HL>'+101H  (with no internal carry prop between bytes)
;
;  and OUT to serial_high sets the serial line high; an OUT
;  to serial_low sets it low, regardless of the contents set to the
;  port.
;
cout:   ld      b,11            ; # bits to send
                                ; (start, 8 data, 2 stop)
        xor     a               ; clear carry for start bit
co1:    jp      nc,cc1          ; if carry, will set line high
        out     (serial_high),a ; set serial line high
        jp      cc2
cc1:    out     (serial_low),a  ; set serial line low
        jp      cc2             ; idle; balance # cycles with those
                                ; from setting output high
cc2:    ld      hl,(bittim)     ; time per bit
co2:    dec     l
        jp      nz,co2          ; idle for one bit time
        dec     h
        jp      nz,co2          ; idle for one bit time
        scf                     ; set carry high for next bit
        ld      a,c             ; a=character
        rra                     ; shift it into the carry
        ld      c,a
        dec     b               ; --bit count
        jp      nz,co1          ; send entire character
        ret
;
;   CIN - input a character to C.
;
;   HALFBIT is the time for a half bit transition on the serial input
;  line. It is calculated as follows:
;    (BITTIM-101h)/2 +101h
;
cin:    ld      b,9             ; bit count (start + 8 data)
ci1:    in      a,(serial_port) ; read serial line
        and     data_bit        ; isolate serial bit
        jp      nz,ci1          ; wait till serial data comes
        ld      hl,(halfbt)     ; get 1/2 bit time
ci2:    dec     l
        jp      nz,ci2          ; wait till middle of start bit
        dec     h
        jp      nz,ci2
```

Figure C.4 (Continued)

```
ci3:    ld      hl, (bittim)     ; bit time
ci4:    dec     1
        jp      nz, ci4          ; now wait one entire bit time
        dec     h
        jp      nz, ci4
        in      a, (serial_port) ; read serial character
        and     data_bit         ; isolate serial data
        jp      z, ci6           ; j if data is 0
        inc     a                ; now register A=serial data
ci6:    rra                      ; rotate it into carry
        dec     b                ; dec bit count
        jp      z, ci5           ; j if last bit
        ld      a, c             ; this is where we assemble char
        rra                      ; rotate it into the character from carry
        ld      c, a
        nop                      ; delay so timing matches that in output
                                 ; routine
        jp      ci3              ; do next bit
ci5:    ret
```

Figure C.4 (*Continued*)

Receiving is trickier. When routine **CIN** detects a start bit it delays for half a bit time to the start's center. This improves timing margins—we always sample the data stream in the center of each bit cell. The code then delays one bit time and reads data bit 0. It repeats the one bit delay and reads the rest of the character.

The principle works with any processor. Balancing execution times between the three subroutines is the most difficult part of a software UART. Intel's "Using the Intel 8085 Serial I/O Lines" application note is the best reference for the math behind the computations.

Notice that all of the operations are independent of baud rate and processor clock speeds. The **BITTIM** measurements are entirely relative. If you know your processor's clock rate you could dispense with the **BRID** routine altogether; just compute (or better, measure) the bit time and plug it into the code. It's a good idea to disable interrupts and DMA while using these routines. Asyncronous activities may skew timing enough to corrupt data transmission.

The code will support 9600 baud transmission if your processor runs at more than about 6 MHz. A very slow clock will necessitate using reduced baud rates.

Autobauding

We can extend the automatic baud-rate detection scheme outlined in subroutine **BRID** for use with a conventional UART. UARTs don't give us access to the raw serial bit stream, so we'll use a different approach.

```
;
;   With a real uart, detecting the baud rate is a bit of a hassle.
;   We set the baud rate generator to 19.2k baud, and read how many
;   characters are read when a space is typed. From that we can figure
;   the rate.
;
brid:    ld      a,baud_19200
         out     (baud_port),a    ; set 19.2 kbaud
auto0:   ld      hl,40000h        ; timeout
auto1:   in      a,(uartstat)     ; read status port
         and     ready            ; if <>0, char ready
         jp      z,auto1          ; wait till char ready
         in      a,(uartdata)     ; clear uart ready bit
         ld      b,1              ; b=# chars read
auto2:   in      a,(uartstat)     ; now count # recvd till timeout
         and     2
         jp      nz,auto3         ; loop till char ready
         dec     hl               ; dec timeout
         ld      a,1
         or      h                ; see if timeout=0
         jp      nz,auto2         ; if timeout <>0, keep getting chars
         jp      auto4            ; j if timeout up
auto3:   ld      hl,4000h         ; reset timeout
         in      a,(uartdata)     ; clear uart ready bit
         inc     b                ; inc char count
         jp      auto2            ; get another char
auto4:
         ld      a,b
         cp      1                ; if 1, 19.2kb
         ld      c,baud_19200
         jp      nz,auto41        ; j if not 19.2 kb
         in      a,(uartdata)     ; be sure by reading the char
         cp      ' '              ; should be a space
         jp      nz,auto0         ; retry if no good
         jp      auto5
auto41:  ld      c,baud_9600
         cp      2                ; 9600?
         jp      z,auto5          ; j if 9600
         ld      c,baud_4800
         cp      4                ; 4800?
         jp      m,auto5          ; j if 4800
         ld      c,baud_2400
         cp      9
         jp      m,auto5          ; j if 2400
         ld      c,baud_1200
         cp      12h
         jp      m,auto5          ; j if 1200
         ld      c,baud_600
         cp      24h
```

Figure C.5 Autobauding with a UART. (*Figure continues.*)

```
          jp     m, auto5        ; j if 600
          ld     c, baud_300
          cp     50h
          jp     m, auto5        ; j if 300
          ld     c, baud_110     ; assume 110
auto5:    ld     a, c            ; prog to send to port
          ld     (baud), a       ; set rate
          out    (baudport), a   ; set rate
          ret
```

Figure C.5 (*Continued*)

Figure C.5 shows Z80 code that detects the incoming rate for speeds up to 19200. It starts off by setting the baud-rate generator to 19200, the fastest supported in this application.

When the user types a space the code counts the characters it detects. If the incoming rate is 19200 it will find only one character. This is not true with data transmitted at lower speeds. At 1200 baud the space will appear to be many, many individual characters. The data processed by the UART will be totally corrupt—after all, we're receiving 1200 baud data while set to 19200! Still, the received character count tells us how fast the data was transmitted.

Different UARTs might behave slightly differently from the 8251 that this code was written for, so you may have to tune the character counts empirically.

Bibliography

Many authors fear that programmers don't read. DeMarco and Lister eloquently make this point in *Peopleware*. The industry changes so fast that we simply must acquire knowledge wherever we can! These are some of the publications I found useful in preparing this book.

Allen, Marc L. Forked interrupt systems. *The C Users Journal*, p. 113, April, 1990.

> Contains a complete discussion of forked interrupt processing, including code written for the 80x88 family of CPUs.

Black, Sol L. Consider testability in your next design. *Electronic Design Magazine*, p. 54, December 27, 1990.

Boehm, Barry. "Software Engineering Economics." Prentice-Hall, 1981.

> The bible of estimating software costs. The famous COCOMO model is developed here.

Boothroyd, J. Chebyschev curve fit. *Communications of the ACM Algorithm Collection, Algorithm 318.*

> This short piece includes complete pseudocode to implement a Chebyschev curve fit that, unlike the algorithms in this book that minimize sum-square errors, minimizes the absolute error over the curve.

Brooks, Frederick P. "The Mythical Man-Month." Addison-Wesley, Reading, MA, 1975.

> Unfortunately, the title has become an idiom in this business. Everyone seems to be aware of Brooks' central tenet: adding programmers to a late project will make it later. While he describes this in lucid detail, much more interesting is his solution of centering a small organization around a single highly qualified programmer. Up to 10 support people may be

needed to relieve the guru of the inevitable tedium associated with the job, leaving him to do what he does best—write specifications and code. This quickly read book is quite thought provoking.

Cassola, Robert L. Floating-point algorithm design. *Computer Design Magazine*, p. 107, June 1982.

An alternative to rational approximations using partitioned polynomials. The article is by no means complete by itself, but it includes useful references.

DeMarco, Tom, and Timothy Lister. "Peopleware." Dorset House, New York, 1987.

Required reading for managers wishing to improve their peoples' productivity. The authors draw on their extensive studies of different organizations to identify the largest bottlenecks to efficient code production. After over a decade of annual, heavily documented "code wars," they discovered a remarkable fact: simply decreasing noise and interruptions generally triples programmer productivity. Very readable and entertaining.

"Developing Managerial Skills in Engineers and Scientists: Succeeding as a Technical Manager," Van Nostrand Reinhold, New York, NY, 1982

"Embedded Applications." Order # 270648-002, Intel Corporation, Santa Clara, CA, 1990.

A collection of algorithms and ideas aimed mostly at the 80196 and 8051 families.

"Doctor Dobbs Toolbook of C." Prentice Hall, New York, 1986.

Complete description of a small C with source in C and with an assembler for the 8088 also in C.

Gilder, George. "Microcosm." Simon & Schuster, New York, 1989.

Explores the directions we can expect this technology to head. Must reading for thinking engineers wondering what this business will be like in a decade.

Hamming, R. W. "Numerical Methods for Scientists and Engineers." McGraw-Hill, New York, 1962.

Hamming's motto is "The purpose in computing is insight, not numbers," which is a theme he carries through the book. While you'll need some math background to fully understand this work, it does present the basis for the most important numerical methods (like least squares) in a fairly easy-to-understand way.

Hart, John F., E. Wicheney, C. L. Lawson, H. J. Maehly, C. K. Mesztenyi, and J. R. Rice. "Computer Approximations." John Wiley & Sons, New York, 1968.

The bible of rational approximations. While not particularly readable, it is encyclopedic in scope.

Lipovski, G. J. "Single- and Multiple-Chip Microcomputer Interfacing." Prentice-Hall, Englewood Cliffs, N.J., 1988.

Excellent introduction to the hardware of simple embedded systems. Newcomers to the field will find Lipovski's work an invaluable introduction to the hardware end of the embedded business.

Knuth, Donald. "The Art of Computer Programming," Vols. 1 through 4. Addison-Wesley, Reading, MA, 1968.

Knuth's mighty tomes are regarded as part of the fundamental lore of programming, despite the fact that few embedded programmers actually read them. The four volumes are chock-full of useful algorithms, but it takes a bit of work to wade through the fairly mathematical explanations.

Morgan, Christopher. "Bluebook of Assembly Routines for the IBM PC and XT." Signet, New York, 1984.

Morris, Michale F. "Computer Performance Evaluation." Van Nostrand Reinhold, New York. Addresses larger systems and complex techniques; stresses modeling, simulation, and after-the-fact tuning methodologies.

Moshier, Stephen L. Computer approximations. *Byte*, April 1986, p. 161.

A readable and interesting discussion of where rational approximations come from.

Nguyen, Toan. Numerical methods in data analysis. *Byte*, May 1981, p. 435.

Gives a fairly complete overview of the theory behind least squares and the Newton–Raphson methods of curve fitting.

Ripps, David. The multitasking mindset meets the operating system. *EDN*, October 1, 1990, p. 115.

Good discussion of data structures in an interrupting environment.

Savitzky, A., and M. Golay. Smoothing and differentiation of data by least-squares procedures. *Journal of Analytical Chemistry* **36** (8), 1607, July 1964.

This seminal paper discusses using convolutions to fit and differentiate curves. Tables of coefficients are included.

Sedgewick, Robert. "Algorithms." Addison-Wesley, Reading, MA, 1988.

A good description of the theory of algorithms, data structures, and sorting and searching techniques.

Silverthorn, Lee. Rate monotonic scheduling ensures tasks meet deadlines. *EDN*, October 26, 1989, p. 191.

A 68000 real-time operating system. *Doctor Dobbs Journal*, January 1986.

Assembly source code of an RTOS for the 68000.

Smith, Erol R. New algorithm calculates e˟, *EDN*, June 20, 1975, p. 164.

A simple and fast algorithm to compute integer powers of *e*.

"Guide to Embedded Languages," Softaid, Columbia, MD, 1989.

This discussion of embedding a language into your product centers around building a BASIC interpreter or compiler into the ROMed code.

Southworth, Raymond, and Samuel Deleeuw. "Digital Computation and Numerical Methods." McGraw-Hill, New York, 1965.

A practical, down-to-earth presentation of algorithms for solving various iterative and matrix algorithms. If you need to fit curves, integrate or differentiate, solve linear equations, or interpolate, this is a worthwhile reference.

Storer, James A. "Data Compression: Methods and Theory." Computer Science Press, New York, 1988.

Toffler, Alvin. "PowerShift." Bantam, New York, 1990.

An interesting complement to Gilder's *Microcosm*. Examines the societal and political shifts we can expect as a result of the new information economy we computer folks have created.

"Using the Intel 8085 Serial I/O Lines." Order # 9800684A, Intel Corporation, Santa Clara, CA, 1977.

No other reference contains so much information about writing a bit-banging UART.

Wo, Lau Siu. Extracting the *n*th root from a binary number. *Byte*, November 1986, p. 115.

An algorithm to take any integer root of an integer number without floating point.

Yourdon, Edward, and Larry Constantine. "Structured Design." Prentice-Hall, Englewood Cliffs, N.J. 1979.

A *must read*. Extremely readable description of the whole process of sane programming. Essential even for small systems.

Index

ISBN 0-12-274880-8

9 780122 748806

90293